STUDIES IN
HIGHER EDUCATION

Edited by
Philip G. Altbach
Monan Professor of Higher Education
Lynch School of Education, Boston College

A ROUTLEDGE SERIES

Studies in Higher Education

Philip G. Altbach, *General Editor*

DOMINANT BELIEFS AND ALTERNATIVE VOICES
DISCOURSE, BELIEF, AND GENDER IN AMERICAN STUDY ABROAD

Joan Elias Gore

Routledge
New York & London

Published in 2005 by
Routledge
Taylor & Francis Group
270 Madison Avenue
New York, NY 10016

Published in Great Britain by
Routledge
Taylor & Francis Group
2 Park Square
Milton Park, Abingdon
Oxon OX14 4RN

Printed in the United States of America on acid-free paper
10 9 8 7 6 5 4 3 2 1

International Standard Book Number-10: 0-415-97457-7 (Hardcover)
International Standard Book Number-13: 978-0-415-97457-8 (Hardcover)
Library of Congress Card Number 2005009582

Library of Congress Cataloging-in-Publication Data

Gore, Joan Elias.
    Dominant beliefs and alternative voices : discourse, belief, and gender in American study abroad / Joan Elias Gore.
        p. cm. -- (Studies in higher education)
    Includes bibliographical references and index.
    ISBN 0-415-97457-7
    1. Foreign study. 2. American students--Foreign countries. 3. Women--Education (Higher)--United States. 4. Higher education and state. I. Title. II. Series.

LB2376.G68 2005
378'.016--dc22

2005009582

Taylor & Francis Group
is the Academic Division of T&F Informa plc.

Visit the Taylor & Francis Web site at
http://www.taylorandfrancis.com

and the Routledge Web site at
http://www.routledge-ny.com

Contents

List of Tables and Figures

LIST OF TABLES

LIST OF FIGURES

Part One
The Status of Study Abroad

Chapter One

The Marginal Role of Study Abroad in American Higher Education

In recent years, the word "internationalization" has been uttered more and more often on college and university campuses across the United States of America. Most members of the higher education world agree with the mission of increasing the international component of their curricula, and many schools have announced new programs and initiatives to do so. The American Council on Education (ACE) has put internationalization high on its agenda since the 1950s. Intent on understanding how effectively this new focus has influenced American undergraduate education in this half-century, in 2000 ACE initiated a study of the question. Study results, titled *Mapping Internationalization on U.S. Campuses: Final Report 2003*, included good and bad news. "Higher education has made some progress in internationalizing the undergraduate experience in the past 15 years," the report stated, "but there is still much work to do."[1]

Agreed, said former Ford Foundation program officer Sheila Biddle in her book *Internationalization: Rhetoric or Reality*. "'Internationalization' became a buzzword in academic circles," wrote Biddle, and "the rhetoric surrounding it ubiquitous."[2] An earlier ACE report, *Public Experience, Attitudes and Knowledge: A Report on Two National Surveys About International Education*, written by Fred M. Hayward and Laura M. Siaya, had found that "Although college and university presidents express stronger commitments to international education than they did a decade ago, that commitment does not seem to translate into an action agenda on campus."[3] Representative of the "weaknesses in internationalization" reported in *Mapping Internationalization* was the finding that "While the number of participants had increased, only a small portion of undergraduates participated in academic programs abroad."[4] The 2003 report recommended that leaders in

American higher education "bridge the gap between attitudes and actions"[5]—that they effect real change to match the calls for increased global understanding and international awareness so often voiced in the discourse of higher education.

Discourse, commitment, and action on the internationalization front must be seen within a social and historical context.[6] An ACE report titled *Beyond September 11: A Comprehensive U.S. National Policy on International Education* stated, "The tragic events of September 11, 2001, crystallized in a single, terrible moment the challenges of globalization and the importance of international research and education to our national security."[7] The ACE survey confirmed that after 9/11, Americans saw the importance of international issues in their lives, parents saw the importance of international education for their children, and almost one-half of college-bound students anticipated studying abroad during their college years.[8]

In this charged political climate, calls to increase support for study abroad ring through the halls of America's higher education community. Students are choosing to study in sites that have not traditionally hosted many American undergraduates, such as New Zealand, South Africa, Cuba, Kenya, Korea, Hong Kong, Morocco, and Vietnam.[9] Study abroad scholarship programs are receiving more applications.[10] The U.S. Congress has proposed increasing expenditures on international education and foreign exchange programs.[11]

All short-term indicators suggest a rise in student interest. But despite the manifestation of public support and student interest, in fact enrollments in study abroad, along with participation in other internationalization efforts, have barely increased over the past decades. While "the majority of students and faculty expressed support for international activities," declared the *Mapping Internationalization* report summary, they "failed to participate in these activities."[12] Again, despite the rhetoric, actions have spoken otherwise.

Repeatedly, policy goals for enrollment and funding have not been met. By some calculations a proportion as small as 1 percent of students in U.S. colleges and universities include a study abroad experience in their undergraduate education.[13] Less than 1 percent of discretionary expenditures for higher education in the combined budgets of the U.S. Departments of Education, State, and Defense goes toward international education and foreign exchange.[14] In *Beyond September 11,* the American Council on Education joined with thirty-three other higher education organizations to emphasize the urgent need to strengthen and to grow enrollment in foreign study programs. "The United States must invest in an educational infra-structure that produces knowledge of languages and cultures," said ACE President David Ward. "Creating true international capacity requires both educational reform and sustained financing."[15] Despite evidence of grow-ing interest and enthusiasm within the international education community itself, study abroad remains at the margins of American post-secondary education. Commenting on foreign study enrollment growth reported in 2004, Alan Goodman, president of the Institute of International Education, observed, "These increasing numbers show that American students are continuing to reach out to the rest of the world . . . However, those who do so are still a very small proportion of all U.S. students."[16]

At the same time, educators hear ever more warnings that "the level of international knowledge and understanding" among Americans is "wanting in comparison with others"[17] and that "as a nation we suffer from a pervasive lack of knowledge about the world."[18] When the National Geographic Soci-ety conducted its National Geographic-Roper 2002 Global Geographic Liter-acy Survey, American students scored next to last, second only to teenagers from Mexico. Of college-age Americans surveyed, 87 percent couldn't locate Iraq on a map of the world, 70 percent couldn't locate New Jersey, 29 percent couldn't find the Pacific Ocean, and 11 percent couldn't even point to the United States.[19] In 2003, a strategic task force on education abroad organized by NAFSA: The Association of International Educators observed in their pub-lication, *Securing America's Future: Global Education for a Global Age, Report of The Strategic Task Force on Education Abroad*, "As a nation we suffer from a pervasive lack of knowledge about the world. There have been periods, indeed entire eras, in our history when Americans have relished their isolation from the world. Some have made speaking only English a point of national pride instead of a disgrace."[20]

In the aftermath of September 11, Vic Johnson, associate executive director for public policy at NAFSA, insisted that "international education is a national security issue," since "the globalization of terror has propelled those of us who promote the globalization of education ineluctably into the policy arena."[21] Calls for international education have been bipartisan, reported Carl A. Herrin, then director of government relations for the Amer-ican Councils for International Education and chair of the Strategic Task Force on Education Abroad.[22] The NAFSA report records former U.S. Secre-tary of Education Richard W. Riley's endorsement of international exchange,[23] and President George W. Bush's sentiment that "America's lead-ership and national security rest on our commitment to educate and prepare our youth for active engagement in the international community."[24]

The American Council on Education survey showed that students and faculty not only continued to express support for international education but in some cases felt that 9/11 made them even more likely to support it.[25] But even as a seeming crescendo of voices builds, uttering the need to "internationalize the campus" and "globalize the curriculum," and even as students, too, express support, study abroad programs still fail to attract a significant percentage of undergraduate students in the United States. As the authors of "One Year Later" note, "Support in the abstract does not necessarily translate into personal action."[26]

What is going on, and why?

THE CURRENT STATE OF STUDY ABROAD

International education leaders have long committed themselves to increasing the number of Americans studying abroad, with policy statements calling for growth beginning in 1960 with the National Conference on Study Abroad Programs.[27] Their calls echoed through to the close of the century. "By the year 2000 ten percent of American college and university students should have a significant educational experience abroad during their undergraduate years," read the 1990 *National Mandate for Education Abroad: Getting on with the Task, Report of the National Task Force on Undergraduate Education Abroad.*[28] In 1998 a further goal was stated, posing the challenge of reaching a level of 20 to 25 percent of undergraduates in study abroad by 2008.[29] In 2000 Richard Riley called for a doubling of the study abroad population by 2010.[30] White papers jointly issued by NAFSA and the Alliance for International Educational and Cultural Exchange in 2000 and 2003 set the goals of 20 percent of American college graduates studying abroad by 2010 and 50 percent by 2040.[31] The late Senator Paul Simon, a member of the 2003 NAFSA education abroad task force, called for the creation of a "Lincoln Fellowship," funded at the level of one-seventh of 1 percent of the federal budget. At that rate, such a program at the end of ten years would ensure half a million American college students some education overseas.[32] Despite all these ambitions, few U.S. students study abroad.

Advocates for study abroad reported remarkable increases in student involvement during the turn-of-the-century decade. Figures from the Institute of International Education's *Open Doors* indicated that between 1991 and 2001–02 (the most recent year for which figures are available), the number of students studying abroad more than doubled, from 71,154 to 160,920, an increase of 126 percent.[33] Such increases are positive signs, but to be more realistic, the numbers must be seen within the larger context of total undergraduate enrollments throughout the United States.

The 2002 *Digest of Education Statistics,* published online by the National Center for Education Statistics (NCES)—the most current comprehensive source for statistics about U.S. higher education enrollments— states that during the academic year 2000–01, 15,312,289 students enrolled in two-year and four-year, public and private, degree-granting institutions throughout the United States.[34] Of that total, 9,009,600 attended school full-time, while 6,302,689 attended part-time.[35] In that same academic year, 154,168 Americans studied abroad.[36] These statistics show that 1.01 percent of all U.S. students, part-time and full-time, participated in study abroad, while 1.71 percent of all full-time U.S. students at two- and four-year institutions studied abroad.

By distinguishing between students attending two- and four-year higher education institutions full-time, the statistics can be further refined. In 2000–01, of the 9,009,600 students attending full-time, 6,792,557 attended four-year institutions.[37] So if the calculation is restricted to only full-time students enrolled in four-year institutions, those engaged in study abroad still represent only 2.27 percent of the entire U.S. higher education student population.

Two additional distinctions can be made. Of all full-time students at four-year institutions, 5,705,882 are undergraduates.[38] With the calculation restricted to this population segment only, the proportion of students choosing to study abroad still amounts to 2.71 percent. The most favorable measure is to calculate the total number of students abroad against one year of an undergraduate class. Using this tactic, one gets the highest percentage reported, as high as 12.44 percent.[39] Not all students go abroad during the same year, however, and this number is an inaccurate reflection of real growth in participation. In short, the record still shows that fewer than 3 percent of all American students chose to study abroad in the academic year 2000–01.

Foreign nations send far more students to the United States than the U.S. sends abroad. In 2000–01, for example, foreign students in the United States outnumbered Americans studying abroad by more than three to one.[40] Trends revealed by IIE's *Open Doors* annual surveys clearly delineate the demographic differences between foreign students who come to the United States and Americans who go abroad to study. Throughout the entire fifty years of IIE record keeping, reported on the CD-ROM *50 Years of Open Doors,* male students have outnumbered female students in the population of international students coming to the United States by as many as four to one in the 1950s and roughly three to one on average over the fifty years since. The proportion of graduate to undergraduate students stayed roughly equivalent through the five decades, with graduate students nearly always representing a good 40 percent or more of the total foreign student population.[41] Foreign nationals, especially those on the graduate level, have come to the United States primarily to study scientific and technical subjects, as shown by the IIE statistics.[42] Over the past fifty years, the typical foreigner coming to study in the United States has been a male undergraduate or graduate student studying science, technology, or business, a pattern sustained in 2000–01.[43]

The population of American college students going abroad contrasts significantly with that of foreign students coming to the United States.[44] In a 1997–98 historical review, IIE's *Open Doors* cited that male students represented one-third of the study abroad population in that academic year, "the inverse of that of the foreign students in the United States," and that "the male-to-female ratio among U.S. students studying abroad has remained stable since the 1980s."[45] No more than 10 percent of Americans studying abroad have enrolled in graduate-level studies, that proportion falling as low as 5.7 percent in 1988–89.[46] The primary fields of study chosen by Americans abroad have remained the social sciences and humanities, preferred consistently at a rate of about three to one over the technical fields throughout the years reported.[47]

In short, the general demographic picture of Americans choosing to study abroad proves to be the converse of that of foreign students coming to the United States. The typical American studying abroad is a female undergraduate majoring in the humanities or social sciences, as borne out in 2000–01, the year of our comparative statistics, when 90 percent of all U.S. study abroad students were undergraduates,[48] 65 percent of them were female,[49] 63 percent chose Europe as their study travel destination,[50] and only 33 percent majored in business, the physical and health sciences, engineering, math, computer sciences, or agriculture.[51] This demographic profile has persisted in the twenty-first century. According to *Open Doors 2003*, "Despite the growing diversity in destinations and majors, the profile of U.S. students abroad remains largely unchanged,"[52] with almost two-thirds of participants continuing to be female, the great majority of students studying at the undergraduate level, the leading destination Western Europe, and the largest number of registrants still studying the social sciences and humanities.[53] All these patterns have shaped the definition of study abroad and contributed to its valuation in the United States.

U.S. international education literature rarely defines "study abroad." Dr. William Hoffa, preparing material for publication about the history of U.S. study abroad, stated the following:

> My working definition of "U.S. study abroad" is that it is *"a program-matic educational activity taking place outside of the United States, often as a group activity, organized either by a U.S. college or university campus, or an overseas campus or agency, which results in the award of academic credit toward the American student participant's U.S. college or university degree"* [Hoffa's italics]. This working definition distinguishes it from all earlier (and many current) traditions of living and learning in a country foreign to the visiting learner. These other forms are, generally speaking, either educational ventures undertaken "abroad" for a variety of individual reasons unrelated to undergraduate degree studies, or involve overseas enrollment for full academic degrees offered by institutions foreign to the sojourner.[54]

It is also possible to extrapolate a working definition from the practices of organizations sponsoring study abroad for American students, and this *de facto* definition stands at the center of most American academics' opinions about study abroad.

The Council on International Educational Exchange (CIEE) is a non-profit, non-governmental organization, known as a world leader in operating undergraduate study abroad programs that are open to every eligible student in the United States. In its literature, CIEE states that its programs "provide credit-bearing semester, academic year, summer, and January-term study abroad programs in a variety of disciplines."[55] Similarly the Institute of International Education (IIE), a non-profit organization with over 800 college and university members in the U.S. and abroad,[56] states in its study abroad guidebook for U.S. undergraduates that "Many programs offer academic credit that may be used in partial fulfillment of requirements for an academic degree. It is usually not possible to complete all course requirements for an academic degree in the period of time covered by [these] programs . . . nor is that their purpose."[57] These descriptions establish some of the necessary conditions for an educational experience to be considered "study abroad" in the American academic tradition: Undergraduate study abroad involves domicile in a foreign country, rarely exceeding a year and always for a shorter term of enrollment than that in the home institution. It results in completion of a portion of the accredited coursework required by the U.S. home institution for the baccalaureate degree.

Until the 1960s, most American students spent the entire junior year overseas, but "the pronounced trend has been away from yearlong programs and toward programs of a semester or less with much coursework taken outside major fields."[58] While the duration of stay has declined substantially, the "junior year abroad" label remains, even for shorter programs. Most students enroll in a study abroad program during the third, and sometimes the fourth, of their four undergraduate years.

In many cases, students enroll in programs designed by U.S. institutions or agencies in concert with foreign host institutions, resulting in a combination of learning experiences, some indigenous and some designed for visitors. Some American students enroll in "island programs" run solely by an American sponsoring institution without any cooperative arrangement with a foreign institution. And some U.S. students independently register for courses at foreign institutions, in which case U.S. institutions scrutinize their offerings and requirements carefully to assure that they fulfill stateside academic expectations. American academics expect foreign study, whether pursued for one week, one month, or one full academic year, to dovetail smoothly with students' programs of study at home. Supporting faculty oversee the choices made, so they can assure the student returning to the United States full academic credit toward the baccalaureate degree.[59]

Through this half-century evolution of study abroad, voices within the U.S. international education community have called attention to its marginal role. They have called to increase program enrollments and to build greater respect for the contribution study abroad can make toward American educational goals. Statistics that represent change over those five decades tell the tale. While the slowly increasing numbers of students going abroad to study may provide reason for optimism, the statistics demonstrate that the nation's goals for internationalizing the curriculum and globalizing education have simply not been met. The question remains: Why not?

COMING TO RECOGNIZE THE PROBLEMS

My interest in understanding why study abroad is not a mainstream activity in the United States, a nation long established as a global power, emerged from my professional work, through which I became an advocate of study abroad. I also became an admirer of the academic commitment of the faculty and students who pursued study abroad and of my overseas colleagues who provided it, and a somewhat surprised observer of the wide disdain in which study abroad programs, sponsors, and participants seem held among members of the American higher education establishment.

From 1972 to 1987, I taught at a major public research university, where I established a study abroad office and administered its advising system. The undergraduates I counseled who wished to study abroad were excellent students, and their supporters were among leading university faculty. The programs the students entered were excellent as well: sound academic courses of study offering great potential for academic and professional growth. During those years my institution was rising to its reputation as a top public university in the country, and I assumed that others in my community shared my sense of the high quality of students choosing study abroad and the excellence of the programs in which they were enrolling.

However, I began to notice that some of my own university colleagues had doubts about study abroad. Some seemed unsure that study abroad represented an academically rigorous education. They doubted that the study abroad experience could contribute to professional development. They seemed to believe that our home campus curriculum provided a much better education than anything a student could get abroad. I was shocked. Even recently, that very sentiment was expressed to me by one of my former colleagues, despite almost one quarter-century of successful academic study abroad pursuits at that person's home institution.

My colleagues, I soon discovered, were not alone in their attitudes. In 1988–89 I participated in the Coalition for the Advancement of Foreign Languages and International Studies (CAFLIS), a federally funded national committee dedicated to expanding the role of international education in all its components at all levels of American education. Established in 1987 as a two-year project, CAFLIS drew together representatives from 165 member organizations, from businesses, state and local governments, and language and exchange groups, to examine international education "and its relation to our nation's ability to cooperate and to compete with the rest of the world in this and the next century," in the words of Frances Haley, chair of the CAFLIS Working Group on State and Local Initiatives.[60] CAFLIS recognized that study abroad was being treated as a peripheral activity in U.S. education, and I appreciated the opportunity to join a group promoting growth in all forms of international education.

Throughout the CAFLIS committee meetings, I heard not only distress at the low level of participation of U.S. college students in international exchange, but repeated evidence as well of negative and contradictory views toward study abroad from the higher education community. Study abroad, many implied, is or should be for the academic or institutional elite, yet U.S. study abroad was described as an academically weak activity pursued by women interested in leisurely cultural acquisition at best and a great shopping trip at worst. Many participants appeared to believe that international education was frivolous, unmonitored, and lacking in academic rigor and purpose. I heard the statement that study abroad programs should *do* something to train students to function professionally and competitively in the modern world, thus implying that they were not already. Even leading members of the international education community who served on the committee spoke in a highly critical way about study abroad and its place and value within the American educational system. Faculty, committee members said, should develop more serious academic goals for their students. Study abroad, they insisted, needed to change in order to make a *functional* contribution to students' education, rather than simply offer a cultural experience.

In my years subsequent to leaving the university, during which time I worked with U.S. institutions of higher education across the country, I continued to hear such statements expressed, sometimes even from foreign language faculty members. Academic colleagues sometimes seemed to assume that when students went abroad to study, they were going on vacation and would experience little significant academic or professional development while away. Those same colleagues believed that faculty members who supported study abroad by participating in overseas programs did so at the risk of promotion or tenure, choosing vacation experiences over serious academic work.

Study abroad, many seemed to believe, was still the old Grand Tour experience, a leisurely trip for the purpose of absorbing culture, enjoyed by the wealthiest of students, primarily women. Some departments refused (and, for that matter, still do) to accept credit from a study abroad experience toward a student's major. The implicit message was that a serious, bonafide education was available only in the United States. That attitude marginalized those within the U.S. higher education community who chose to participate in or support study abroad.

These realizations continued to shock me. The opinions I heard did not match the evidence I had before me of strong students engaged in challenging and valuable academic and professional work abroad. I wondered if I had misjudged the quality of study abroad, at least as it had been practiced in the past. And I began to question more generally how the American higher education community viewed study abroad and, further, how those views corresponded with the experiences themselves, articulated by the students and sponsors committed to study abroad. I wondered to what extent these opinions dominated how study abroad was understood and if they helped explain why so few students were going overseas.

My investigation began first, then, by taking note of my colleagues' expressions of belief and next by observing organizational efforts to develop policy effective in encouraging interest in international education. Policy statements—official consensus documents describing study abroad and articulating goals for its improvement and growth within the U.S.

academy—abound from the last decades of the twentieth century, and it occurred to me that this policy discourse might also provide a rich field of study. This collection of texts conveys both historical descriptions and prevailing attitudes about study abroad. A study of these documents might help uncover beliefs about study abroad and help explain why study abroad has not become a central part of American higher education.

POLICY DISCOURSE AND BELIEFS ABOUT STUDY ABROAD

Contemporary policy discourse about study abroad in U.S. higher education began with Stephen Freeman's October 1960 report summarizing the goals of the National Conference on Study Abroad Programs, held that month in Chicago.[61] Freeman's report was the first in nearly half a century of efforts and policy formulations in American education designed to promote international education generally and, in some cases, study abroad specifically. In 1971, the National Association of Foreign Student Affairs upgraded its committee on study abroad, first formed in 1963, and established SECUSSA, the Section on U.S. Students Abroad.[62] In 1978, President Jimmy Carter formed the President's Commission on Language and International Studies, which published the report, *Strength Through Wisdom: A Critique of U.S. Capability.*[63]

The 1980s saw an upsurge in research and policy developments. In 1983, the National Commission on Excellence in Education, convened by the U.S. Department of Education, submitted its Report to the Nation and the Secretary of Education, titled *A Nation at Risk: The Imperative for Educational Reform,*[64] one of a number of mid-1980s reports and publications from government agencies and educational organizations, including Richard D. Lambert's *Points of Leverage: An Agenda for a National Foundation for International Studies* and, five years later, his *International Studies and the Undergraduate,* published by the American Council on Education.[65] In 1988, Craufurd Goodwin and Michael Nacht published *Abroad and Beyond: Patterns in American Overseas Education,* sponsored by the Institute of International Education.[66] In 1989 the Higher Education Panel of the American Council on Education published a policy statement titled *What We Can't Say Can Hurt Us: A Call for Foreign Language Competence by the Year 2000,*[67] the Task Force on International Education from the National Governors' Association published *America in Transition: The International Frontier,*[68] and the Coalition for the Advancement of Foreign Language and International Studies published a report and recommendations from its Working Groups.[69] The 1980s ended and the 1990s began with two policy reports about study abroad: *Educating for Global*

Competence (1988)[70] and *A National Mandate for Education Abroad* (1990), previously cited.

"Globalization" became the watchword of the 1990s. Policy reports included *Exchange 2000: International Leadership for the Next Century,*[71] Barbara Burn's *The Contribution of International Exchange to the International Education of Americans: Projections for the Year 2000,*[72] and the American Council on Education's *Educating Americans for a World in Flux: Ten Ground Rules for Internationalizing Higher Education.*[73] *International Education in the New Global Era,* published in 1998, reported the proceedings of a national policy conference.[74]

Reports on the future and significance of international education continued to dominate the discussions of the twenty-first century.[75] Thanks to efforts on the part of NAFSA and the Alliance for International Education and Cultural Exchange, bipartisan resolutions supporting international exchange were introduced in the 107th Congress and passed by the United States Senate.[76] The American Council on Education published *Beyond September 11,*[77] and in 2002 NAFSA created its Strategic Task Force on Education Abroad, with representatives from across the American higher education community, to "spearhead a comprehensive national initiative to expand U.S. student participation in education abroad."[78] In January 2003, Duke University hosted a conference titled "Global Challenges & U.S. Higher Education" to "evaluate the current and future national needs for international and foreign language competence," stimulated by the pending reauthorization of the Higher Education Act.[79] In October 2003, ACE published its report, *Mapping Internationalization on U.S. Campuses,* previously cited, which clearly reflected how far colleges and universities are from reaching the goals of internationalization that they have so long stated.

In short, for more than four decades, scores of statements, speeches, articles, books, proceedings, and reports have appeared nationally, all addressing the status, significance, and future of U.S. study abroad. These publications reflect growing interest in international education and a prospect for expanding study abroad beyond traditional boundaries. They call for internationalization in multiple realms of higher education, mentioning faculty exchange, research collaboration, inbound student populations, and curricular globalization. These publications analyze the status of international education generally, or study abroad specifically, with the goal of making recommendations about its future development. They have been commissioned by either federal or state governmental agencies and/or by higher education or international education agencies with membership from across the entire American higher education community. For the purposes of this book, they will be considered "policy statements," their authors will be considered "policy makers," and the dialogue within them will be seen to represent policy discourse. Together these policy statements address, either directly or indirectly, the role and value of undergraduate study abroad within the larger effort to internationalize U.S. higher education. They represent a wealth of material manifesting discourse on the subject of U.S. study abroad.

Out of this nearly half-century of discourse, three examples stand out most clearly as crystallizing all the prevailing ideas expressed about study abroad. These are the period's three comprehensive policy statements devoted solely to the topic of study abroad: *Educating for Global Competence* (1988), *A National Mandate for Education Abroad* (1990), and the newest policy statement, *Securing America's Future: Global Education for a Global Age, Report of The Strategic Task Force on Education Abroad* (2003), emerging from the aforementioned 2002 NAFSA Strategic Task Force. These three texts represent a body of discourse which, when analyzed in detail, can reveal beliefs about study abroad—beliefs that may underlie some of the dreams but may also reveal some of the obstacles to progress in U.S. higher education.

The first, *Educating for Global Competence: The Report of the Advisory Council for International Educational Exchange,* was published in 1988 by the Council on International Educational Exchange (CIEE), whose membership includes educational leaders and policy makers in international education. Any report from CIEE is both reflective and formative, representing the predominant beliefs of leaders in U.S. study abroad programming and wielding influence in the academic community.

This report's primary calls for development were predicated on the need, so it stated, to "counter the serious flaws in the preparation of American education for an interdependent world."[80] The report recommended:

1. The number of college students who study abroad should be increased to at least 10 percent of enrollment by 1995, with a schedule set for a further increase into the next century.
2. Special efforts should be made to identify and encourage both students from under-represented academic and social groups and students with potential leadership ability, to incorporate study abroad in their academic programs, and to do so in a greater range of subject areas.
3. Study abroad in developing countries and those outside the traditional Anglo-European settings should be a matter of high priority,

with special attention to creating educational exchange programs in the Western Pacific Rim, as well as in the rest of Asia, the Middle East, Africa, Latin America and Eastern Europe.

4. Responsibility for implementing increased internationalization should be vested at the highest institutional level.[81]

Similar objectives were expressed in *A National Mandate for Education Abroad: Getting on with the Task,* the 1990 report of the National Task Force on Undergraduate Education Abroad, published by the National Association for Foreign Student Affairs (now called NAFSA: Association of International Educators). NAFSA draws members from every U.S. state and eighty-four nations, primarily administrators and supporters of foreign study programs.[82] Thus the NAFSA membership also represents leaders and policy makers within the field of study abroad, and a NAFSA report, like a CIEE report, both reflects and forms opinion in the field.

The 1990 *National Mandate* proposed five major recommendations designed to "greatly enhance the contribution of overseas study abroad programs to the internationalization of the higher education experience of undergraduates."[83] The report summarized its recommendations:

> *Expansion of Education Abroad.* By the year 2000, ten percent of American college and university students should have a significant educational experience abroad during their undergraduate years. Achieving this will require substantial growth in the number and type of opportunities provided and a more pervasive integration of education abroad into institutional strategies aimed at strengthening the international dimension in U.S. higher education.
>
> *Increased Diversity.* As number and opportunities are expanded we urge that greater diversity be a major goal for all aspects of education abroad: greater diversity in participating students, in foreign locations, and in types of programs.
>
> *Curricular Connections.* The study abroad experience must be integrated into regular degree programs in many different fields including professional schools. In some fields, study abroad should become a requirement, for example, for future foreign language teachers in elementary and secondary schools.
>
> *Major Inhibitors.* A variety of factors inhibit expansion of numbers and diversity in undergraduate education abroad. Some are historical; others are tied to negative perceptions. We urge that all be vigorously addressed. They include:

- Insufficient institutional commitment to international education.

- Negative views of some faculty members.

- Restrictive curricular requirements.

- Foreign language deficiencies.

- Inadequate study abroad support services on campuses and abroad.

- Inadequate information about education abroad opportunities and their relative quality.

- Financial regulations and shortfalls.

Financial Options. While lack of money is not always the main obstacle to program development or student participation, expanded funding from both private and public sources will be essential if the academic community is to diversify the types of institutions, students, and experiences involved in study abroad in the years ahead.[84]

The third policy statement arises out of NAFSA's twenty-first-century Strategic Task Force on Education Abroad. Beginning to meet in 2003, its charge was to look "strategically and holistically at the subject of U.S. student participation in education abroad programs and articulate a coherent strategy for increasing such participation."[85]

The task force was charged to:

1. Articulate the importance of education abroad programs, both in terms of the benefits to students and the U.S. national interest, for the American public as well as institutional and governmental policy makers;

2. Define and prioritize the major barriers that inhibit the participation of U.S. post-secondary students in education abroad programs, e.g. financial constraints, curricular limitations, insufficient proficiency in foreign languages, lack of awareness about opportunities, and failure of institutions to encourage students;

3. Identify issues that need further analysis, data collection, or research;

4. Develop a coherent, comprehensive set of concrete recommendations, which would result in substantially increased participation in education abroad programs, including short- and long-term study abroad, reciprocal exchanges, internships abroad, discovery-based learning activities, etc.; and

5. Identify critical sectors, organizations, and groups that need to be
    involved in the proposed national initiative to expand participa-
    tion in education abroad (e.g., the federal government, state and
    local governments, the business community, foundations, higher
    education institutions, schools, parents, etc.) and develop a plan
    to involve them.

Further, the task force was asked to remain faithful to "SECUSSA's longstanding commitment to 1) enhancing diversity within study abroad participants, 2) expanding educational abroad programs beyond traditional
destinations in Western Europe, and 3) involving students from science,
applied science and other subjects not traditionally participating in education abroad programs."[86]

Responding to post-9/11 urgent concerns to increase international
awareness, the strategic task force identified these goals and in some ways
echoed the earlier CAFLIS report:

> The challenges of the new millennium are unquestionably global in
> nature. This reality imposes a new and urgent demand on Americans,
> one this country has been all too quick to ignore: international knowl-
> edge and skills are imperative for the future security and competitive-
> ness of the United States. The rhetoric of a decade attests to the
> widespread recognition of this fundamental truth, yet concrete steps to
> fulfill this need have been few. Strong leadership and a coherent policy
> are still lacking, and the cost of inaction grows ever greater.
>
> To address this serious deficit in global competence, the report of
> NAFSA's Strategic Task Force on Education Abroad proposes a national
> effort to promote study abroad. We strongly believe that the events of
> September 11, 2001, constituted a wake-up call—a warning that Amer-
> ica's ignorance of the world is now a national liability. Americans in vastly
> greater numbers must devote a substantive portion of their education to
> gaining an understanding of other countries, regions, languages, and cul-
> tures, through direct personal experience . . . Here is what must be done:
>
> • The president and Congress must articulate this urgent national
>   priority, provide a legislative framework and resources appro-
>   priate to the urgency of the problem, and remove regulatory
>   barriers to study abroad.
>
> • Governors and state legislatures must make international educa-
>   tion an integral part of their strategic planning for enhancing
>   state economic development and competitiveness.

- College and university presidents must implement strategies to encourage study abroad on a school-wide basis. They must involve the faculty, ease curricular rigidities, counter financial disincentives, and create new study abroad models and diverse study abroad options that recognize the changed demographics of U.S. higher education today and make study abroad accessible to the broadest possible spectrum of students.

- The private sector must do more to encourage and assist schools in producing the globally competent workforce it requires.

- Professional licensing and accrediting agencies must build global competence into the curricular standards that they set for professional schools.

It is the hope of the task force that this report will stimulate a long-overdue dialogue among these parties and lead to a national effort to ensure that far greater numbers of American students pursue part of their higher education abroad.[87]

Indeed, stated the authors, the mission of the task force was to establish these recommendations in order to implement the calls made in the 2000 and 2003 white papers from NAFSA and the Alliance for International Educational and Cultural Exchange, which proposed a new international education policy that would:

- Set an objective that 20 percent of American students receiving college degrees will have studied abroad for credit by 2010, and 50 percent by 2040.

- Promote ethnic, socioeconomic, and gender diversity in study abroad.

- Promote the diversification of the study abroad experience, including: increased study in nontraditional locations outside the United Kingdom and the rest of Western Europe; increased study of major world languages—such as Arabic, Chinese, Japanese, Portuguese, and Russian—that are less commonly learned by Americans; and increased study abroad in underrepresented subjects such as mathematical and physical sciences and business.

- Promote the integration of study abroad into the higher education curriculum, and increase opportunities for international internships and service learning.[88]

Task force members concluded by pledging to go beyond simply a call to action, considering it a road map for making policy a reality.[89]

These three study abroad policy statements show how certain ideas recur and govern the discussions about U.S. study abroad. All three iterations call for increased numbers and increased diversity in the student body going abroad and increased diversity in the locations to which they go. Many urge more professionally focused programs; some argue for increased academic rigor in study abroad programs; and all clamor for increased financial aid.

Certain recurrent ideas arise from this wealth of discourse about study abroad, if one reads in their calls for change implied attitudes about the status quo. They imply that existing study abroad programs do not provide coursework applicable to a professional education. Calling for higher academic standards, they sometimes imply that study abroad does not already demand academic rigor. Even the call for financial aid, which can be taken as a healthy request for more program funding in general, also implies that currently, primarily wealthy students study abroad, an observation sometimes specifically made.[90] In short, these policy documents, representing a consensus of the membership of the American international education community and echoing many more policy statements from over the years, manifest a cluster of common assumptions about study abroad.

To be blunt, international education policy discourse often reflects a perception that study abroad programs attract wealthy white women to academically weak European programs. It assumes programs to be defined by the liberal arts tradition and questions their capability to prepare students for work and the professions. Policy discourse calls for initiatives to diversify the population of U.S. students abroad, not only to increase the participation of students from racial and ethnic minority groups but also to diversify the gender of students abroad. Since Americans studying abroad are now and have perennially been in the majority women, the call to diversify gender can be translated into a call for more male study abroad participants.

An underlying, yet unspoken, assumption accompanies many of these recommendations: if study abroad were redesigned by expanding the fields of study available abroad, broadening study abroad to include professional training, and increasing financial support, it would enjoy an improvement in the quality of programs and thereby might attract more male students. Like the comments of my own colleagues and the attitudes I heard expressed in a policy formulation group, the assumptions invested in this discourse reflect a commitment to study abroad growth but at the same time cast serious doubt on its current worth and function. I realized that I, too, had come to assume that prior to my experience, study abroad must have been an academically weak activity for the wealthy.

To examine these assumptions, I embarked on a more thorough analysis of discourse about study abroad, believing that it could illuminate how this educational endeavor is perceived and valued within the American academic community and among those who have endowed its definition with these derogatory attitudes. Such an analysis can also provide an interesting vantage point from which to consider the voices of students and their faculty sponsors, such as those I have come to know in my professional life, whose experiences and attitudes seem to contradict the skepticism. This counterpoint in discourse might, in turn, offer some suggestions as to why study abroad has grown slowly and what might be needed to encourage growth more effectively.

This book represents the results of that analysis. Using the method of discourse analysis, it investigates perceptions and attitudes found in discourse within the academy, asking what definition of study abroad faculty and students hold, whether that definition devalues foreign education, and how that definition contributes to the marginalization of study abroad as part of American higher education.

THE PRACTICE OF DISCOURSE ANALYSIS

Discourse analysis examines how things are understood and how they come to be valued. Discourse, or rhetorical, analysis studies not events or things themselves so much as the discussion about them—how events or things come to be perceived, understood, and valued. Discourse analysis is done not to document the historical evolution of events but to glean how those events were perceived and how, in turn, those perceptions have made an impact on the events themselves.

Rhetorical analysis has a long history. From Plato and Aristotle onward, it has been central to Western pedagogy.[91] In the Platonic tradition, discourse reveals truth, so that rhetorical analysis becomes the search for and exposure of the truth revealed through discourse. In the Aristotelian tradition, though, discourse is the art of persuasion, performed as a speaker addresses an audience and accomplished by establishing *ethos* (the credibility of the speaker), *pathos* (an emotional appeal about the issue that resonates with the audience), and *logos* (a logical argument). All strands of discourse—ethos, pathos, and logos—must resonate with the audience in order for a discourse to make sense and to be persuasive.

In modern times, the concept of discourse has broadened in scope to include text, dialogue, action, events, and symbols, as well as formal public speaking. While the traditional definition of "rhetoric" as "the art of using language so as to persuade or influence others" still holds,[92] the word "rhetoric" has come to encompass both language and action, involving not only the interaction of speaker and audience but also the interaction of public discourse, actual and symbolic, with values in broad social contexts.[93]

Modern rhetoricians like Kenneth Burke, Wayne Booth, and the French theorists use the analysis of discourse to explore how social values emerge in society. These theories focus not on "the art of persuasion" but on constructions of reality. Some, like Benjamin Whorf, argue that language, thought, and perception are interrelated, and that their interactions define for each of us what we understand as reality.[94] Others include the interactions of language, perception, and culture as part of the process that not only individuals but also groups and societies undergo as they construct their shared sense of reality.[95] This contemporary concept of discourse and its study in all its forms and functions plays a central role in the work of the French theorist Michel Foucault. Foucault's theories encompass language, culture, events, and action in the creation of reality and explore how this reality affects the constituent members of the society who created it.

Much of Foucault's work hinges on an overriding theory that discourse has the power to generate beliefs about people, things, events, and activities of common concern to the community.[96] These dominant beliefs, as they are called in this book, describe that "group of statements" belonging to the same discursive formation. These beliefs are statements for which "conditions of existence" can be defined.[97] They are bound historically, and it is possible to explore the conditions that produced them and empowered them all to be believed as descriptions of reality. Shared within a social group, these beliefs can interact to form an "episteme"—a powerful and overarching definition that controls perceptions about events, institutions, and individuals. As Foucault says, when statements coalesce with a common theme and become a "dominant" vision, they cross the "threshold of epistemologization" and together form an episteme—a definition that gains acceptance as a powerful "truth."[98]

According to Foucault, the episteme is a conception developed through community discourse which "provides man's everyday perception with theoretical powers, and defines the conditions in which he can sustain a discourse about things . . . recognized to be true."[99] An episteme forms the "fundamental code" of a community, framing that community's reality.[100] Discourse forms rules of inclusion and exclusion—what is good or bad, right or wrong, accepted or ignored. [101] In a sense, Foucault's ideas here bridge the gap between contemporary and Platonic conceptions of rhetoric: Discourse does convey truth, but it is a socially constructed truth, unconsciously created by those who share it.

These concepts offer a methodology with which to analyze the discourse of the American academy, to evaluate whether the clichés and assumptions reflected in discourse about study abroad represent a set of dominant beliefs with the power to endow or withdraw validation.[102] Foucault's method of inquiry is to explore both the historical context in which specific discourses took shape and also the roots of power and marginalization in a community. For Foucault, historiography is not the stuff of fact. Instead, discourse itself is the object of study.[103] The purpose of inquiry is to expose the foundations of power endowed through discourse, a process Foucault labels "archaeology," by which the inquirer "brings to light" the foundations of a powerful episteme.[104] Archaeology is a "dig"—an investigation into the deeper meanings embedded in discourse, leading to a diagnosis of how a culture has established its own truths.[105]

Foucault's methodology also facilitates the exploration of the discourse of groups disenfranchised by prevailing belief—any discourse that describes an alternative vision. Foucault labels this exploration of invalidated discourses "genealogy."[106] Genealogy likewise "brings to light" ignored beliefs. In this case, it illuminates the discourses marginalized by the empowered and normalized beliefs. In other words, it raises the volume on alternative voices that have been excluded and hence unheard.[107]

Foucault draws attention to how beliefs are formed: whose voices are normalized and empowered as the dominant voices, and whose voices are excluded, unheard, and unrespected in an alternative discourse. In educational settings as well as in other settings, as he describes, validated discourses have been empowered and invalidated discourses disenfranchised.[108] For Foucault, analysis of this kind—identifying the foundations of empowered discourses and the existence of alternative voices—carries with it the potential to introduce new concepts into the discourse and, ultimately, to transform existing beliefs and attitudes.[109]

THE PURPOSE OF THIS STUDY

This book adapts Foucault's theories to an analysis of the discourse about study abroad in American higher education. It investigates the clichés emerging in academic discourse about study abroad, seeking to understand how they have informed widely and deeply held dominant beliefs about this weakly supported form of American education. It explores how a constellation of dominant beliefs has coalesced to form an episteme held by the U.S. higher education community: an episteme that defines study abroad as academically weak and without significant functional purpose, a prevailing definition that has marginalized study abroad in the U.S. academic community for decades.

To begin, this discourse analysis delineates the emergence of the clichés as they clustered into dominant negating beliefs about study abroad. By conducting a Foucault-like archaeological "dig" into the roots of these beliefs, the study will investigate the power they had and continue to have to define study abroad. Dominant discourse suggests that study abroad programs are perceived as attracting wealthy women to academically weak European programs established in a frivolous Grand Tour tradition. It suggests that these programs are defined by the liberal arts and suspect for their lack of rigorous and serious preparation for work and the professions. These beliefs have coalesced into the episteme, effectively disenfranchising advocates of study abroad. The coming chapters of this book consider each component belief: the Grand Tour tradition in chapter 2, the roles of women and wealth in chapter 3, and the liberal arts tradition and its academically weak stepchild, study abroad, in chapter 4.

Having laid out the dominant beliefs, next the book turns to consider alternative voices, conducting a genealogical "excavation" of the marginalized beliefs about study abroad. Chapter 5 considers the voices of faculty members who support study abroad both for its academic rigor and for the professional preparation it offers. Chapter 6 reveals the voices of students, including and especially the female students who compose the majority of all study abroad participants, as they articulate their academic and professional motives and their dedication to study abroad as a significant part of their undergraduate education, even when they are studying in difficult times and places.

Ultimately, this book explores how dominant beliefs have marginalized study abroad, on the one hand, and how alternative voices, although disregarded, have expressed its value. It is my hope that this book will offer a new sense of the interaction of dominant beliefs and alternative voices about U.S. study abroad from its origins after World War I to the present. Likewise, it is my hope that the book will help inform the discourse in the academy about the role of study abroad in U.S. higher education and will encourage a new way of hearing and responding to the many calls for study abroad to become a vital and central part of the American undergraduate experience.

Part Two
Dominant Beliefs

Chapter Two
Dominant Beliefs: Study Abroad Is a Grand Tour

Analysis of policy discourse suggests that underlying clichés characterize study abroad as a leisurely experience pursued by wealthy women who travel to Europe and enroll in academically weak programs in the liberal arts to acquire a general and genial familiarity with a foreign culture. This chapter will conduct an "archaeological dig" into the belief that study abroad is for general and genial purposes of cultural acquisition—or, in other words, that study abroad constitutes a "Grand Tour." This chapter will seek to uncover perceptions including: What do Americans mean by the "Grand Tour"? How has the term been associated with study abroad in the discourse of the academy? What are the roots of this association? And how has it developed as a dominant belief contributing to an episteme that study abroad is academically weak and without serious and professional purpose, thus helping to marginalize study abroad in American higher education?

AMERICAN CONCEPTIONS OF THE GRAND TOUR

In American educational discourse, study abroad has long been associated with the term "Grand Tour." The phrase was first used in 1648, in the writing of Richard Lassels, a Catholic priest and traveling tutor of the seventeenth century.[1] The English term derives from the French for "great circuit" and is defined as "a tour of the principal cities and places of Europe, formerly supposed to be necessary to complete the education of young men of position."[2]

The tradition of the Grand Tour as an essential ingredient of higher education arose within British upper-class culture during the first half of the eighteenth century. Defining characteristics of a Grand Tour were "a young British male patrician (member of the aristocracy or gentry), a tutor who accompanies his charge throughout the journey, a fixed itinerary that makes Rome its principal destination, and a lengthy period of absence (2–3 years)."[3] While the Grand Tour was considered an educational and cultural experience, it often included an element of leisure, even libertinism: "In actual practice, of course, many of these young men merely frittered away their time in the fleshpots of Europe, agreeably cultivating each other's company."[4] The Grand Tour was regarded as an essential part of a young man's coming of age, and each individual made of it what he might, some cultivating serious international understanding and others pursuing a simple pleasure jaunt.[5]

Americans quickly adopted the tradition of the Grand Tour as part of the educational imperative for up-and-coming young men. In 1815, George Ticknor of Boston confessed a lack of curiosity about travel in his own country but an urgent desire to travel in Europe. Like Ticknor, young American men traveled to Europe, particularly Britain, France, Germany, and Italy, as part of their culminating education.[6] Visions of Europe steeped the minds of emerging American literati. In the novels of Henry James, Europe became "not so much a real place as a very commodious signifier" of culture and romance.[7]

Many of these same characteristics come into play when the words "Grand Tour" are used among Americans today to describe a European travel experience for college-age youth. The term is used primarily as a derogatory description of international study, loosely connoting the travel experiences of the young and wealthy, intended to broaden their cultural horizons, but often suggesting leisurely, desultory, elitist, unintellectual, and unprofessional aims. These beliefs have been buffeted through political conflicts, as Americans' post–World War I valuation of European culture evolved into a post–World War II nationalistic suspicion of Eurocentrism.

Through all these years, many study abroad experiences may not have matched the prevailing definition of the Grand Tour, but that has not affected the growing power of this belief to define study abroad. As Foucault argues, in the discursive construction of belief, historical accuracy is irrelevant.[8] Some wealthy American students have studied abroad; some students have turned their study abroad enrollment into a leisurely, non-productive experience. It can and does happen in human culture, as Foucault has shown, that a set of particulars is generalized into a single notion about all related examples, despite contradictory particulars. When that happens, the resulting generalized idea emerges as belief and obscures the contradictory examples. Such a process has occurred in the evolution of the associations between the Grand Tour tradition and study abroad in the United States.

PERCEPTIONS OF STUDY ABROAD AS A GRAND TOUR

From the colonial era through World War II, when Americans studied abroad, they did so almost exclusively in Europe. "Europe beckons," wrote Asa Briggs and Barbara Burn in their book, *Study Abroad: A European and an American Perspective, Organization and Impact of Study Abroad,* "and it beckons to non-Europeans, particularly, perhaps, Americans."[9] In the one history of U.S. study abroad that has been written, *Educating American Undergraduates Abroad: The Development of Study Abroad Programs by American Colleges and Universities,* author John E. Bowman notes the cultural associations accruing to the European travel experiences undertaken by American youth. Early travelers included both earnest youth seeking professional training and wealthy young people sent abroad for general cultural edification, yet the image of the latter imprinted a defining character on all in the discourse.[10]

"The continental 'grand tour' with which young British gentry capped their formal education a century and more ago before entering public life can be seen as an early prototype of experiential learning abroad," noted Briggs and Burn.[11] In 1971 Herbert Maza, at that time with the Institute for American Universities, wrote a book chapter titled "Backlash in Education Abroad" in which he noted that many students, though presumed to be studying abroad, "are actually there on travel programs" and reaping only "superficial knowledge."[12] Craufurd D. Goodwin and Michael Nacht, in *Abroad and Beyond: Patterns in American Overseas Education,* granted the tendency to associate features of this historic precedent with modern study abroad by arguing against it: "A good deal of the skepticism of study abroad is based, we conclude, on a rather careless assumption that it is still simply the grand tour for the well-to-do . . . rather than a valuable, or even vital, feature of higher education. This belief explains symbolic rules in one state university prohibiting use of public funds for foreign travel, or even for transoceanic phone calls!"[13] Nevertheless, Goodwin and Nacht suggested, some students were attracted to study abroad chiefly because they and their families perceived it would provide a Grand Tour experience. While they no longer expressed this motive outright, the perception nonetheless remained, "lurking in the shadows, especially at the more expensive liberal arts colleges and private universities."[14]

Briggs and Burn recognized that the contemporary social context for study abroad was very different from that of the eighteenth century, but they still saw similarities between the Grand Tour two centuries ago and study abroad today. "As far as [this] motivation for mobility, the quest for experience, is concerned, it still guides the travel of tens of thousands of students—and teachers—from very different backgrounds within the highly organized educational complexes of the twentieth century as much as it guided the travel of scores of young gentlemen during the golden years of the Grand Tour," they wrote. "It is the economic, political, social and institutional context that has changed, not the motivation itself."[15]

Other modern discourse manifested continuing associations between study abroad and the undirected cultural exploration of the Grand Tour. Archer Brown, former deputy executive director of NAFSA, quoted a report written by two Thai students from the University of Minnesota, saying that "whereas the foreign student comes to the United States in fulfillment of a purpose, the United States student goes abroad in search of one."[16] In an oral history video interview with the late Lily Von Klemperer, a leader in study abroad development, Tom Roberts, then Butler College's international programs officer, labeled both pre– and post–World War II study programs as Grand Tour experiences.[17]

Some reports within the higher education community, including those calling for change, have criticized study abroad for being a Grand Tour experience. In 1991, prompted by faculty and administrators at Beloit College in Wisconsin, an ad hoc group of liberal arts schools formed the International 50, joined by a common commitment to international education as part of their curricula. In 1992, the group published a report, titled *In the International Interest,*[18] which commented that "Many of the early programs, both at International 50 colleges and elsewhere, were structured 'like finishing schools' focusing on the 'inculcation of cultural attitudes appropriate for a particular class and station.'"[19]

The CIEE 1988 report, *Educating for Global Competence: The Report of the Advisory Council for International Educational Exchange,* intimated less than serious motives for study abroad by saying that the American "Junior Year Abroad . . . focused on the European cultural heritage." While this traditional focus was applicable to liberal arts and humanities students, the CIEE report continued, "now global competence for our citizens requires us to expand study abroad into other areas."[20] When such a report must argue a move away from the dominant belief, then it manifests the existence and influence of that belief.

In his 1989 report for the American Council on Education, Richard Lambert recognized a common opinion that study abroad is frivolous travel, made for personal cultural experience rather than serious academic accomplishments, when he stated that limits were put on students' international experiences because "study abroad is seen as a diversionary frill, interrupting the flow of the real educational process that is presumed to take place on campus."[21] The popular press still echoes derogatory definitions of study abroad today. Setting the tone for the entire piece, an article in the February 7, 2003, *Wall Street Journal* began like this: "Ashly Hanna recently enjoyed a week in the French Alps, skiing by day and dancing in trendy nightclubs after dark. The best part: It's included in her semester abroad at Boston College. 'It felt like a five-star vacation,' says the 20-year-old junior."[22]

Although the article went on to say that "exotic locales like Cuba and Vietnam are joining the old European standbys," it emphasized that American colleges and universities are adding cultural entertainment features into their study abroad programs in order to attract more students. "Far from cutting back these days, a surprising number of colleges are taking study-abroad programs to a whole new level of high-end learning," wrote staff reporter Elizabeth Bernstein. The article included a chart showing six new examples of the "increasing number of colleges" that are "beefing up their overseas-study programs." The newspaper titled the chart "Grand Tour."[23] Similar implications about the entertainment and leisure quotient of current study abroad experiences arose in another *Wall Street Journal* article, appearing in the "Personal Journal" section and titled "Sex, Drugs and Junior Year Abroad: Doctors Work to Protect Travelers."[24]

In another report Ben Feinberg, a faculty member at Warren Wilson College, wrote an article for the *Chronicle of Higher Education's* "Point of View" column titled "What Students Don't Learn Abroad."[25] Criticizing the content of the study abroad experience, Feinberg reported that, rather than discussing the academic challenges of their experience and the insight it provided them, students returning from overseas often discussed their personal growth (sounding, Feinberg said, like heroes of a Nike commercial) or made comments reflecting that they had experienced no change in media-received definitions of overseas locations. He commented on one student:

> The responses from Peter, who had spent 10 weeks studying and working on service projects with a group in South Africa, Zimbabwe, and Lesotho, were representative. When asked what he had learned from his African experience, Peter used the first-person pronoun seven times, eliminating Africans: "I learned that I'm a risk taker, um, that I don't put up with people's bull, uh, what else? That I can do anything that I put my mind to. I can do anything I want. You know, it's just—life is what you make of it."
>
> Peter didn't mention that Zimbabweans live in an impoverished dictatorship where 25 percent of the population is HIV positive, and thus they cannot do anything they put their minds to—a lesson he evidently didn't learn. Instead, like so many other traveling young people, he

claimed to have learned about himself, and talked about group dynam-
ics; students' transgressive behavior, like drinking too much; and
bungee jumping at Victoria Falls—rather than southern Africa's cultures or social problems.

Suggesting that students do not report on the academic experience, Feinberg went on to say:

> Students like Peter talk about interactions with outsiders only in vague
> abstractions, while expostulating brilliantly about the nuances of Ameri-
> can students' interactions with one another. Even the few individuals who
> left their peers to engage the outside world explained that move as an
> individual rejection of the group and still found it easier to discuss their
> fellow students than the generically defined "friends" they met at bars.[26]

Reports like this reinforce the conception of study abroad pursued for less
than serious purposes.

Influential analyses and popular representations of study abroad continue to echo one another. Over and over, U.S. study abroad has been
described as a Grand Tour experience. Each such discursive event further
associates travel and cultural acquisition with leisure. Study abroad is portrayed as a personal experience designed not to gain purposeful knowledge
so much as to gain social standing and enjoy private pleasure.

Everyone in a community is formed in some way through that community's discourse. Even the opinions and perceptions of study abroad participants can be constrained by dominant beliefs and the resulting episteme.
This phenomenon was in evidence in the results of an alumni survey conducted among past participants of the United States's oldest ongoing study
abroad program, the Junior Year Abroad program operated by Sweet Briar
College. This program originated in 1922, when the University of Delaware
began sending students to Paris to study, and was transferred to Sweet Briar
after World War II. A wealth of research material is available from this venerated coeducational program.[27]

When women who had participated in Sweet Briar programs were
asked to identify (for the entire group, not for themselves individually) "the
primary reason for WOMEN participating in study abroad," 93.2 percent of
respondents chose "their cultural interests" first. Participants saw others, if
not themselves, to be pursuing cultural interests—an example of the power of
the belief to define the experience they imagined others to be having. (For a
summary of survey responses to this question, see Appendix, Table 2–1.)

Both men and women were asked, "Why do you think it has been
more frequently undergraduate women rather than men from the United

States who have studied abroad?" The largest proportion of both male and female respondents, with only a slightly higher percentage of males, chose as their answer: "Women more frequently than men are interested in understanding and supporting art and culture." (See Appendix, Table 2–2.)

Almost an equal percentage of men and women believed that "Women feel overseas living and study is an important opportunity for self-development and independence which men can usually attain within their U.S. environment." Even when the motivation is identified as "self-development and independence," study abroad can be perceived as a culturally enriching experience more than an academic or professional one.[28] A greater percentage of males believed men need to stay in the U.S. to focus on career development, a belief which again can reinforce a view of study abroad as a cultural, not a professional training, experience.

Further, answering a survey question that asked their reasons for going abroad, men and women agreed that they went to Europe to broaden their cultural horizons. While this reason does not confirm a Grand Tour-like motivation for study abroad—and indeed the data in the table shows other motives strongly expressed by many respondents—it may well reinforce the perceptions students have of their peers, if not themselves. These associations are further reinforced by the focus on Europe, both in American culture and in study abroad. (For a summary of the responses to Question 13, see Appendix, Table 2–3.)

Writing in 1940, Gertrude Stein recognized the long-held American adulation of things European within the intellectual community before World War II:

> everybody, that is, everybody who writes, is interested in living inside themselves in order to tell what is inside themselves. That is why writers have to have two countries, the one where they belong and the one in which they really live. The second one is romantic, it is separate from themselves, it is not real but it is really there.

> The English Victorians were like that about Italy, the early nineteenth-century Americans were like that about Spain, the middle nineteenth-century Americans were like that about England. My generation, the end of the nineteenth-century American generation, was like that about France.[29]

After World War II, in the academic community, this adulation dissipated, and criticism of Europe as the site for undergraduate study abroad began to emerge. Sometimes criticism of the episteme unintentionally confirms and prolongs it, however. Commenting in 1990, Richard D. Lambert, director of the National Foreign Language Center, cited that in the 1980s, 79 percent of students going abroad still went to England and Western Europe. "In a world in which the non-European world is playing a greater and greater role in global affairs," wrote Lambert, "our continued fixation on Western Europe is striking."[30] The editors of the first edition of *NAFSA's Guide to Education Abroad for Advisers and Administrators,* published in 1993, expressed similar concern. Decrying the lack of diversity, Hoffa, Pearson, and Slind regretted that the majority of students going abroad chose to study in a relatively small number of Western European countries.[31]

Calling for a change from this prevailing Eurocentrism, the authors of *Educating for Global Competence* argued that to ensure international capability, "Study abroad in developing countries and countries outside the traditional Anglo-European settings should be a matter of high priority."[32] The Report of the National Task Force on Undergraduate Education Abroad likewise recommended that more diverse locations be a priority in American undergraduate study abroad.[33] The most recent task force pronounced the same goal.[34]

The federally funded National Security Education Program Scholarship Fund began funding undergraduate and graduate study in non–Western European locations worldwide, reflecting the commitment of the U.S. government to support new geographical regions for American study.[35] In the mid-1990s, the Council on International Educational Exchange surveyed international education administrators at 1,500 schools in the United States, seeking to ascertain the scope and nature of institutional support for study abroad activities.[36] The results of that baseline survey described increasing interest in world regions beyond Western Europe, with advisers reporting particular interest in Latin America, Eastern and Central Europe, Southeast Asia and Japan, and Oceania.[37]

While the higher education community and the federal government have expressly encouraged study abroad in alternative world sites, Europe still predominates. In its most recent survey, the Institute of International Education (IIE) identified that 62.9 percent of all U.S. students studying abroad went to Europe.[38] The extent to which reports have called attention to European locations reflects how much this characteristic forms a part of the defining discourse about U.S. study abroad. This persistent concern, while urging a change from the norm, may have also, if unintentionally, reinforced the perception that study abroad is and for a long time has been a European Grand Tour.

THE ROOTS OF THE BELIEF: STUDY ABROAD IS A GRAND TOUR

From policy documents and influential analyses to popular representations, over and over U.S. study abroad has been described as a European Grand Tour pursued by students for personal cultural enrichment, considered insignificant, rather than for any serious academic or professional purposes. To adapt Foucault's archaeological method to learn more about how this dominant belief contributes to the episteme, the first step is to inquire into the discourse field from which the belief emerged, seeking the context within which it developed its power to negatively define study abroad. In this case, it is valuable to recall the historical context in which the pertinent discourse arose, associating American foreign study with the devaluing conception of the European Grand Tour.

Study abroad can be documented as a Western European educational practice since the Middle Ages, and perceptions of it have not always been flattering. In *The Rise of Universities,* Charles Homer Haskins noted students moving from one western European country to another to study and revealed ancient suspicions over the value of such movements: "Nigel 'Wireker' satirises the English students in Paris in the person of an ass, Brunellus—'Daun Burnell' in Chaucer—who studies there seven years without learning a word, braying at the end as at the beginning of his course, and leaving at last with the resolve to become a monk or a bishop."[39]

Nonetheless, study experiences in other countries have for centuries played an important part in European higher education, adopted as well by students in the earliest years of American higher education, throughout the colonial and post-colonial years. Early American educators and administrators looked to Europe, and particularly to Germany, for models as they shaped all their institutions of higher learning.[40] "Looking at Europe, they saw what they needed," wrote educational historian Laurence R. Veysey.[41]

Early study abroad in the United States was a critical avenue for professional training for young men. Men training for the ministry, for medicine, and for other professions typically traveled to Great Britain, Germany, France, and Austria to study.[42] Valued as a preprofessional commodity, study abroad was sometimes even necessary for men who wished to assume leadership in early American culture because of the lack of strong professional training opportunities within American institutions in those years.

The interest in study abroad was manifest in the respect Americans held for the German university, especially in the latter half of the nineteenth century. American scholars particularly appreciated the opportunity to go to Germany to study the sciences in a way that was perceived to be unavailable in the United States.[43] Indeed, from the beginning of the eighteenth century until 1914, it is estimated that approximately ten thousand American students studied in Germany alone.[44] Carol Gruber counted almost nine thousand Americans studying abroad between 1820 and 1920,[45] drawn by intellectual concerns: "The prestige of the German doctorate was very high, and the degree was relatively easy to acquire. Americans were drawn by the intellectual vitality of nineteenth-century German university scholarship and by the reputation of individual scholars."[46] By the end of the nineteenth century, a small proportion of those seeking professional training and/or graduate study abroad were women, for whom graduate education was frequently unavailable in the United States.[47] Before World War I, however, study abroad for Americans remained predominantly a male experience, conducted to gain entry into the professional world.

Late in the nineteenth century, regard for German universities began to decline, and the concomitant opinion developed that American universities were providing adequate, perhaps even better, educations.[48] Indeed, by the end of that century, Americans perceived their own institutions of higher education as better than many in Europe. Fewer men went overseas to study, preferring professional training at home. The era of male graduate and professional study abroad was at an end in United States history.[49] Thomas Jefferson had lamented prophetically, one century earlier, that young men traveling overseas came to no good—a regret that led him to found the University of Virginia, the United States' first full-fledged state university, so that young American men could study at home. By the beginning of the twentieth century, Jefferson's vision had materialized, and America's "young men no longer regarded study in Europe as the preferred professional training," according to Bowman.[50]

American men turned to domestic institutions for professional training, and education became accessible to men from across the socioeconomic strata.[51] Wealthier American women carried forward the genteel custom of the Grand Tour. They began to travel in more organized institutional ways. Earlier in the century, young women might have traveled to Europe with families or chaperones, but "By the late nineteenth century," according to John Bowman, "professors at several institutions were conducting groups of young ladies on educational tours in Europe, visiting museums, cathedrals and the like."[52]

In her book on the history of women and higher education in America, *In the Company of Educated Women,* Barbara Miller Solomon argued that travel overseas for women in the U.S. was early on linked to the idea of cultural acquisition. In fact, wrote Solomon, study abroad was indeed supported by a wealthy socioeconomic group that disdained formal education for its daughters: "The established eastern elites—Boston Brahmins, Philadelphia Main Liners, and Hudson Valley New Yorkers—preferred to educate daughters privately at home, in boarding school, and through travel abroad." Travel abroad for these wealthy young women took on a distinctive character, due to their socioeconomic status. "New rich millionaires obsessed with making good marriages for their daughters imitated the patterns of the older families, dismissing college as preparation for women who had no option but to be schoolteachers. Both sets of families prepared daughters for a life of leisure, not work."[53]

So by the onset of World War I, the picture of study abroad in the United States had shifted from that of earlier years. Young men no longer went abroad in great numbers, reflecting their belief that their professional training needs could best be satisfied at American universities. Those who continued to study abroad were the male children of wealthy Americans, able to afford to follow the Grand Tour tradition, or female students, accompanying professors abroad to explore western European culture. In this historical context at the start of World War I, the modern discursive associations about U.S. study abroad began to form.

After World War I, the structure of U.S. study abroad changed radically.[54] Many young men had seen Europe because of military service during the war. Even after the war ended, many American troops remained in France. As troops demobilized, they had time on their hands. French institutions organized special programs to teach French language and culture, and the "Cours de Civilisation" emerged.

Established by the Sorbonne, the Cours de Civilisation was a set of special courses for foreign students seeking to study about and within another country. It became a model and set important study abroad precedents.[55] The program allowed study abroad without direct enrollment and integration into the foreign institution. It offered an opportunity for students who might not otherwise gain access to a European university (still the case in the 1920s for many women) or who did not seek to complete a degree abroad. It allowed students to study even without foreign language fluency, since courses were specially taught to non-native speakers. Finally, it accommodated students from educational systems different from those of the host country. In other words, students studying abroad did not have to be at the same academic level or share the same background or skills as their host-country peers. Without a traditional European or American academic structure, without full integration into degree-granting activities, and without a clear place in an academic sequence, the Sorbonne model contributed to suspicion within the American higher education community. It was perceived as a program designed not to capitalize on the strengths and depths of European education but rather to ease the discomforts of Americans in a foreign culture.

Nonetheless, for many American undergraduates, the Sorbonne model created a new and unique opportunity.[56] The Cours de Civilisation established a new academic model for students seeking foreign study experience, soon institutionalized as the "Junior Year Abroad." It was adapted to the academic training and language level of an American college undergraduate. Offered by an accredited academic institution, it was designed to award degree credit within the American home institution, not the foreign host institution.[57] It offered an innovative outlet for some members of the higher education community, while by others it was criticized as a frivolous way to travel abroad. The Sorbonne model marks the inauguration of modern study abroad programs.[58]

In 1923, the first study abroad program modeled on the Sorbonne structure was established at Delaware College (later the University of Delaware). Returning from military service in France with the idea that American students could study abroad in an organized fashion, Professor Raymond Kirkbride founded it. The University of Delaware program, designed to send students to Paris, initially enrolled eight students—all men—although the program was open to women as well. Within two years, the majority of participants were women, a gender mix that remained every year thereafter. (See frontispiece for photographs illustrating the first class, with its all-male membership, and the class ten years later, clearly dominated by women participants.) It was this program, referred to earlier in this chapter, that transferred to Sweet Briar College in 1947.[59] (See Appendix, Table 2–4, University of Delaware Foreign Study Plan, Paris Program Gender Analysis, 1923–24 to 1939–40.)

In that early era, a small number of other institutions followed this model in their study abroad programs as well. These programs were all established by women's colleges, which meant that, at least initially, enrollment was limited to female students.[60] Marymount College in New York established a program in Paris in 1924. Smith College established a program in Paris in 1925. In the same year, Rosary College established a program in Fribourg, Switzerland. Before World War II began, Marymount, Smith, and Delaware had established programs in other Western European countries as well.

Smith College helped consolidate the tradition, initiated in the Sorbonne programs, of study abroad as a year-long experience during the third undergraduate year, a configuration that continues to influence U.S. study abroad programs today. "Smith College pioneered the Junior Year Abroad concept, sending third year undergraduates to study in Paris for an academic year, primarily to strengthen their foreign language proficiency and for cultural immersion," wrote Barbara Burn. Once again, with this practice cultural values were discursively associated with the study abroad experience, building dominant beliefs: "The several junior year programs launched by women's colleges in the 1920's gave to study abroad an image which has clung over the decades, namely that it is primarily a private college phenomenon, is predominantly for women and in humanities fields, and tends to be expensive,"[61] generating doubt about the utility and worth of liberal education pursued in overseas settings.

Rosary College, a Catholic women's college located in River Forest, Illinois, began its study abroad program in 1925. Rosary College women resided and were taught at the Institut des Hautes Études in Fribourg, Switzerland, studying French, literature, religion, philosophy, history, and English. The program was suspended during World War II but revived afterward, through promotional efforts exemplified by a bulletin published by the college in 1947.

The Rosary College bulletin promoted the program in a variety of ways, including offering it as "a way to become better acquainted with Europeans and Old World culture" and to improve foreign language skills. "The aspect of the Foreign Study Plan that perhaps excites the most interest among young women & their parents is the opportunity offered for travel abroad," the bulletin read.[62] It identified as an equally central mission of the program furthering women's professional careers as teachers. Travel opportunities and serious academic and professional benefits were described together. Nonetheless, the use of the Grand Tour idiom within the discourse articulated with suspicions about the quality and value of study abroad.

Early programs were established in Western Europe. This European focus dominated the discourse about study abroad. [63] The majority of programs were initially located in France, and that pattern held until well after World War II. "America was very interested in Europe in the 1920s," wrote Bowman, noting that this early European focus reflected the "dominant role which European art and literature plays in American culture and in the curriculum of American universities."[64]

Subsequent shifts in program locations reflected geopolitical events. Barbara Burn called the Fulbright plan, the post-World War II international exchange initiative, the equivalent of the Marshall Plan in education, broadening American educational vision.[65] In the 1960s the Peace Corps brought fuller awareness of developing nations and their issues into the American academic community.[66] U.S. military training brought men and women into broader contact with diverse foreign languages, expanding American higher education contacts with the Third World.[67] And since World War II, the trend has been to diversify destinations for U.S. study abroad.[68] Nevertheless, while the numbers of participants and diversified destinations keep growing, the trend has not eroded the predominantly European focus of study abroad, nor muted the criticisms about that focus.

THE GRAND TOUR IN DISCOURSE ON STUDY ABROAD

Far from being just a cliché, the belief that study abroad is a general and genial Grand Tour undertaken for purposes of cultural acquisition has become a core component of the episteme dismissing study abroad as academically and functionally irrelevant. The primary destination for U.S. study abroad remains Europe, as it has been from early in the nineteenth century when educators looked to the Continent as the parent culture. The two world wars in the twentieth century produced discourse questioning the value of that tradition. The United States gained ascendancy among world powers, sending its sons and daughters to Asian and African as well as European theaters of war. Prevailing educational opinions regarded Europe less and less as the repository of educational wisdom. The United States' education system granted itself world ascendancy at the same time that Americans became more interested in non-European traditions.[69] The growing disdain for European institutions associated with suspicions about the Sorbonne model and with the conviction that U.S. education had become superior to that available abroad. Males stayed at home for serious education and professional training, while wealthy women, most often from private institutions, it was believed, went abroad for cultural acquisition.

All these factors reinforced the dominant belief that study in Europe, heir to the Grand Tour tradition, was pursued for personal rewards. Gradually, American undergraduate study abroad came to stand apart as an aberration within the male-dominated norms of higher education as they developed in the early twentieth century. Meanwhile, more and more undergraduate women continued to study abroad, forming the majority of American students doing so. It is to those female students—women presumed to have wealth and little professional ambition; women who pursued the twentieth-century American Grand Tour—that this study now turns.

Chapter Three

Dominant Beliefs: Study Abroad Is an Insignificant Pursuit by Wealthy Women

"La Dolce Semester," heralded a recent *New York Times* headline about study abroad,[1] conjuring up the image of the Grand Tour and reinforcing the belief that study abroad is a leisurely experience for the sake of general and genial cultural edification. At the same time, study abroad has been seen as primarily a woman's pursuit. In this chapter, we will continue the process of archaeology, as Foucault would call it, delving into the role that women and their foreign education practices have played in building the episteme that study abroad is neither academically rigorous nor professionally relevant.

In almost every year since 1923, when institutionalized undergraduate credit-bearing programs were first offered to American students, more women than men have chosen to study abroad. In their earliest years, study abroad programs were more frequently supported by private and costly women's colleges than by coeducational institutions; and, ever since, study abroad has drawn more female students, whether they attend all-female or coeducational institutions. This chapter will consider how attitudes about women's roles in society and beliefs about the purposes for educating women linked to other emerging conceptions about study abroad and ultimately contributed to its marginalization. Two clichés deserve special consideration: the notion that since study abroad is a venture predominantly undertaken by women, it is academically insignificant; and the notion that study abroad is for wealthy women from wealthy institutions. Analyzing the discourse within the academic community, this chapter will explore these clichés, observing their emergence as dominant beliefs that have contributed to a devaluing episteme of study abroad.

THE PREDOMINANCE OF WOMEN IN STUDY ABROAD

The most recent data available on study abroad enrollments indicate that almost 65 percent of all participants are female—a preponderance of women that has held relatively constant from the earliest years of American study abroad activity, as will be demonstrated in this chapter.[2] A review of academic discourse confirms that this persistent demographic has been a defining trait of U.S. study abroad.

Comments from leaders in the field, such as Richard D. Lambert, reflect the defining characteristics associated with study abroad: "The prototypical person most likely to go abroad is a white, female, middle-class, full-time student majoring in foreign languages, in history, or in social sciences, and registered at a liberal arts college."[3] NAFSA's newest study abroad policy report calls for the promotion of not only ethnic, racial, and socioeconomic diversity in study abroad but also for "gender diversity" in study abroad.[4] Students deem the gender disproportion worth discussing, manifest in a 2004 Boston College newspaper article headlined, "Gender difference in study abroad: BC sends more women than men abroad."[5]

This interest in gender and study abroad is grounded in a long history of female predominance among study abroad enrollees. Only in the years just after World War II did the number of men even approach the number of women involved in the Delaware/Sweet Briar program, for example (see Appendix, Table 3–1, Summary of Sweet Briar Junior Year in France Groups, 1948–49 to 2003–04). The strength of males in the 1948–1949 program reflects the first impact of the GI Bill (as the Servicemen's Readjustment Act of 1944 was called popularly), which supported veterans after World War II and encouraged them to attend school rather than flood the job market and create unemployment.[6] From 1949 on, however, women consistently outnumbered men. Participant records from the period after World War II and on show that 75 percent of participants in this, the oldest of U.S. study abroad programs, have been female.

More empirical evidence over time can be summoned to back up the general sense that women have predominated as participants in U.S. study abroad. For example, in 1987, in research conducted in cooperation with the Council for International Educational Exchange (CIEE), Jolene Koester conducted a study of 5,600 U.S. purchasers of the international student identity card. She concluded that "international study, travel, and work abroad is an educational experience populated by women," while the "causes and consequences of this uneven interest" she found to be "purely speculative."[7] Council on International Educational Exchange data confirm this predominance in study abroad to the present day. Since its first programs, established in 1973 in France and Spain, through its most recent programs operating worldwide, CIEE has reported that 67 percent of its enrollment is female and 33 percent male.[8]

Records from other longstanding programs mirror this gender proportion. The Institute for the International Education of Students (IES) is a global non-profit educational organization that began fifty-three years ago working with a consortium of more than 150 highly selective U.S. colleges and universities and offers programs in twenty-two cities throughout Asia, Australia, Europe, and South America. IES data for nearly the past decade have reflected 69 percent to 72 percent female enrollees annually. A survey of some 17,000 IES alumni studying abroad from 1950 to 2000 showed that among their respondents, 28.7 percent were male and 70.6 percent female. Enrollment analysis by gender reported for the years 1958 through 1983 confirms this pattern of distribution.[9]

More recently, in the late 1990s at the University of Minnesota Global Campus (now the Learning Abroad Center), a project was initiated to develop new ways to integrate study abroad into the curricula and increase interest in this form of study. Developed across the system's statewide campuses, the program has received extensive funding from organizations including the Archibald Bush Foundation and the U.S. Department of Education,[10] and these efforts have in fact increased participation in study abroad. Data collected on the three campuses where study abroad was most substantial (Minneapolis, Duluth, and Morris, listed in order of enrollment total) allowed a comparison of enrollments from the start of the project in 1997–98 through 2003. In that time, enrollment increased threefold at Duluth; by more than 50 percent at Morris; and, on the primary sending campus, Minneapolis, from 770 to 1,294 students in the five-year period. Female enrollments remained the majority consistently throughout this growth, with women outnumbering men almost two to one from the Minneapolis campus and more than that on the other campuses.[11]

These representative sources indicate that from the inception of modern undergraduate study abroad programs in the United States to the present day, between two-thirds and three-quarters of participants have been female in programs whose records are accessible and provide data over the last half-century of study abroad activity.

PERCEPTIONS OF WOMEN IN STUDY ABROAD

Many academics have gone a step further with the awareness that women predominate as study abroad participants. They associate that recognition with the cultural assumption that women's search for education is not as serious as that of men. These associated beliefs have had an impact on the episteme about U.S. study abroad, as Briggs and Burn have pointed out: "That more women than men study abroad as undergraduates and more in humanities than in professional fields may exacerbate the perception that undergraduate study abroad lacks in seriousness of purpose."[12]

Educators who hold this view have formed a link between the predominance of women as participants in U.S. study abroad and the presumption that a female study abroad experience is a Grand Tour experience, pursued for cultural enrichment. John E. Bowman, for instance, stated: "The Junior Year Abroad programs prior to World War II were, with one exception, operated by women's colleges and, at first, enrollment was limited to women. They were, *thus,* in part, a transformation of the European tour for young women into an academic experience" [emphasis added].[13] Women were assigned the role as "guardians of the culture"[14] while men had to earn a living, support families, and find professionally relevant educational experiences. All these associations reflect deeply held cultural assumptions on the part of American academics. As Foucault notes, these kinds of associations become perpetuated in discourse, including the discourse defining study abroad for faculty and students.

Explaining why more women than men from the United States study abroad, Stephen Cooper and Mary Anne Grant conjectured that "the imbalance reflects American cultural values. Societal and parental expectations in the United States have traditionally inculcated young men to pursue 'serious' career-oriented degrees, while young women are encouraged to 'cultivate' themselves and/or prepare for marriage. Given the prevalence of such sexism, and the notion that a study abroad experience is somehow frivolous, we can see why more women than men have traditionally studied abroad."[15]

In another forum representative of the pervasive academic view, William Hoffa initiated Internet discussions in 1997 on SECUSS-L, the national study abroad advisers online discussion list operated by NAFSA: Association of International Educators. By raising the question as to why more women than men continue to go abroad to study, Hoffa elicited a flurry of responses that help to reveal current opinion in the American academy. Hoffa began, "Since the number of male undergraduate students, generally speaking, is roughly equal to the number of female students, there must be some reasons for these differences. What are they?" Hoffa tried to fend off the most stereotypical of responses by including, with his original query, the following statement:

One view commonly put forth is that men have tended to major in academic areas (science, business, pre-law, etc.) less prominently featured in study abroad programs. Another is that male students have feared that their professional pursuits would be jeopardized if a period of ("dilettantish," "frivolous") study abroad was seen on their academic record—whereas, the argument went, women students, not pursuing such careers, were "freer" to "cultivate" themselves through a foreign sojourn. Given recent expansions of program options across the curriculum, plus the nominal "liberation" of both men and women from such gender politics, neither of these explanations would seem to have much credence, these days.[16]

Hoffa posed his general question in three parts:

THREE QUESTIONS FOR A SECUSS-L FORUM DISCUSSION:

1) What then accounts for the fact that more than 6 out of every 10 students studying abroad continue to be women?
2) Since there are bound to be exceptions, institution to institution, program to program, location to location, what are these exceptions and can we learn anything from them?
3) Are there advising strategies or institutional policies which can make a difference? If so, what are they?[17]

Hoffa's statement and questions themselves reiterated the importance of female dominance as a defining element within the higher education community's episteme of study abroad. He echoed prevailing explanations for past statistical consistencies and reflected the continuing debate about study abroad's academic significance, given that it has attracted primarily women.

Ironically, his question elicited responses reporting or reflecting the beliefs he had disclaimed. For example, George Boyd at Trinity University reported that an "esteemed colleague at a major study abroad institution" had "several times told me of her problem with finding an 'undemanding' London program that won't crimp travel, shopping, and socializing for her sorority women who go abroad in big groups."[18]

Cheryl L. Darrup, marketing director with the North American Institute for Study Abroad, offered the opinion that male students themselves, as well as their advisers, had fallen into the trap of gender stereotyping, disregarding study abroad as an educational option because they feared that their own professional futures would be put in jeopardy if their academic histories included time spent studying abroad.[19]

Those very presumptions—that male students regard study abroad and the professional aspect of their education to be mutually exclusive—were expressed online by SECUSSA subscriber Cameron Beatty:

> We might also consider the possibility that men are less likely to do study abroad because in general they feel they have to focus on their careers as a goal for the immediate future and haven't been convinced that the contribution made by a study abroad experience would justify the time and expense required. Note that I'm NOT saying that women don't have career goals (heaven forefend), but cultural expectations vis-à-vis careers and their importance are somewhat different for men than they are for women. Looked at from that perspective, it could be claimed that women are more likely to participate in a study abroad program because they are in general LESS developed emotionally, or intellectually, or whatever one calls it, than college-age men in general seem to be.[20]

Not all respondents seemed, like this one, to accept the dominant beliefs regarding the gender-specific appropriateness of U.S. study abroad. For example, Marvin Slind, professor and former study abroad professional, bemoaned the stereotyping voiced in answer to Hoffa's question:

> What concerns me even more, however, is the basic nature of those theories: gender-based stereotypes. For example: on the one hand, we learn that males are less mature or less socially developed. On the other, they have stereotypically been more directed toward career or "real-life" issues. I think that while both extremes may contain some accuracies, but [sic] they also are dangerously broad.
>
> I shudder to think of the wave of hostile reactions that would have descended upon anyone who made similar gender-based stereotypes about female students. A wide range of unpleasant—and inaccurate—examples comes to mind. For example, on a few occasions, I have had to take issue with people who suggested that women study abroad when men don't, because men have to work to pay for their own educations, while women have their parents pay for such frills as cute little red cars and study abroad programs.[21]

Yet, despite remarks like Slind's, the discourse evoked by Hoffa's questions reflected that beliefs associating gender with academic quality continued to frame judgment, including that of some faculty who advise students going abroad.

The predominance of women remains an ongoing topic for discussion. William Hoffa raised the topic again in the summer of 2004 in a new representative venue: the Discussion Board of the Forum on International

Education, an organization of close to 150 leading study abroad institutions and institutional supporters.[22] He introduced a new hypothesis into the discussion, suggesting role models as yet another reason for the predominance of women in study abroad. "Students are influenced by the role model presented (indirectly) by their campus adviser, and such a person is likely to be a woman (who, of course, studied abroad)," said Hoffa. "Look around you at your next SECUSSA session. Current male/female imbalances in the education abroad profession, in other words, perpetuate the gender divide."[23] In short, the very presence of women in the study abroad profession may itself have an unintended and troublesome impact on students' perceptions—an idea addressed in the next chapter of this book.

Students may well imbibe gender-related perceptions about their study abroad interests. For example, in the Sweet Briar Alumni Survey, Question 10 (cited in chapter 2), a majority of men and more than 40 percent of women reported that they believe more women than men go abroad because men must remain in the U.S. to prepare for their careers. Some alumni comments echoed the adviser discourse described above, as seen in these written responses to the question:

> Men do not generally prefer what is foreign to them.
>
> I think, for this age group (20–22), women for the most part are more focused on long-term goals.
>
> Men get too comfortable in the cocoons of frats and sports. They tend to follow the easy path.
>
> Perhaps women are more adventurous when it comes to creating a new group of friends.
>
> Women are more comfortable taking risks in experiences that might affect their identity.

(See Appendix, Table 3–2, for more written responses to this question.) Only a small number of alumni reported suspicions about study abroad expressed to them by faculty advisers; but of those who did, more than 50 percent of the women reported hearing that study abroad was not academically beneficial (and both genders reported that, at least occasionally, faculty with whom they spoke about study abroad perceived them to have no career goals).[24] (See Appendix, Table 3–3, for comments on impediments to study abroad.) This contrasts with the students' own reality, as they reported in Question 13 (cited in chapter 2), when over three-quarters of both men and women reported they went abroad to enhance their career skills.

The predominance of women participants in modern credit-bearing study abroad programs is a defining trait within the higher education community. Because of it, value judgments about women's cultural roles and educational goals have attached to judgments about their participation in study abroad. These bundled judgments then go to form the prevailing episteme of study abroad itself, leading academics to question the seriousness and functional significance of overseas education.

THE ROOTS OF THE BELIEF: STUDY ABROAD IS FOR WOMEN AND THUS NOT ACADEMICALLY SIGNIFICANT

A Foucault-like archaeological investigation of this bundle of negative judgments about female participants in study abroad uncovers its roots in the broader history of American higher education. Some form of what could be considered higher education for women began in the United States at the end of the eighteenth century. Following the American Revolution, the United States was developing a new identity based on a republican ideal. The purposes for male education included the creation of an educated male citizenry capable of making responsible electoral decisions. Women did not vote or take part in the democratic process, nor was there concern at the time that they should. As wives and mothers—but not as voting citizens—women exerted influence on their sons, the republic's future decision makers: "Republican wives and mothers gained a special role in the creation of an informed citizenry," wrote Barbara Miller Solomon. "Though not citizens themselves, they would train their young male offspring for citizenship. . . . thus Republican motherhood furnished a utilitarian motive for educating women."[25] Additionally, because men might be away from home for lengthy periods of time, the education of the children might devolve upon the woman—another reason for providing a woman some education of her own.[26]

Institutions of higher learning designed exclusively for women began appearing in early nineteenth-century America. Founded to help women develop independent intellectual skills, they were intended not to controvert so much as to enhance their roles as spouses and helpmates.[27] The trustees of Randolph-Macon Women's College in Lynchburg, Virginia, writing in 1891, expressed this sentiment in establishing "a college . . . where the dignity and strength of fully-developed faculties and the charm of the highest literary culture may be acquired by our daughters without loss to woman's crowning glory—her gentleness and grace."[28]

At first, higher education attracted less wealthy women who sought socioeconomic advancement through education. The "serious, hardworking daughter of the middle class preparing to teach—often dubbed the 'calico girl'—formed the backbone of the early classes," wrote Helen Horowitz in her history of the design and function of American women's colleges.[29] Women from wealthy families had other options available. By the end of the nineteenth century, though, colleges were increasingly attracting women from all socioeconomic classes.

Additionally, in the latter nineteenth century, the curriculum changed. Newly established liberal education programs expanded the opportunities to pursue humanistic studies and the social sciences. These changes sparked further debate about the purpose of education for women. Men could study the new liberal arts, the new humanistic disciplines, and the new social sciences and still advance toward a professional future, but already "Liberal culture for women was held up as learning for its own sake, detached from professional motives," reported Solomon.[30]

Leaders of education as prominent as Charles W. Eliot, president of Harvard University at the end of the nineteenth century, were suspicious of the purpose of educating women. Eliot "scandalized academic women," wrote Horowitz, "by a speech at Wellesley suggesting that the great traditions of learning from the time of the Egyptians were the creation by and for men and served as no guide in educating women."[31] Eliot's observations reflected the public devaluation of higher education opportunities for women, an attitude that was reinforced by the increasing belief that college women were motivated by the "pursuit of happiness," not the motives of professional or occupational advancement that had in fact been articulated by college women between 1860 and 1890.[32] Serious academic intentions were articulated by those three earliest generations of U.S. college women, Solomon noted, but the male educational leaders and creators of significant discourse did not fully recognize or respect their intentions.[33]

With the emergence of the flapper after World War I during the 1920s, the perception continued to evolve that women attended college in pursuit of happiness. The earlier image of the college woman as serious of purpose, destined to achieve academically and then to serve, gave way to the image of the fun-loving woman pursuing higher education for frivolous reasons.[34] Young women still learned that the educated had an obligation to society, but they were often reluctant to make commitments to future activities. They behaved "as if college were a four-year moratorium from real life," suggested Solomon.[35]

Even though the voices of college women expressing serious motives for pursuing education re-emerged in the 1930s Depression era,[36] it was in the exuberant period just after World War I that the idea of the Junior Year

Abroad was born. As Foucault argues, chance circumstances can attach particular characterizations to an event or action. Those random associations get systematized in ongoing discourse, gaining the power to define. Just such a process occurred in the founding of the Junior Year Abroad programs. College women of the 1920s, no matter what their own conceptions, were believed to be more concerned about enjoying their college years and focusing on their futures as cultural guardians, playing a secondary and supportive role in American culture, while college men developed professional acumen and leadership skills.[37] These distinctions arose from the tradition that even serious women students were to be educated as handmaidens, not as leaders—a tradition that disenfranchised women and their education just as it empowered men and theirs. Discursive associations through time bundled up these judgments and projected them onto study abroad as a whole. Thus study abroad earned a reputation as a frivolous experience for women, providing marginal or trivial cultural enrichment, not serious academic or professional advancement for the students involved.

Despite this milieu, women enrolled in college and women elected to study abroad. Clearly they were finding value in both experiences, but their discourse of personal motivations and valuations was marginalized. No matter what their excluded discourse might have expressed, dominant discourse within the academic community perpetuated the notion that they attended school for personal enjoyment and traveled abroad for cultural enrichment. That discourse informed the dominant belief that study abroad, since its programs serve primarily women, is not a significant academic pursuit. Value judgments did and still do adhere to study abroad as a result of the predominance of females among its participants.

PERCEPTIONS OF WEALTH IN STUDY ABROAD

Within the discourse of the American higher education community, the perception that study abroad is an academically insignificant Grand Tour for women who could travel for leisure and be frivolous about their education linked with the belief that study abroad is an activity pursued by the wealthy. Altschuler's recent *New York Times* article proclaimed, "The programs, featured prominently in college admissions literature, have become nothing less than an expectation among upper-middle-class teenagers, like braces and a car."[38] And, indeed, a dominant belief has emerged that study abroad programs are intended expressly for wealthy women attending wealthy institutions.

Academic literature, reports, and public statements assert repeatedly that wealthier students are the primary participants in U.S. study abroad.

The first report of the National Task Force on Undergraduate Education Abroad included the statement that "Opportunities for such experience abroad are still confined to a small fraction of American undergraduates, *mainly upper middle class*" [emphasis added].[39] The 2003 NAFSA Study Abroad Task Force report reiterated this concern, connecting wealth with race: "We underscore the importance of making study abroad a reality for all college students, not just the white and the wealthy."[40]

The perception dates back decades. In 1960, new interest in study abroad brought over 500 academic representatives to the National Conference on Study Abroad, organized by the Association of American Colleges, the Council on Student Travel, the Experiment in International Living, and the Institute of International Education.[41] This pivotal meeting found it important to call for low-cost programs and study abroad scholarships "to avoid limiting the programs to those with greater financial means."[42] In the 1980s, Goodwin and Nacht still considered study abroad to be the bastion of more privileged students.[43] More recently, the late Barbara Burn bemoaned the image of the "junior year, rich woman."[44]

Many students have likewise held the belief that study abroad is for the well-to-do among them. "Prohibitive costs—real or imagined—are one reason students do not consider education abroad as an option in undergraduate studies," found Nancy Stubbs of the University of Colorado, author of the chapter on financial aid in NAFSA's *Guide to Education Abroad*.[45] The CIEE Baseline Survey conducted in the mid-1990s also showed cost considerations to be a top concern among students,[46] as did a 1995–96 market analysis of U.S. college student interest in study abroad, supported by CIEE and conducted by students in the Darden Graduate School of Business at the University of Virginia.[47] In fact, that study found that students choosing not to study abroad overwhelmingly cited cost as a reason. Results from the Darden survey and the CIEE Study Abroad Baseline Survey reveal that finances were perceived to be both students' top concern and also their primary reason for choosing not to study abroad.[48]

Study abroad advisers often hear these reasons expressed.[49] Twenty-first century surveys have confirmed that students continue to perceive study abroad as an activity for those with funds to spare. Part of the University of Minnesota curriculum integration initiative described above, Evaluation of Initiative surveys reported that cost continued to be perceived as a barrier to study abroad, with between 67.5 and 74.4 percent of student respondents identifying cost as a barrier.[50] Faculty surveyed reported that more than half of the time, students explaining their decisions not to study overseas gave financial concerns as their number one reason.[51] Evidence from a number of sources confirms that the prevailing belief, held by academic leaders and students alike, is that study abroad is costly and hence an experience for the wealthy—and female—student only.

Closely akin to the dominant belief that wealthy women participate in U.S. study abroad is the assumption that predominantly wealthy institutions advocate, initiate, and maintain study abroad programs for American students. U.S. study abroad programs did originate largely at Eastern colleges,[52] particularly private women's colleges. Briggs and Burn pointed out that the origin of the Junior Year Abroad at predominantly women's colleges continues to influence belief in study abroad as a women's "private college phenomenon."[53] Goodwin and Nacht articulated the belief as well. Even as they reported growth among study abroad programs and increased diversity among the institutions supporting them in the 1980s, nonetheless they described study abroad before the growth phase as an experience that drew primarily "juniors at elite liberal arts colleges."[54] And the recent *New York Times* article quoted above stated that "Since students also have to pay for travel and can't get work-study jobs overseas, most participants come from elite, expensive private institutions."[55]

These beliefs persist, particularly since they resonate with the other dominant beliefs, such as that of the Grand Tour tradition with its upper-class origins and its implications of wealth and leisure. Despite empirical evidence to the contrary, the perception of study abroad as an expensive experience, only for the wealthy, has assumed a central role in forming the episteme of study abroad in the American higher education community.

THE ROOTS OF THE BELIEF: STUDY ABROAD IS FOR WEALTHY WOMEN FROM WEALTHY INSTITUTIONS

To understand fully the ongoing discourse of wealth as a defining characteristic of the study abroad experience, it must be viewed within the larger history, as part of the institutional development of study abroad programs and in association with beliefs about the function of education in women's lives.

Modern study abroad programs developed just after World War I as many more Americans of both genders began attending college and as the idea of women attending college became more socially acceptable. Ironically, those historical moves paralleled the already described decline in the image of college women as serious-minded. Travel, too, carried with it pejorative connotations. Travel for personal enrichment was a leisure-class activity, as noted early on by Thorstein Veblen, who argued that "modes of behavior and sets of values motivated by the privileged classes" who need to convert excess time and money into prestige become "standards of 'decency' for entire cultures."[56] In this context, "the social benefits of 'honorific waste' were added to the very real personal pleasures and satisfactions of European travel," writes William W. Stowe in his book on American travel to Europe in the nineteenth century, *Going Abroad.* "The trip to Europe, a luxury made possible by the accumulation of excess capital, became a token of bourgeois respectability."[57] As beliefs about study abroad began to arise during the same period, such valuations of women's education and travel informed the developing episteme.

Many believed that most American students engaged in study abroad in the 1920s were wealthy women. Robert C. Pace, in his study of participants in the Delaware/Sweet Briar programs, observed that by and large women from wealthy homes were the students most able to attend these programs.[58] Data from Sweet Briar confirm the image to some extent. Sweet Briar study abroad alumni considered themselves at least middle-class or upper-middle-class, with almost half the women—more than the men responding—identifying themselves as upper middle class, and as many as 10 percent of the women seeing themselves as upper class. (See Appendix, Table 3–4, for answers to Question 11 in the Sweet Briar survey regarding socioeconomic status at time of study abroad.)

From early on, though, faculty and administrators sought ways to make study abroad financially feasible for a wide range of students. President Walter Hullihen of the University of Delaware, a primary supporter for the nation's first program, expressed his hope from the start that the experience would not prove too costly.[59] According to John A. Munroe in his history of the University of Delaware, Hullihen wanted the program to cost no more than 20 percent above the regular fees of University of Delaware enrollment, but it was not possible to keep the costs that low.[60]

Jean Brown, University of Delaware archivist, has found that participants in these seminal programs were not always the wealthiest students. The record indicates that some were receiving scholarship funding.[61] Scholarships for students who wished to go abroad, made possible by donations from the DuPont family and others,[62] amounted to $300 apiece and "were offered to students who could not afford to go without financial aid," according to the 1931 *Bulletin of the University of Delaware*.[63]

In his study of the Sweet Briar program, *Twenty-Five Years on the Left Bank,* John Matthew found that during the years 1948–49 through 1971–72, an increasing effort was made to support lower-income students: "As the number of participants increased from year to year, 67 in 1948–49 to 106 in 1972–73, so too did the number of worthy students who were granted scholarship awards who otherwise might not have been able to participate."[64] While scholarship development began slowly, with "one scholarship awarded the first year, 3 or 4 the second year, 14 the third year, the program has continued to give scholarship awards as funds have become available." In 1971–72, 28 students out of 106 received aid of some kind, and 18 of them received awards directly from Sweet Briar Junior Year in France funds.[65]

Scholarship and aid use is reported throughout the Sweet Briar program to the present day. Former director Emile Langlois reported that between 15 percent and 19 percent of students received financial aid from the time of computerized recordkeeping in 1992 through 1996.[66] Current director Margaret Scouten noted that "Whoever shows a need base receives a hefty scholarship."[67] While some of the data from the Sweet Briar survey suggest that especially women received financial contributions from their families, thus reinforcing the stereotype of the wealthy woman, still, when calculating responses measuring how many students of all survey respondents received financial assistance, almost 15 percent received scholarships and almost 13 percent received financial aid from federal or state loan programs. Fourteen percent worked to contribute to costs and 32 percent combined support from two or more sources. (See Appendix, Table 3–5, for answers to Question 12 regarding methods of financing study abroad.)

So while many students going abroad did (and still do) come from relatively well-to-do households, not all have been wealthy. With the effort to develop low-cost programs and with federal and state aid, an increasingly diverse socioeconomic group now goes abroad.[68] The Institute of International Education reported that 56 percent of its responding institutions allowed all forms of financial aid to be used for study abroad, with the remainder allowing some forms of aid to be applied.[69] Gail Hochhauser, senior director of special programs at NAFSA, observed that more students are now able to apply their federal financial aid to study abroad costs.[70] And the 2003 ACE report, *Mapping Internationalization on U.S. Campuses,* reported that 35 percent of its survey institutions helped fund study and work abroad programs.[71] Program providers subsidized needier students with aid as well.[72]

When financial issues are reduced by making scholarships and aid available, it is still, according to accessible data, most often women who utilize that support and study overseas. For example, in the Sweet Briar program, of the 64 students awarded financial aid between 1992 and 1996, only five were men.[73] Margaret Scouten confirms that it is in the majority women, rather than men, who apply for Sweet Briar scholarships, and it continues to be, in the majority, women who receive them.[74] CIEE confirms exactly the same phenomena, even with its many diverse disciplinary and geographic programs worldwide.[75] Financial aid does not necessarily affect the gender ratio of participants, in other words. Even with this leveler, no new evidence presents itself to shake the perception that the women who participate must be wealthy.[76]

Just as it is believed that elite female students go abroad, it is also perceived that study abroad programs are sponsored by elite institutions. The demographics changed dramatically following World War II. Private eastern women's colleges tended to be the earliest institutions sponsoring study abroad programs, but that profile changed rapidly in the second half of the twentieth century. Figures vary but generally agree. The first U.S. census of students abroad was done by the Institute of International Education in 1954–55.[77] In *Study Abroad, New Dimensions in Higher Education,* Irwin Abrams and W. R. Hatch asserted that from 1919 to 1955 about 2,000 students in all studied abroad, with strong growth in the 1950s. One thousand registered in 1956–57 alone. As evidence they cite IIE reports.[78] John Bowman counted ten 1950 programs in Europe; thirty 1960 programs. During the 1960s, a period of rapid growth, one hundred new programs in Europe opened.[79] William Allaway counted half a dozen programs in 1950 and over three hundred in 1970.[80]

Regardless of some variation in data, the growth in program numbers is clear. This expansion attracted new higher education institutions into foreign exchange activities. Large private and public universities became actively involved in sponsoring diverse international education programs, in contrast to the early sponsorship pattern, in which small, private, predominantly Eastern, women's liberal arts colleges or Catholic women's colleges with European ties were most often the sponsors.[81]

Explanations for the growth of study abroad that began in the 1950s are varied. After two world wars, post-war reconstruction and interest in finding a path to world peace directed attention abroad.[82] John Wallace noted that as former Fulbright faculty returned to their overseas locations, bringing their students with them, they contributed to the growing interest in study abroad.[83] The Cold War brought new emphasis to foreign language and area studies; Russia's launch of Sputnik, the world's first satellite, aroused concern about American competence and prompted calls for better domestic and foreign education to keep America competitive.[84] Legislation—including the Higher Education Act (HEA) of 1965 (Title VI), the Mutual Educational and Cultural Exchange Act of 1961 (Fulbright-Hays), and now the National Security Education Program of 1991—helped colleges and universities develop international programs and encourage student interest in them, even though funding was insufficient.[85]

The Peace Corps contributed to a new sense of the importance of foreign travel and living abroad as part of a young person's education.[86] Trade and investment abroad, together with, in Clark Kerr's words, "the emergence of multinational companies as a 'sixth continent,'" developed as a motive for interest in international education in the 1960s and 1970s, as did the specter of national security.[87]

In the 1980s, the themes of global awareness and responsibility dominated discourse concerning the value of study abroad, as stated in *Educating for Global Competence:*

> Despite our position of international leadership for almost fifty years, we are ill-prepared for the changes in business, manufacturing, diplomacy, science and technology that have come with an intensely interdependent world. Effectiveness in such a world requires a citizenry whose knowledge is sufficiently international in scope to cope with global interdependence.[88]

And after September 11, 2001, the new NAFSA task force on study abroad, for reasons of national security, urged the United States to recognize that:

> *We are now in another Sputnik moment. . . . It is time to launch a major national effort to ensure that every U.S. college student graduates with both an understanding of at least one foreign area and facility in at least one foreign language. For that to happen . . . study abroad must become the norm, not the exception, at higher education institutions in the United States.* [italics in original][89]

In this climate of global concern, the number of programs abroad and the number of institutions supporting study abroad has grown dramatically. The Institute of International Education's 33rd edition of semester and year study abroad programs, published in 2004, listed over 2,900 programs offered to U.S. students, 75 percent of which are sponsored by accredited colleges and universities in the United States.[90] The Institute listed 2,700 summer programs, 60 percent of them operated by U.S. institutions.[91]

At the same time, the array of institutions sponsoring study abroad has diversified. "In the 1950s and 1960s, formal academic programs were conducted primarily by four-year, private liberal arts institutions," wrote Archer Brown; "in the 1970s there was a sizable increase in the number of state universities and two-year colleges offering study abroad options."[92] Programs came to be found in all types of institutions, "from the community college to the high-powered technical research university, institutions that are public and private, rural and urban, secular and church-related."[93]

According to the American Council on Education surveys reported in 2003 in *Mapping Internationalization on U.S. Campuses,* 95 percent of research institutions administered undergraduate study abroad programs.[94] Further, 88 percent of comprehensive universities, 80 percent of liberal arts colleges, and 38 percent of community colleges reported that they administered foreign study programs.[95]

Private liberal arts colleges have continued to support international education extensively. Liberal arts college students participated in study abroad programs "to a greater extent than many of their counterparts at other types of institutions . . . (18 percent)," reported the 2003 ACE survey report.[96] Although liberal arts colleges represent only one type of all schools offering or encouraging study abroad, their presence in the mix tends to confirm the normalized image of study abroad as an experience for the wealthy, ignoring the possibility that financial aid might enable the less wealthy to participate. One example of the predominant presence of upper-echelon private colleges is manifest in the International 50, which provided international activities resources "far greater than their comparatively small enrollments would suggest."[97] The International 50 schools reported initially that while fewer than one percent of all American college students and just 2.1 percent of undergraduates at research universities were studying abroad in a given year, fully 8.5 percent of International 50 liberal arts college students participated in study abroad programs annually.[98] Over one-third of all International 50 students had some sort of academic experience abroad before graduation, a figure four times the Higher Education Research Institute's national figure of 8.9 percent.[99] They stood forth as models of study abroad activity, blotting from view those schools that did not match the wealthy private-school image.[100]

Evidence exists to challenge the prevailing view that it has been primarily upper-tier liberal arts colleges that have sponsored study abroad. The Institute for International Education's figures have suggested significant diversity among the institutional supporters of U.S. undergraduate study abroad,[101] and ACE has reported that more students from research universities pursue study abroad programs than from any other type of higher education institution, including liberal arts institutions.[102] As the number of U.S. colleges and universities involved in study abroad has increased, so has the number of public and lower-cost institutions.[103]

Yet, in keeping with the theories of Michel Foucault, in institutions such as universities, discourse creates and sustains persistent definitions that reinforce traditional allocations of power.[104] Those persistent definitions forcefully exclude ideas or evidence that challenge existing belief.[105] Diversification of institutions supporting study abroad and socioeconomic diversification of participants has been ongoing within the U.S. higher education community for four decades. Nevertheless, these developments, including efforts from early on through to today to subsidize poorer students, have not eroded the dominant belief that study abroad is the prerogative of wealthy women from wealthy institutions.

WOMEN, WEALTH, AND EDUCATION IN DISCOURSE ON STUDY ABROAD

Most of the pre–World War II study abroad programs were sponsored by small, somewhat elite women's colleges. From that situation, the dominant belief emerged that only wealthy women from wealthy institutions participated in study abroad. This belief blended with the belief that study abroad is a Grand Tour, enjoyed for cultural enrichment by the leisure class. In a setting where the purpose of women's education was presumed to be the cultural enrichment of guardians and helpmates, the belief grew even more strong and complex: Study abroad provides broad cultural enrichment for women with no concern for professional preparation and no interest in significant academic experiences.

Alternative discourses about the function and worth of study abroad were developing in parallel, but alternative discourses by their very nature, as Foucault has argued, remain marginalized and often invisible.[106] Indeed the first study abroad program, at the University of Delaware, was not even housed in or sponsored by a private women's college. Early sponsoring institutions were most often women's colleges, but since the end of World War II, the list of American schools involved in study abroad reflects a growing diversity, broadening to include feeder institutions and sponsoring institutions, including a large percentage of lower-cost public institutions. From the start, efforts have been made to diversify program participation with financial assistance. In recent years, the demographic characteristics of students involved in study abroad have broadened as well. Despite all these developments, the belief remains dominant that it is wealthy women from wealthy institutions who study abroad. This belief links neatly with the belief that, since study abroad is pursued predominantly by women, it must be academically unimportant. And both bundle with the other dominant belief, explored in chapter 2, that study abroad is a frivolous Grand Tour experience, providing no serious academic or professional benefits. Together these beliefs have, through the course of this past century of discourse, integrated into an episteme that continues to devalue study abroad as academically weak and functionally purposeless.

Chapter Four

Dominant Beliefs: Study Abroad Offers a Nonprofessional Course of Study Inferior to American Education

In 2004, editors of *IIE Passport,* an annual review of study abroad opportunities now in its 54th edition, renamed their summer program guide *Short-Term Study Abroad,* abandoning the old title, *Vacation Study Abroad.* In making this change, they sought to ensure that the book "more accurately describe[d] the directory's focus and content, and . . . the academic integrity of its programs."[1] The new title moved away from the associations between U.S. study abroad programs and the elitist Grand Tour, designed for wealthy women and grounded in the liberal arts tradition. At a time when the new American university was on the rise to educate men for leadership, liberal education was evoking more distrust. Doubts about the quality and utility of liberal education coalesced into powerful beliefs and generated even greater doubt in the value of study overseas. As the old Harvard adage put it, "If you are already at the best in the world, why go anywhere else?"[2]

This chapter will explore how attitudes about liberal education, its role and its worth, linked to beliefs about American higher education and the role of women in it. As these perceptions and definitions coalesced, the episteme matured within the academic mind, portraying study abroad as an avenue devoid of useful professional training and as the weak stepchild within a vigorous higher education system.

PERCEPTIONS ABOUT THE LIBERAL ARTS TRADITION, CAREER PREPARATION, AND STUDY ABROAD

Many comments in the discourse convey the belief that since students abroad pursue liberal arts studies, they must not be interested in serious and professional education. Liberal arts institutions today still express concern about how the relevance of their education is perceived, as revealed again when the *Chronicle of Higher Education* reported on the 2004 annual meeting of the Association of American Colleges and Universities: "Many of them [the 1,300 liberal arts academicians attending] were eager to discuss why studying philosophy—or . . . German, or Wallace Stevens—is important, and how to . . . explain that to the rest of the world."[3] A similar impulse must have spurred Marshall Gregory, professor of English, liberal education, and pedagogy at Butler University, to write "A Liberal Education is Not a Luxury," in which he recognized that the liberal education discourse of the last century "implicitly concedes the strongest ground in any discussion of educational aims to faculty members from professional and pre-professional programs."[4]

With regard to study abroad, Kathleen M. Reilly, former foreign study director at Seton Hall University and 1997–98 chair of NCISPA, the Title VI Holders Division of the International Studies Association, observed that:

> Study abroad has long been considered a worthwhile, if only tangential, academic activity for the personal development and cultural exposure of college students. Usually associated with the affluent, study abroad was most often considered the domain of women in the liberal arts. . . . Students and administrators still frequently view study abroad as the cultural dabbling of dilettantes despite dramatically changed social, economic and political conditions that are making international experience critically important.[5]

Within this single statement about prevailing opinions among students and administrators, Reilly encapsulated the dominant beliefs already identified in this book—that study abroad is considered a Grand Tour, for "personal development and cultural exposure"; that study abroad is "considered the domain of women"; and that study abroad is "usually associated with the affluent." Reilly identified another related perception, saying that many consider study abroad "tangential," concerned only with liberal arts—an education considered "the cultural dabbling of dilettantes."[6] Briggs and Burn summarized this view as well when they decried the reputation of study abroad as an elitist female pursuit and observed that this image derived in part from association with the study of humanities.[7]

Even when the liberal curriculum is respected as important, still it is suspected of not delivering useful education. Speaking after 9/11, Karen Jenkins, then president of Brethren Colleges Abroad, and James Skelly, senior fellow at the Baker Institute, Juniata College, and academic coordinator of the Peace and Justice Programs at Brethren Colleges Abroad, wrote that education abroad programs fail to encourage effective global citizens.[8] Jenkins and Skelly particularly assailed the assumption that the past and present content of study abroad—including its cultural content and the experience it offers—creates students who can more likely help forge international peace through increased understanding. Contributing to *Rockin' in Red Square,* John and Lilli Engle denounced study abroad, especially its liberal arts content, as failed, frivolous, weak, and without serious professional purpose in an article they titled "Neither International Nor Educative: Study Abroad in the Time of Globalization."[9]

For some, if not all, these beliefs articulate with one another: The notion that study abroad involves liberal study for cultural pursuit, defined as insignificant or trivial and not for serious or professional purposes, links with the dominant belief that study abroad is predominantly for women and therefore of lesser significance. "The arts are tinged with effeminacy in the popular thinking," stated Mabel Newcomer, emeritus professor of economics at Vassar College. Men apologize for their interest in the arts, while women find such an interest to be "natural."[10] In the mid-twentieth century, Newcomer found women to be "often credited with preserving the liberal arts tradition in a period when technical training was increasingly demanded by the new and the monetary value of higher education was emphasized."[11] Catherine R. Stimpson, feminist scholar and dean of the Graduate School of Arts and Sciences at New York University, observed the link between the liberal arts and gender stereotypes when she wrote in 1998 that "There may be a bias against the liberal arts, a feeling that real men don't speak French, that in the 20th century these are women's topics."[12] Male and female alumni responding to the Sweet Briar survey wrote, for example: "I found in studying French that most men find French to be a 'sissy' language," and "It is more accepted (culturally) for the female gender to have an interest in arts and culture" (see Appendix, Table 3–2).[13]

These prevailing beliefs within the academy frame the valuation of foreign language and overseas study. "United States study abroad has traditionally focused on language and culture, rather than on the acquisition of specific knowledge in other fields," wrote Archer Brown.[14] The Engles argued that U.S. study abroad is pursued as "the extension via field learning of classroom study in such domains as the arts, international relations, or archaeology; language study as much for liberal arts curricular breadth as for later professional use; enhanced cultural awareness through host culture interaction."[15] They postulated that inbound students take their academic work much more seriously than do U.S. students—an opinion not altogether unsurprising given their view of what U.S. students encounter in study abroad programs. "At this point an honest look at what 'comes out' of most experiences abroad would make us blush," they continued, "but then, as most study abroad is structured, we can hardly expect students to get much of their experience when they are required to put so little into it: little academic work, to be sure, even less in the way of prior required language preparation, host cultural contact often restricted (literally) to pragmatic mini-conversations with waiters, post office workers, and train conductors."[16]

Believed to be as such, study abroad—with its liberal curriculum and its association with devalued female education—appears to carry no focused or significant career-oriented aid to the student. Employers, too, seem to doubt the value of overseas education experience. "Currently, very few employers specifically recruit candidates with an overseas study experience, unless they require either cross cultural skills or a job specifically requires it," observed the authors of a recent study conducted by the Institute of International Education.[17] Study abroad advisers report hearing with some regularity student comments such as "Going abroad will never do anything for my career!" and "The professional bodies in my field are opposed to it."[18] Indeed, students as well as employers, faculty, and administrators express doubt about the usefulness of the overseas education experience as preparation for the world of work.

THE ROOTS OF THE BELIEF: STUDY ABROAD OFFERS A LIBERAL ARTS PROGRAM OF STUDY INAPPLICABLE TO PROFESSIONAL DEVELOPMENT

Liberal education had early on performed the function of training men for careers in colonial and post-colonial America,[19] a function that substantially gave way in the mid-nineteenth century to a practical curriculum offered at land-grant colleges and universities. The new practical focus energized the American education movement and gave rise to some suspicions about liberal education, although full-fledged professional education did not receive university status until the end of the nineteenth century.[20] A new formula for the modern American university developed, exemplified by numerous universities established in the latter half of the nineteenth century. These schools were designed to collect the best of European educational traditions and yet add something uniquely American: "the rationalism and empiricism of the Enlightenment, the impact of the American and French revolution, the influence of the resurgent German universities of the nineteenth century, and the utilitarian need for incorporating new fields of knowledge, such as science and modern languages, into the curriculum to serve the needs of an expanding society,"[21] as Ernest L. Boyer and Fred M. Hechinger put it. Indeed, nineteenth-century female scholars contributed to the influence of the German universities in U.S. higher education, as some 1,350 North American women sought graduate study at German institutions, often because they were denied access to the highest-quality training at home.[22] As author Sandra Singer observed, many of these women's stories "have been lost to history" and little has been written about them, probably because they were ignored at the time.[23]

In the nineteenth century, females were not considered a serious constituency within the college student population. College administrators sought to serve their male students, who in that era were the obvious and only pursuers of professional goals.[24] That many of the German universities, too, excluded or discouraged women was an argument used by many leaders at U.S. institutions to sustain their belief that they were creating the best of all educations for their male students.[25] By 1900, men found greater value in American higher education, while many women continued to search for educational opportunities overseas.

By the end of the nineteenth century, the shape of a college curriculum had changed as well. The idea of electives emerged, supplanting the concept of a single classical course of study for all students. Harvard University led the way, radically relaxing course and curriculum requirements. The social sciences were developing as significant fields of study, and courses in those new disciplines took the place of some of the core courses in the old liberal arts curriculum. The core that had once included religion and philosophy now contained economics, sociology, psychology, history, and government.[26]

These new courses in the social sciences attracted men and women equally. But at that historical moment, since male education was seen as professional and female education was not, some reacted against women who chose the new fields of study. Some feared the "feminization" of the new electives—a derogatory term meaning that women, whose studies were presumed not to have serious purpose, were devaluing the courses available to men. As a result, there was some effort to develop courses oriented more toward women. A new sort of college curriculum emerged within American institutions, with courses that emphasized skills like calisthenics and disciplines like home economics.[27]

At the end of the nineteenth century, to support a serious commitment to the education of women, another type of "women's curriculum" developed at the Ivy League women's colleges, stronger in the arts than its male counterpart and, "in fact, more intelligent, human, and 'progressive' than the curriculum in such places as Yale and Princeton," as Page Smith put it in his book, *Killing the Spirit: Higher Education in America*. [28] The zeal at women's colleges in the late nineteenth and early twentieth centuries was generated by a sense that women and women's colleges were part of a great venture in the spirit of the suffrage movement gaining steam: "To them, women's colleges were an important if not essential aspect of God's plan for the emancipation of their sex and the redemption of the world,"[29] wrote Smith.

However, as the pre–World War I vision of education for unmarried or career-oriented women disappeared, supplanted by more devaluing opinions of the role of women as pleasure-seeking flappers while in college,[30] cultural perceptions also shifted to consider the study of a diminished liberal arts and sciences curriculum to be women's proper education.[31] In 1924, in a representative example offered by Helen Lefkowitz Horowitz, Vassar took the steps "to establish a program which adapted the arts and sciences to homemaking."[32] Women nonetheless persisted in their expression of interest in the new social science and humanities courses. New courses held "broad appeal at women's colleges as well as at comparable men's schools," reported Solomon. "Yet this change in academic climate had different implications for women and men students."[33] Women, it was assumed, would eventually marry and bear children and thus "waste" advanced education.[34] The modern university curriculum developed, based on the assumption that male studies, even within the liberal arts, were pre-professional, while female studies were edifying in nature.[35] "One consequence of coeducation for women," wrote Page Smith, "was the tendency to head them into the liberal-arts curriculum and to charge them with the responsibility for 'culture.'"[36]

This definition of the purpose for female liberal arts study linked with the beliefs constituting study abroad as a Grand Tour clothed as a traditional liberal education and a cultural pursuit undertaken by wealthy women. Together, these beliefs further devalued overseas education. This devaluation has been nurtured by the persistent perception of the dominance of the liberal arts as the content of study abroad.

Evidence of how extensively programs abroad have supported liberal arts study can be gathered both from the academic majors of students involved and from the courses of study offered. Robert C. Pace's 1959 study of the Delaware/Sweet Briar Paris program found that participants by and large majored in foreign languages and literature, a pattern consistent to the present day in the Sweet Briar program.[37] Surveys conducted by the Institute of International Education have indicated an increasing number of students with diverse majors participating in study abroad in recent years, especially from business and management. Nonetheless, the IIE results also demonstrated a consistent core group of majors in the social sciences, humanities, foreign languages, and fine or applied arts who attend study abroad programs.[38] *Open Door's* 2003 editors reported that "the traditional majors still represent the largest proportion of U.S. students abroad (Social Sciences, Humanities, and Foreign Languages)."[39]

These data indicate what students are majoring in before leaving for study abroad but do not tell what types of programs they choose overseas. There are indications that the majority of students enroll in liberal arts programs, even as more diverse majors choose to study abroad. A mid-1990s analysis of statistics provided by Peterson's publications showed that three of the top four program types offered were history, political science, and social science; business was the fourth.[40] An analysis of CIEE's most recent records showed that from fall 1992 to fall 2004, only 9.2 percent of all enrollments—in programs including business, engineering, health, and science—were outside the humanities and social sciences.[41] These enrollments suggest that the majority of students overseas have concentrated in programs in the humanities and social sciences.

Even with the disciplinary diversity that has occurred, *Open Doors* editors noted, "the profile of U.S. students abroad remains largely unchanged in terms of gender."[42] The preponderance of women participants and of liberal arts majors, the large number of humanities and social science study abroad program themes, the effort to exclude women from the new curriculums and assign to them the world of liberal education, the sense of the liberal arts as a lesser cultural study pursued by women, the presumption that women were uninterested in a professional life regardless of what curriculum they pursued, the belief that their liberal study was solely edifying, the discursive association of women's interests with elitism, wealth, leisure, and travel for pleasure—all these ideas have coalesced to formulate and sustain the dominant belief that study abroad programs offer a liberal arts experience primarily of interest to women and unrelated to professional preparation.

PERCEPTIONS ABOUT THE PRE-EMINENCE OF AMERICAN HIGHER EDUCATION AND THE MARGINAL WORTH OF INTERNATIONAL EDUCATION

According to Foucault, institutions construct their self-images through discourse informed by historic circumstance. Those self-images define the visions and opinions that institutions empower.[43] Since the early twentieth century, the discourse of American faculty has most often exhibited the belief that serious academic work can best be done in the United States, not abroad. Just as this belief raised doubts about the professional usefulness of overseas study, it also contributed to questions about its quality. This discourse of superiority empowers domestic education and marginalizes education abroad.

Even during America's post-colonial era, as the founders of educational institutions looked to Europe for models, a mistrust of the academic worth of Old World institutions was articulated. When Thomas Jefferson founded the nation's first full-fledged state university, the University of Virginia (intending, as mentioned earlier, to provide a more rigorous educational setting than he believed could be found overseas), he recruited five Europeans among his seven first professors. He explained to fellow patriot John Adams that with so few American scholars to choose from in the young republic, he preferred hiring "foreigners of the first order to natives of the second."[44] Despite this rationale, Jefferson received criticism from newspaper editors who accused him of insulting the American people by this act of intellectual "importation."[45]

Nationalistic challenges continue today to confront American higher education institutions. Philip Altbach, director of the Center for International Higher Education at Boston College, has observed that "American faculty seem to feel that U.S. higher education is at the center of an international academic system."[46] Goodwin and Nacht reported that many U.S. faculty believed that "foreign education systems are derivative, teach mainly rote learning, and stifle creativity."[47] Josef Mestenhauser identified as a barrier to internationalization an "academic ethnocentrism that we are the best and do not need to import knowledge from other sources."[48] William Hoffa commented, "If U.S. faculty assume that little of lasting educational value can happen outside of the classroom on their own campus, one can be sure that they are even more suspicious of such experiential doings on foreign soil."[49]

Faculty often look with suspicion on internationalization in general and study abroad in particular. The authors of *Promising Practices: Spotlighting Excellence in Comprehensive Internationalization*, a 2002 ACE study of effective internationalization at eight higher education institutions, argued that internationalization is only possible when faculty support it, since "academic change is the domain of the faculty. And neither making international perspectives real nor infusing the curriculum with those perspectives is a given for U.S. faculty." The Carnegie Foundation's fourteen-nation study of the academic profession, they pointed out, found American faculty far less committed to internationalism than their counterparts elsewhere. Investment in faculty support for internationalism is a prerequisite to its acceptance, but unfortunately, they commented, "budget tightening and the ever-present suspicion that international travel is a boondoggle make this important investment vulnerable to cutbacks."[50]

"Travel as boondoggle" reflects longstanding suspicion in the academy about overseas activities. In the mid-1990s study abroad researchers reported similar views. Benjamin Urbain de Winter reported in *Overcoming Barriers to Study Abroad: A Report of the New York State Task Force on International Education* the attitude "that educational programs abroad are simply not as good as those found in the U.S.," even those programs teaching foreign languages, literature, and culture. De Winter reported hearing some administrators state opinions such as, "The best work in German literature is done in the U.S."[51] In the late 1980s, Goodwin and Nacht likewise encountered some language instructors "who claimed that foreign languages could better be taught at home without all the 'impure' distractions of an overseas setting," although that was a minority opinion.[52] The "boondoggle" perception is evidently a well-entrenched view of international education activity abroad and a perception that effectively marginalizes it within the academic community.

Beliefs as to the primacy of the American educational system are further manifested in the sometimes sparse amount of international research and academic travel activities conducted by faculty at U.S. colleges and universities. ACE surveys of faculty attitudes are somewhat encouraging, indicating that a majority of faculty at surveyed institutions supported internationalization and have some type of international academic experience.[53] Yet most faculty, when they travel, go for one month or less to English-speaking countries (the same criticism many faculty levy against students), and some travel just to the countries adjacent to the United States. Looking at the data through a less than optimistic lens, among the surveyed faculty 80 percent had not submitted to or published in a foreign journal during the past three years; 75 percent had not worked collaboratively with a foreign-born scholar; 73 percent felt international work would not be considered in their promotion and tenure reviews; and, although in the minority, still 36 percent felt that "The more time spent teaching students about other countries, cultures, and global issues, the less time is available for teaching the basics."[54] These statistics reflect what Goodwin and Nacht identified in the late 1980s as "a good deal of indifference in some quarters and a high level of skepticism, even hostility, among many faculty, administrators, and friends of higher education" toward international education.[55] Echoing the "boondoggle" idea, Goodwin and Nacht reported that many American faculty felt that those colleagues who were developing programs overseas were engaging in "faculty frolic," "creating lucrative playpens," and indulging in "an irrelevant distraction on the road to professional careers."[56] They reported attitudes that, in some cases, despite the gains reported in the ACE *Mapping* survey, mirror views still held by some today.

Judgments about the worth of international education compared to domestic education are also expressed through resource allocation.[57] Although the CIEE Baseline Survey in the mid-1990s found that, on average, advisers considered their institutions to be committed to international education,[58] funding decisions often did not echo that commitment. Thirty-eight percent of institutions reported charging beyond regular tuition and fees to support study abroad administration.[59] The 1995 New York State Task Force on International Education decried this approach as marginalizing study abroad: "Study abroad offices are often established with funds which are not allocated as part of the regular college budget." The report recommended institutional support, not self-support, for study abroad activities, in part to reduce "the distorted image of study abroad as a nonessential dimension of education."[60] At the end of the century, the Association of International Education Administrators (AIEA) reported that even when an international education office did receive institutional funds, those funds rarely covered as much as two-thirds of operating expenses, and the typical office had to generate "significant proportions of total revenue."[61]

Sheila Biddle, author of *Internationalization: Rhetoric or Reality*, has suggested that until colleges and universities commit "not just rhetoric but resources and rewards" to faculty who engage in internationalization, neither they nor their students will support it.[62] These resources have not been forthcoming and, complementing funding deficits, a lack of institutional dedication to foreign study is yet another arena where beliefs about study abroad's marginal value reside.[63] The 2003 *Mapping* survey reported erratic administrative support of international education. Some institutions reported no office charged with the support of international education as either part or all of its charge. Others reported that the offices charged with this mission fulfilled other responsibilities as well or that employees within them had multiple charges. Some institutions did report offices with full-time employees dedicated to international education.[64] Perhaps surprisingly, given their featured role in beliefs about study abroad, few liberal arts colleges reported full-time offices for international education.[65] The majority of liberal arts colleges reported only part-time staff in their offices charged with international responsibilities, with most offices fulfilling other duties as well.[66]

But offices either fully or partly dedicated to international education do not themselves manifest an increase in eminence or an end to perceived marginalization. As Goodwin and Nacht wrote, "It is important to have study abroad well woven into the total fabric of the institution, and the administrator responsible for the function should be firmly in the academic sector, rather than in student affairs, student services, general administration, counseling, or some other more distant part of the educational hierarchy."[67] Yet no survey has yet reported widespread success in grounding study abroad in fully staffed and financially supported offices located within the heart of the academic world. Without resource allocation and institutional support, study abroad programs, the faculty who operate and support them, and the students interested in them continue to be diminished in the discourse of the academy. Programs cannot build numbers, quality, influence, or reputation. And study abroad continues to founder in comparison to American higher education.

THE ROOTS OF THE BELIEF: STUDY ABROAD PROGRAMS ARE ACADEMICALLY WEAK AND INSIGNIFICANT IN COMPARISON TO U.S. EDUCATION

Today, says Jane Guyer, Johns Hopkins professor of anthropology, "internationalization is constantly in danger of running aground on one or another implication of America's mutating sense of its own uniqueness in the world."[68] Still, it was not a given that study abroad would be perceived as weak just because U.S. education came to be perceived as strong. This validation of domestic over foreign education, and its reflection in the lack of support for international education, has formed through practices that include the emergence of the multidisciplinary university in the United States, described earlier,[69] the structure of study abroad program models, and institutional choices that bear an impact on how study abroad is perceived.

The preference for domestic education can be found in some of the earliest discourse about modern study abroad. When Smith College began its program in the 1920s, the faculty railed against the idea, reports Patricia Olmsted, director emeritus of Smith's Office of Study Abroad. According to Olmsted's retrospective, the French Department in particular questioned the feasibility of the Junior Year Abroad model, given their students' inability to integrate into the French university system.[70] The Smith faculty voted against what they deemed a "wild" proposal.[71] Olmsted reports a Smith College dean as saying:

> The Junior Year is in large part a tool of general educational experi-
> ence; language, places, museums, general know-how; not the develop-
> ment of critical powers and fine discriminating judgment on literary
> questions. The French Department at Smith can develop these powers
> for its students; in a comparable degree the Paris faculty cannot . . . [72]

A set of mutually exclusive values soon attached to the Junior Year Abroad.
As discussed earlier, the model was on the one hand connected to the elite
Eastern women's colleges where such programs first took shape. John Bow-
man described these early programs as, "in part, a transformation of the
European tour for young women into an academic experience."[73] The
Junior Year Abroad soon became associated with an elite population study-
ing less than serious academic subjects in the Grand Tour tradition.

Admiration was also expressed from early on, though. A Junior Year
Abroad provided a significant opportunity to immerse students in another
culture and language.[74] Goodwin and Nacht reported that when faculty
have articulated support for foreign study, it has often been support for the
junior year immersion model, "defended with almost religious zeal by its
supporters, who are mainly faculty members and study abroad directors at
the institutions of origin . . . in prestigious highly selective colleges and universities."[75] Concerns that students spend too short a time abroad have
been voiced for decades, the most skeptical represented by the Engles, who
wrote recently that "the message of short terms and undemanding language
requirements seems clear: anyone, apparently, can 'Access the World.'"[76]

Nonetheless, whether short-term or full-year, it is the quality of the
experience that raises suspicions. As Benjamin De Winter stated in the mid-
1990s, "The traditional partner universities in Europe place less emphasis on
the results of a particular semester. In fact, there may be almost no work
required to receive credit, and credits often do not even exist. European students are expected to study more on their own, in preparation for all-impor-
tant comprehensive exams after 6 or 10 semesters." De Winter went on to
state that "American students who enter such a system for just one or two
semesters perceive a lighter work load. Unprepared as juniors for highly independent study methods, and distracted by the adjustment to a new environment, they appear to do less 'academic' work than their friends back home.
Professors, too, may share this perception, looking at study abroad programs
as opportunities to get away from campus, with fewer responsibilities and a
reduced workload abroad."[77] Attitudes within American higher education
toward the Junior Year Abroad contradict one another, in other words. The
model stands on the one hand as an example of high quality and extended
valuable study and on the other as an academically weak and frivolous

Grand Tour experience for wealthy women uninterested in advancing to a career.

Host country faculty have contributed to the discursive formation of the beliefs that devalue the Junior Year Abroad as academically unchallenging. Historically, some have questioned the serious intent of these college juniors, younger than the majority of students at European universities.[78] As Barbara Burn noted, many professionals in U.S. and overseas higher education "remain convinced that graduate study abroad is far more important than undergraduate," because undergraduate education, and in particular undergraduate education abroad, does not involve the same focus, goals, or value.[79] As expressed by the authors of *The Brave New (and Smaller) World of Higher Education: A Transatlantic View,* a document emerging from the 2001 Transatlantic Dialogue sponsored by the American Council on Education, the Association of Universities and Colleges of Canada, and the European University Association, "Rarely does an American student enroll at a foreign university in the same way that foreign students enroll at U.S. institutions."[80] They further observe that U.S. study abroad is primarily for undergraduates, three-quarters of whom study in English and many of whom are taught by American faculty with American classmates, all limiting their exposure to their host community.[81] Doubts about undergraduate purpose and program quality continue to adhere.

This dismissal of the quality of U.S. study abroad reveals that post–World War II changes in study abroad models have not necessarily improved its valuation within the American academy. Since World War II students have been offered choices for their length of study. During this period, though, the number of students going abroad for a semester or a summer has come to exceed by far the number of students studying abroad for a full academic year, and indeed almost half go on short-term programs less than a quarter of a year in length.[82] As the first Report of the National Task Force on Undergraduate Education Abroad concluded, "Faculty often do not recognize the academic legitimacy of the students' activities abroad."[83] Perhaps this is especially reinforced when these experiences last only a few weeks, as these days they often do. These new models have left unchanged expressions of suspicion about the quality of study abroad programs, and in some cases have increased them.

One post–WWII program innovation has substantially added to this discourse of invalidation, as *The Brave New (and Smaller) World* authors noted: studies abroad conducted in the English language. Some researchers have noted that the foreign language skills of American students determine the level at which they may enter a host country's educational system, and foreign language skills have steadily declined among American students in recent years.[84] "Foreign-language enrollments as a percentage of higher education enrollments have declined from 16 percent in the 1960s to a current average of less than 8 percent," wrote Engberg and Green in *Promising Practices*.[85] Only 7.9 percent of study abroad students are reported to be foreign language majors.[86]

Responding to this longstanding problem, educators established special, separate courses for U.S. students abroad, taught in English, to ensure that more students could study overseas. According to the survey conducted for the 1997 editions of *Peterson's Study Abroad* and *Peterson's Summer Study Abroad*, English was the primary language of instruction in 59 percent of all programs that year.[87] Among CIEE programs established prior to 1990, 37 percent, or three out of eight, were taught in English.[88] As of 2003–04, 38 of CIEE's 60 programs, or 63 percent—nearly two out of three—were taught in English. [89]

Although designed to encourage more American students to study abroad, English-language programs have been perceived as weakening the academic quality of offerings overall. Briggs and Burn reported this suspicion in the early years of English-language programs and recommended steps to improve student skills, such as providing "intensive language programs prior to their departure from the U.S. or on arrival in their host country." The alternative approach of "organizing special programs for American students in foreign language countries which are mainly conducted in English and also teach elementary or intermediate skills in the host country's language," they found, "has the basic deficiency of insulating the Americans from the local students and culture."[90]

Both the domestic lack of support for foreign language study at all levels and the persistence of study abroad in English continue to influence perceptions of the worth of study abroad programs. David Maxwell, president of Drake University and former National Foreign Language Center director, and Nina Garrett, director of Yale University's Center for Language Study, wrote that "for most of the past century, the United States has wallowed in the complacency of linguistic and cultural myopia, firmly convinced that it is not important for us to understand other languages or cultures, since much of the world speaks English and they're all trying to emulate us anyway. We are, in Richard Lambert's wonderful description, the most devoutly monolingual populace in the world."[91] For those with this perspective, foreign language study is not a valued commodity, whether pursued domestically or overseas.

On the other hand, many worry that there continues to be insufficient language preparation for study abroad. Sheila Biddle observed that while there is lots of resolve to increase the number of students going abroad, little language learning is going on.[92] Likewise the newest members of the NAFSA Task Force on Education Abroad focused on the lack of foreign language competency in their report.[93] Arguing for the value of going abroad for foreign language training, the report implicitly if not intentionally criticized the current state of study abroad. The Engles included the increasing number of English language programs in their denunciation of the quality and worth of study abroad.[94]

In short, efforts by some to make study abroad appeal to a broader student base have drawn criticism from a different direction.[95] By increasing English-language offerings, study abroad coordinators have simultaneously inserted a new element in the discourse that draws disparaging comments, sustains derogatory beliefs, confirms the normalized view, and systematizes with other institutional issues and practices reflecting negative views about study abroad.

In addition to forms of study programs, those administering study abroad themselves may sometimes be viewed as less than academic or as exercising skills not central to the mission of the institution, which generates devaluing associations about the worth of the product they oversee. Josef Mestenhauser noted that in the last decades of the twentieth century, American faculty rarely respected their colleagues' cross-cultural and international educational skills, sometimes expressing that appointments in the field of international education had been made in a serendipitous fashion because, for example, someone was available locally who had a Ph.D. in some glutted field, but not because someone had expertise in international education. Further, he observed, gender and credential evaluation of administrators could be another discursive component in judgments about study abroad, somewhat in parallel to Hoffa's observation that the gender of study abroad advisers may discourage male prospects. "We are a female-dominated profession numerically," said Mestenhauser, "but this doesn't mean we are a profession which supports women in senior positions. Because of the serendipitous nature of appointments and peripheral role of international education within higher education, secretaries or lower-level administrators are often promoted to administrative positions, perpetuating the non-academic, 'mother hen' image of international education advisors."[96]

His observation was confirmed by a NAFSA survey of its membership at the time,[97] then reinforced in 2004 when NAFSA again surveyed its membership. Among its 8,900 members at all appointment levels from the U.S. and abroad, women still dominated. While two-thirds of members were female, only 14 percent held the Ph.D. degree and only 2 percent held senior administrative positions.[98] Within SECUSSA, the study abroad section of NAFSA, 64 percent of the membership was female; 21 percent held a B.A., 69 percent an M.A., and 9 percent a Ph.D. or J.D.[99] The gender breakdown mimicked the gender proportions among participants in study abroad. Regardless of the actual competence study abroad practitioners may exercise, the absence of the Ph.D. within the international education profession prompts distrust from faculty about the academic judgment of these professionals and the programs they supervise.

Study abroad advisers and sometimes even the most senior study abroad appointees often find themselves low on the higher education pay scale, further confirming the marginality of their work and worth in the eyes of their peers.[100] As of 2004, the median salary for a study abroad adviser, $35,291,[101] was even lower than the lowest faculty rank salary, $38,501.[102] Among median salaries for mid-level college student services administrators in 2003–04, the category of study abroad adviser ranked only six positions from the bottom. Study abroad advisers earned less than food service unit managers.[103]

International educators at the most senior levels of appointment, with comprehensive duties including but not exclusive to study abroad, present a somewhat different picture. In 1999 the Association of International Education Administrators (AIEA) reported that office heads most often held the Ph.D.; that more than 40 percent held faculty appointments; and that its 81 survey respondents reported an average salary of $83,750, more than twice that of staff identified as study abroad advisers.[104] At this most senior level of the professional spectrum, where there are greater opportunities to wield power, the majority of employees were male.[105] Still, the AIEA survey also revealed that international educators did not always hold positions of power. The majority of respondents (64.2%) held the title "Director," with only 14.8 percent appointed "Dean," 13.6 percent "Associate/Assistant Vice President," and 3 percent "Vice President."[106] Even at this most senior level at most colleges and universities, in positions where the average age of the jobholder was almost 55 years old, a wide range in salary was reported, from $40,000 to $150,000 per year.[107]

Lack of powerful appointment status and lower salaries for the vast majority of those working in international education confirm the belief that these forms of education, study abroad included, are not of sufficient worth to command high recognition or reward. Josef Mestenhauser wrote recently, just

as he had more than fifteen years before, that international education professionals remain unrespected, with their lack of authority "reflected in the hier-
archical relationship between faculty and non-teaching staff involved in
administering international programs."[108] This includes study abroad advisers, who hold positions in "the lower rungs" of institutional respect.

Even at institutions with a centralized office headed by a senior
appointee, study abroad development itself may not be centralized. On
many campuses it is initiated by individuals acting on their own rather than
in concert with a staff appointed and supported by the central administration.[109] According to Anders Uhrskov, Denmark's International Study Program director, within the more than 150 colleges and universities in its
consortium, it has often been an energetic faculty member who has spurred
a program, an approach that can effectively promote new interest in study
abroad on a campus.[110] Despite the contribution a faculty member might
make to his or her own campus, however, as Briggs and Burn pointed out,
this approach can sometimes have negative rhetorical consequences. A fac-
ulty-initiated study abroad program might be considered "entrepreneurial," "decentralized," and, they argued, "denigrates the need for
professionalism and institutional commitment."[111]

This lack of institutional commitment is reflected in the tenure and
promotion policies. Goodwin and Nacht chronicled many instances of
parochialism, distrust, or intellectual arrogance among American faculty,[112]
noting that international education accomplishments did not contribute
toward promotion and tenure. Many faculty believed they would actually
harm professional progress: "Since international travel connotes both
wealth and dissipation to many Americans, any overseas experience suggests the danger of incipient if not actual moral decay."[113]

This fear persists. Despite their avowed interest in things international—and, from some, an expressed hope that these activities would be
recognized—most faculty surveyed for *Mapping Internationalization*
doubted that international work would count in tenure and promotion
decisions.[114] *Promising Practices* authors reported that only 4 percent of
surveyed higher education institutions specified international work or experience in tenure and promotion decisions.[115] With direct regard to study
abroad, the newest NAFSA study abroad task force reports:

> Colleges often provide too few incentives for faculty to work closely with
> students on planning, supervising, and assessing the study abroad experi-
> ence. Apart from faculty-led study tours over summer or winter break,
> few colleges dispatch their own faculty to teach courses overseas. . . .
> Moreover, junior faculty may be reluctant to take on assignments that cut

into the time available for writing and research, activities that colleges do reward with tenure and promotion. Without faculty respect and institutional advocacy, internationalization activities like study abroad remain invalidated.[116]

By definition, that which is excluded as important in tenure and promotion decisions is defined as less significant in, even peripheral to, higher education practices. These professional practices—budgetary limitations, low salaries, gender- and credential-associated devaluation, and faculty anxieties about recognition and reward for international efforts—associate with suspicions about short-term and English language programs, weak overseas institutional practices, and more broadly with perceptions that study abroad is a woman's liberal education pursuit, insignificant to academic and professional training, both of which are better pursued at home. All coalesce to perpetuate the definition of study abroad as a less significant, lower-quality alternative to domestic education, worthy of neither respect nor support.

LIBERAL ARTS, NATIONALISM, PROFESSIONALISM, AND THE CONFLUENCE OF DOMINANT BELIEFS IN DISCOURSE ON STUDY ABROAD

Foucault argues that men govern by instituting practices that reinforce a defining episteme.[117] They hold on tight to practices that sustain their visions of themselves,[118] define what is acceptable and unacceptable, and support the power of the norm.[119] American educators have been empowered with a vision of the superiority of their institutions over any others in the world, and of their work as more significant than that of their colleagues who would bring an international dimension to the education they offer. Those visions marginalize study abroad.

Indeed, this marginalization is confirmed and perpetuated by each of the dominant beliefs that have been unearthed so far in this book. Common themes weave together; they systematize and cross that "threshold of epistemologization" described by Michel Foucault.[120] In short, discourse generates an episteme that contains the dominant beliefs that study abroad is a Grand Tour; that study abroad is an insignificant pursuit by wealthy women; and that study abroad offers a nonprofessional course of study inferior to American education.

Dominant beliefs about study abroad stand forth as the inverse of notions of normalized domestic education. In a young nation energized by the mission to grow toward world greatness, educational institutions became partners in its "manifest destiny."[121] The energy and vision within

American institutions—dubious about Europe from the start, even if dependent upon it to educate leaders—gave rise to a revolution in higher education, generating a new and sometimes uniquely American curriculum, grounded in the need to train men to solve the problems of the nation.[122] As American universities emerged and gained the respect of those in power within the culture, Europe was rejected as the necessary site for education. American men stayed at home, and at home, men from many walks of life had access to higher education. Egalitarianism spread, if not to gender, at least to social class.[123] By the end of the nineteenth century, the tradition of male European study abroad had ended, and the European experience was relegated to women who sought culture and social status through an elitist Grand Tour tradition. This tradition was anathema to the emerging domestic philosophy of education and to America's vision of itself as a truly "New World."

It was within this cultural context, after World War I, that modern study abroad programs emerged. Offering training through the liberal curriculum, study abroad returned in academic content to colonial and early nineteenth-century forms of education—training grounded in liberal study. Its female constituency was perceived as frivolous, certainly not the audience for whom the new developments in domestic education were being developed. And the institutions most frequently supporting study abroad—the private women's colleges—were viewed in the dominant discourse as secondary because they were not training men for a public life.

Study abroad programs, created most frequently by the private and expensive women's colleges, offered a Eurocentric liberal curriculum. They appeared to turn their backs on the new pride and excitement in quality American education. In short, these programs, so avidly supported by the institutions that created them, flew in the face of America's emerging vision of itself and its educational system. The traits that were perceived to define the programs, through discursive association, condemned them. The episteme devaluing study abroad as academically weak and lacking in professional training emerged, unchallenged by any voice of power.

This book's first chapter described the urgent hopes articulated recently by policy makers that study abroad would become central to the mission of American education. Yet study abroad continues to play at the periphery. It has not yet found support from within the empowered academic community.

Foucault suggests that archaeology, excavating the roots of belief in an episteme and bringing the component parts of belief to consciousness, might lead to epistemic change and the reallocation of power.[124] Such a reallocation of power is likewise the goal of policy makers, who wish their voices to be heeded and their advocacy of study abroad to be embraced and funded. Yet power is endowed by dominant beliefs, and that allocation of power affects individuals' lives[125]—in particular, in this arena, the academic sponsors and participants of study abroad. The faculty and administrators who have supported study abroad programs and the students who have participated in them have been disenfranchised by the status quo. The value they might perceive in their experience has so often gone unacknowledged within their communities. They offer alternative discourses about the nature of an education outside domestic boundaries. Although their voices are diminished or excluded by the normative power endowed by the episteme, their discourse challenges the national vision. The next two chapters of this book explore those alternative discourses in order to hear the beliefs of sponsors and participants about the nature and value of study abroad.

Part Three
Alternative Voices

Chapter Five
Alternative Voices: Discourse and Belief among Faculty Sponsors of U.S. Study Abroad

The prevailing view may be disdain toward study abroad as academically weak and functionally irrelevant, but alternative discourses do exist within the American academy. The vast majority ignores those marginalized voices. This chapter will explore the discourse of those faculty advocates of study abroad who see it as both an academically demanding experience and an important avenue for professional preparation. Involved faculty and administrators see a unique role for study abroad, too, as a form of education that can contribute to international peace.

Michel Foucault recognized the existence of alternative discourses and recommended their exploration to identify the unique and often obscured knowledge locked within them. He encouraged the historian to listen to the voices of the time, labeling this investigation "genealogy."[1] Genealogy includes inquiry conducted to identify dissenting views, which often go unrecognized and invalidated. It is an inquiry that illuminates the beliefs of participants in an event, and particularly the beliefs of those whose knowledge is counter to the norm and thus not respected.[2] The faculty and administrators who have organized or supported programs overseas and the students who have participated in those programs hold dissenting views about study abroad and thus are candidates for a study modeled on Foucault's method of genealogy.

Adapting such a perspective, this chapter and the next will illuminate these alternative beliefs about American study abroad. This chapter will examine the goals and expectations of faculty and administrators committed to study abroad. The next chapter will turn to the student participants, considering their dedication, motivations, and expectations as revealed in discourse from the early twentieth century to the present. The discourse of female study abroad participants, around whose presence the episteme has been constructed, will be of particular interest.

Genealogical inquiry gives voice to those excluded from power and often reveals the contradictory beliefs excluded by the majority. For Foucault, these methods of inquiry carry with them the possibility for change in what is believed and who has power.[3] By bringing into the discussion the alternate beliefs of sponsors and participants of study abroad, perhaps some change can be made in the effectiveness of discourse designed to strengthen study abroad in the American academy.

ALTERNATIVE VOICES ON ACADEMIC QUALITY IN STUDY ABROAD

The discourse and practice of faculty and administrators who have created or supported study abroad programs is largely ignored in an academic world where ninety-seven out of one hundred undergraduate students complete their entire education in the United States. To bring to light alternative beliefs about the academic quality of study abroad, this chapter will examine the academic abilities of students for whom sponsors created programs; the stated academic goals and standards of early and contemporary programs; program admission and foreign language requirements; and the academic caliber of institutions sending students abroad. These inquiries will help illuminate beliefs within the marginalized community of supporters, beliefs that define women as capable and serious students, at home and abroad. In this community of belief, overseas study programs are held to offer high-quality educational opportunities not available in the United States.

First, two historical cases will be examined: the University of Delaware/Sweet Briar College study abroad program and Smith College's overseas program. The program begun by Delaware and continued after World War II at Sweet Briar College offers the most thorough set of data, anecdotal and statistical, to be found on the history of study abroad. Discourse on this coeducational program offers the opportunity to discover faculty beliefs about the quality expected of such a program for both men and women. Smith College presents a program almost as long-lived as that of Delaware/Sweet Briar, yet established and maintained by a women's college for female participants only. Discourse on this program offers the opportunity for an analysis of the beliefs of sponsors about the purposes of women's education through study abroad.

PROGRAM ORIGINS AND A DISCOURSE OF ACADEMIC QUALITY: THE UNIVERSITY OF DELAWARE MODEL

Just as dominant beliefs about study abroad began to form with the emergence of the modern programs after World War I, so an alternative discourse began developing at the same time. From the start, this discourse conceived of women participants as academically capable students.

In his history of study abroad, John Bowman observes that the Junior Year Abroad program established during the presidency of Walter H. Hullihen in 1923 at Delaware College (later the University of Delaware) was an exception to the rule that only women's colleges established study abroad programs.[4] Indeed, one critical decision considered at Delaware was whether to include women in the program. That decision was made deliberately and in full awareness of the academic rigor of the courses being planned. Writing in 1923, Professor R. W. Kirkbride, program founder, addressed the question of admitting women and noted that there was no reason not to, as they would benefit as much as men and their needs would be accommodated with the same academic offerings.

Kirkbride noted that the female candidates for the program were of the highest academic ability. "I know of two Women's College students who would probably make the trip, Miss Catherine Dougherty and Miss Mary Kreuger. Both are brilliant French students . . . I also have an application from a brilliant girl student of Westminster College, New Wilmington, Pa."[5] He did not differentiate between the academic prowess of male and female students, and he expected the highest achievements from both.

The historic record reflects the concern expressed by the Delaware program founders about academic rigor. As Francis M. Rogers pointed out, American colleges were wary of granting credit for work not done within their walls, so "The institution sponsoring the group . . . was expected to maintain the highest standards and to assure the student's American college that a year's work had in fact been satisfactorily accomplished."[6] Delaware sponsors instituted practices to ensure supervision for the program and to immerse students in several months of language training at the University of Nancy prior to their enrollment in the specially designed Cours de Civilisation at the Sorbonne.[7] The University of Delaware archivist, John M. Clayton, Jr., summarizing the materials from that institution's early foray into study abroad, stated that Hullihen decided to start a study abroad program because of the nation's great economic, commercial, and political growth.[8] Hullihen's intent was a strong academic program with purposeful career preparation training.[9]

Delaware's first group studying abroad numbered eight men. They were chosen for their "intellectual gifts, mature character, industrious habits and linguistic ability."[10] In the second year, the program enrolled seven students, four men and three women, two doing graduate work.[11] The program grew quickly, in part because it attracted participants from other schools, to the point that University of Delaware students represented a minority. In those early years, the program was considered an important service provided by the University of Delaware to the higher education community.[12]

The Delaware plan for an academically rigorous program was reflected in student evaluations of the program in the first decade. In 1933, the University of Delaware Committee on Foreign Study surveyed its alumni, hoping to identify the benefits and most important features of the Foreign Study Plan. They contacted the 383 members of the Association des Anciens Étudiants des Groupes Delaware en France, 245 of whom were women; 127 of those women responded to the survey. Of those, 112 women (88.19%) responded positively to a question that asked whether the program provided a scholastic benefit, representing for the Delaware program sponsors the fulfillment of their goals. [13]

PROGRAM ORIGINS AND A DISCOURSE OF ACADEMIC QUALITY: THE SMITH COLLEGE EXAMPLE

Deliberately mirroring the University of Delaware's success,[14] Smith College began a program in Paris in 1925,[15] organized at the instigation of Smith's Scottish-born and Scottish-educated president, William Allan Neilson.[16] Neilson's discourse reflects a commitment to quality education and to education for quality students. He created a "Smith Special Honors" plan, which became an influential model for honors programs. As part of his vision of education for the strongest of students, Neilson proposed a Junior Year Abroad program.[17]

Neilson himself had come to North America in pursuit of education,[18] and he wanted the new study abroad program to be designed for top-quality students. For Neilson, personally involved in developing the program, "The Junior Year Abroad was another device for the better education of the better student," arising out of "expanding internationalism in American thinking after World War I."[19] Neilson visited Paris during the program's first year and frequently thereafter. By 1931, Smith College had established a Junior Year in Spain; by 1932, a Junior Year in Italy.[20]

From the first, the students involved in Smith College's Paris program were described as academically serious. A letter from Hélène Cattanès, a Smith College professor of French whom Neilson appointed to organize the program, described the students as joyful, ready to observe, and avid to learn and understand.[21] For these students, the new Sorbonne model (as described in chapter 2) was implemented. The Sorbonne designed an array of humanities courses in French civilization, literature, history, art, the history of science, philosophy, as well as social science courses on political and social institutions, all conducted in French. Students also spent two months in intensive language study at the University of Grenoble. They lived with families, an arrangement intended to plunge them into French life while still upholding Smith's strict standards of conduct and academic quality.[22] In the words of Smith's French Department Chair, Jean Collignon, the early Junior Year Abroad in Paris offered "intellectual adventure,"[23] solidly academic through careful coaching by faculty.[24]

Smith students, like those from Delaware, enrolled in the Sorbonne's Cours de Civilisation Française. Smith administrators coordinated their Sorbonne work so that all credits would transfer and contribute toward the baccalaureate degree. Thus the Smith program, designed as an honors experience,[25] transcended the Grand Tour tradition: It set high academic standards and expectations for its participants. And it was a program designed with these features to serve an entirely female constituency.

PROGRAM ORIGINS AND A DISCOURSE OF ACADEMIC QUALITY: THE SWEET BRIAR PROGRAM

Smith College's program exerted a formative influence on discourse and practice in early U.S. study abroad. The model—a strong academic program for capable students at a women's college—continued, and institutions including Yale and Harvard expressed support as the Institute of International Education's Committee on Study Abroad supervised the transfer of the program from the University of Delaware to Sweet Briar College, an all-female liberal arts college in Virginia.[26] Both Meta Glass, college president when Sweet Briar initiated the takeover of the Delaware program, and Martha B. Lucas, her successor, went on record to express commitment to strong academic programs. These two administrators supported Joseph Barker, the French professor who had before World War II served as a resident director of the University of Delaware program and who developed it further for Sweet Briar College. Barker believed the program, whether Delaware or Sweet Briar sponsored it, offered academic quality and professional development for strong students.[27]

Sweet Briar maintained an "enviable record for academic vigor," according to college President Harold B. Whitman, Jr., reviewing the program in 1973.[28] Whitman continued:

Sweet Briar is blessed to have had persons with the foresight to continue the program at a moment when it was threatened with disappearance; we are also blessed to have had persons with the standards and the fortitude to make it into an extremely valuable educational experience for all its participants, as well as one of the College's greatest assets.[29]

The stated principles of the Sweet Briar program—which, like Delaware and Smith, influenced many future programs—included "careful selection" of undergraduates, educational counseling while overseas, registration in regular courses at the foreign university as well as special courses for program participants, and periodic tracking of student progress by the home institution.[30] Students were required to have achieved at least a 3.0 average (on a 4.0 scale) in French courses and a minimum 2.5 average in college work as a whole.[31] Today Sweet Briar maintains its program for higher-achieving students and admits only students with a 3.0 average or better in all courses, continuing to articulate the conception that study abroad should be designed to serve academically superior students.[32]

PROGRAM ORIGINS AND DISCOURSES OF ACADEMIC QUALITY: MARYMOUNT AND ROSARY COLLEGES

Founders of the other early study abroad programs established at American women's colleges—Marymount College and Rosary College—described motives similar to those stated by founders at Sweet Briar College and at Delaware and Smith before them. Marymount College, a Catholic women's college in Tarrytown, New York, initially decided to establish a study abroad program in 1921. The Marymount nuns faced difficulties, including real estate problems.[33] They persisted, feeling that the program was important to their school, and finally established "Marymount in Paris" in 1924.[34] According to Sister Rita Arthur, international education director emeritus of Marymount College, their study abroad programs were always set up with an emphasis on high academic standards, offering, some claimed, a much more focused scholarly program than any at Marymount itself.[35]

Rosary College, a women's college organized by the Dominican Sisters in River Forest, Illinois, established a study abroad program in 1925. Participants resided in Fribourg, Switzerland, and studied French, literature, religion, philosophy, history, and English at Fribourg's Institut des Hautes Etudes. World War II interrupted the program, but plans to reopen in 1947 inspired the publication of a college brochure, describing the program and giving a glimpse at the academic expectations of its sponsors. "Who should study abroad?" the brochure asked, answering: "A Serious Student." The brochure then addressed the association with the Grand Tour tradition directly:

> The Junior Year Abroad should not be confused with the traditional Grand Tour. It is not a 12-month holiday devoted to the accidental assimilation of culture and the deliberate enjoyment of leisure.

> Only students who can convince themselves and their teachers of the seriousness of their work should consider the Fribourg Foreign Study Plan.[36]

Appropriate candidates, the brochure stated, "must be young women of character and of studious habits. They must have completed, as better-than-average students, at least two years of college work and be disposed to do earnest studying while abroad."[37] Rosary College administrators and faculty evidently sensed the nascent dominant belief that study abroad provided a dilettantish Grand Tour experience, and they felt the need to make clear that their intentions, and thus their program, were quite different.

Indeed a review of scholarly articles prior to World War II by and for those interested in study abroad revealed no discourse describing these junior year abroad programs as cultural enrichment experiences in the Grand Tour tradition.[38] Instead the discourse of faculty and administrators who sponsored all these early programs—Delaware, Smith, Rosary, Marymount, and, after World War II, Sweet Briar—consistently defined them as academic experiences designed to challenge the most able students, including the women.

POST–WORLD WAR II DISCOURSES OF ACADEMIC STANDARDS

Interest in strong academic programs resumed after World War II in the discourse and practice of programs like the Delaware/Sweet Briar model and continued in U.S. study abroad program development thereafter. The record of Beaver College, now called Arcadia University, provides an example. Beaver College historically admitted more U.S. students to British university programs than any other U.S. institution. Today it enrolls 1,800 students annually in all its programs worldwide and requires a grade point average of 3.0 for admission to the majority of those programs. Arcadia describes its commitments, past and present, to the highest quality in study abroad programs:

As part of a University that has more than 50 years of experience in international education, the Center for Education Abroad maintains that study abroad is fundamental to a liberal education and enhances an individual's ability to live in a global society. Since our beginning, we have been committed to providing high-quality, academically sound and experientially rich study abroad programs.

Our early entry into the field—when just a few American institutions sent students overseas to study for credit in fully integrated programs—has made us the vanguard in study abroad. Through the years we've proudly honored this mark of distinction. Since our beginning, we have continued to evaluate overseas programs and regularly expand our offerings to include those that demonstrate a commitment to high quality education. Additionally, we believe in a firm philosophy of quality improvement and regularly assess our services to ensure that they fully meet the needs of program participants and study abroad professionals.[39]

The Institute for the International Education of Students (IES) also expresses its academic vision, stating that in its 53 years of offering programs, now in 22 locations in Asia, Australia, Europe, and South America, IES has remained "Committed to quality." IES is a consortium composed of more than 150 highly selective U.S. colleges and universities, and states that "because IES admits only top students (90% of whom come from this consortium), each IES program is filled with outstanding achievers."[40] Serving 17,000 students from 1950 to 1999, the period encompassed by its most recent alumni survey, IES requires a 3.0 or higher admissions prerequisite to all its programs, with a 3.2 requirement typically for honors programs.[41]

The CIEE Baseline Survey of international education administrators asked study abroad advisers which criteria counted the most heavily when they evaluated student program applications. Important criteria included faculty recommendations, previous language study, personal attributes, and essay writing, but the most frequently cited criterion was academic standing, reflected in grade point average.[42] Today, offering sixty study centers in twenty-nine countries and providing "a rewarding and respected academic experience through creative curricular design, discriminating selection of host institutions and courses, careful hiring and training of CIEE teachers, and diligent continuous self-assessment of program elements," CIEE programs typically require a grade point average of 2.75 or better for admission.[43]

Finally, an analysis done near the close of the twentieth century compared data from Peterson's *Study Abroad* guide and IIE. It involved an examination of grade point averages required for admission into study abroad programs, and revealed that those schools sending the greatest number of students abroad demonstrated a commitment to their stronger students, typically establishing GPA requirements for admission into study abroad at B-minus or higher.[44] These examples from the past and present suggest that academic ability is and always has been a criterion by which students have been selected to participate in study abroad.

Literature describing students as academically competent also forms part of the discourse that sustains a belief within the sponsor community that study abroad is for capable students. In a 1990 study, Elinor G. Barber and Barbara B. Burn found that "study-abroad students, especially those in academic year programs, exhibit above-average scholastic performance and consider themselves strong academically."[45] Study abroad students were reported to be superior academically during the whole of their college career as well as in the year in which they pursued foreign study. *NAFSA's Guide to Education Abroad for Advisers and Administrators* included a description of program participants as very capable: "study abroad students exhibit above-average scholastic performance." For admissions, the guide continued, "most programs require a minimum of a 3.0 grade point average."[46]

To program participants, the voices of their faculty sponsors come through loud and clear, describing study abroad as a rigorous and rewarding intellectual experience. The survey of Sweet Briar alumni revealed that the 75 percent of women participants identified academic interest as their primary motivation for study abroad. (See Appendix, Table 5–1, for responses to Sweet Briar survey, Question 19, Deciding Factors.) Both male and female participants sought academic guidance to identify which program to attend, turning typically to academic faculty to help them as they made their decisions. (See Appendix, Table 5–2, for a quantitative summary of responses to survey, Question 23, How did you hear about the Sweet Briar program?)

Not all data, however, reinforce the alternative belief that study abroad is a challenging venture for the strongest students. A survey of institutions offering study abroad programs in 1996–97, based on data collected for *Peterson's Guide* that year, provided a mixed message. Of the study abroad programs listed, 58.7 percent required a grade point average of 2.5 or higher for admission. Of those, 46.1 percent of all programs required a grade point average above 2.75.[47] Yet slightly over 40 percent of programs accepted students with below a 2.5. These figures can convey different messages. Compared with decades in the early twentieth century, programs have expanded to include students with lower academic grade point averages. The presence of these students conforms to dominant beliefs about the academic weakness of study abroad. Nonetheless, the alternative discourse describing study abroad as an activity for students with academic strengths remains persistent. Indeed, some researchers have cited this discourse as one of the primary obstacles to expanding enrollment in overseas education, since faculty advocates of overseas education are reluctant to support weaker students in their study abroad applications.[48]

Despite the persistence of these alternative voices, as Foucault argues, information that fits the norm is heard while that which does not fit the norm remains marginalized and unheard.[49] Descriptions of weaker students in study abroad programs support the majority view. The episteme describing study abroad as academically weak still stands, even as programs identify important academic missions for their programs and set high admissions standards for entrance into them, as schools sending students abroad in large numbers often require students to have higher GPAs, as advisers cite the GPA as the most important admission criterion, and as literature reports the academic strength of American students overseas.

DISCOURSE AND PRACTICE: FOREIGN LANGUAGE REQUIREMENTS AND ACADEMIC QUALITY

Debate about foreign language prerequisites for study abroad turns out to be another arena where evidence that reinforces the devaluing episteme is recognized, while that which challenges it is often ignored, especially in discussions about the role of foreign language learning in study abroad.

The earliest of programs, Delaware and Smith, required prior language training. A certain level of language ability was in fact considered essential:

> The theory behind the junior year abroad program was admirably simple and defensible. After two or three years of foreign language study in high school, plus an additional two-year's study in college, the student had reached the point where his accent, his vocabulary, his knowledge of the country and its language, all stood to benefit by a year spent in a foreign environment. As a foreign language major he was intensely motivated for this type experience since it obviously presented him with a linguistic experience superior to that which he could attain on his own campus.[50]

In the aftermath of World War I, the academic community took the opportunity to assess the value of work going on in the various disciplines. This assessment prompted the increased emphasis on spoken as well as written foreign language study in the United States,[51] the pedagogical environment within which U.S. study abroad first emerged and study in the foreign languages first became valued. Sweet Briar College continued the Delaware tradition by requiring prior foreign language training of students attending study abroad programs, and continues this practice to the present day: Two years of pre-college French and the equivalent of two years of college French, including one or more intermediate college courses in literature, language, or civilization, are required to qualify for study abroad. Further, students must show no lower than a B average in college French.[52]

Foreign language study has not only been a requirement: It has, in fact, been a component of the discourse of motivation throughout the development of U.S. study abroad. University of California programs were established in order to teach foreign languages:

> The lag in foreign language instruction in the American schools and colleges became a source of alarm in the late 1950's. Americans realized that they had failed to appreciate the sense of cultural empathy created when men speak the same language. The epithet "Ugly American" . . . has come into everyday usage as a summary of the frustration, . . . and contempt is to be expected when the linguistically and emotionally provincial American goes abroad.[53]

An Education Abroad Program for the entire University of California system was established in 1962, and soon the Regents approved a Junior Year Abroad at the University of Bordeaux. By 1967, the program had expanded to ten countries and was described as "one of the most ambitious programs for overseas study in American higher education." Students admitted to the program had to show two years of prior language study and a B average,[54] a level of expectation that continues to the present in California's immersion programs.[55]

Discourse describing language study as a motivation for study abroad has continued into the twenty-first century. The new NAFSA study abroad task force called September 11, 2001, "a wake-up call,"[56] emphasizing the need to educate students not only internationally but in other languages. "Our adversaries around the world may well speak English in addition to their mother tongues, but we can be sure that they will not be planning attacks against American interests in the one language we are capable of deciphering."[57]

Yet despite this persistent valuation of foreign language training as part of a worthwhile education abroad, those who are organizing programs in non-English speaking countries continue to express uncertainty about foreign language competency as an entrance requirement. Currently some programs forgo such requirements in order to encourage students from disciplines that often do not include foreign language training—technology, science, or business—to study abroad. Other programs are designed for students with no prior language training, to encourage them in language and international education. Data collected for the 1998–99 edition of Peterson's *Study Abroad* showed that about half of programs taught in non-English speaking countries—544 out of 1,100—required some level of foreign language competency for admission.[58] CIEE, committed to foreign language study, did not require it for admission, so as not to exclude able students, but instead required that all participants study the host country language. A substantial number—38 of the 60 CIEE programs offered in 2003–04—were taught in English.[59]

There is the danger described in the previous chapter that these figures will be interpreted to mean study abroad programs are lowering their standards when they do not require previous foreign language study for admission or allow study in English only, yet they can be evaluated in another light. Given current trends in study abroad, these data represent the efforts of program sponsors to expand study abroad venues to locations whose native languages are infrequently taught domestically, to encourage language learning among those who have not before pursued it, and to expand participation by students in majors outside the liberal arts.[60] As William Hoffa put it, while acknowledging faculty distrust of English-language and short-term programs: "the holistic, traditional full immersion in the language and culture of a given country may no longer be possible for most U.S. students and programs, due to the combination of (a) a lack of linguistic and intellectual preparation, (b) the brevity and circumscribed conditions of most programs, (c) the poly-cultural populations now found within most national borders, and (d) the emergence of a global culture. The value of what students have experienced and what they have learned about the current and future world as it *is* is no less significant, however [italics Hoffa's]. This knowledge is both real and essential to their understanding of the changing realities of the world in which they will live. . . . They and we realize that staying home makes it considerably less likely that these essential lessons will be learned."[61]

While the increasing number of English language programs affirms for many their suspicions about study abroad, for others these programs form part of the discourse that validates foreign education. They play a central part in the effort to enhance the importance of study overseas and do not erode its academic quality.

DISCOURSE AND PRACTICE: SUPPORT FOR STUDY ABROAD AND ACADEMIC QUALITY BY HIGHER-RANKING INSTITUTIONS

Despite its devaluation, study abroad has been supported by the strongest of academic institutions, "especially those in the upper tier of prestige," as Philip Altbach put it.[62] A statistical analysis of academic rankings of U.S. institutions published annually in the 2003 *U.S. News and World Report* edition of *America's Best Colleges,* comparing these rankings to the numbers of students abroad from U.S. institutions as reported by the Institute of International Education, confirmed this claim. In the top-ranked 120 public and private American colleges and universities, an average of 20.1 percent of undergraduate students participated in study abroad. Of these, the top ten showed an average 21.4 percent rate of participation, while the bottom ten showed only 8.3 percent. Looking only at public institutions, the top-ranked institutions sent an average of 16.3 percent of their undergraduate students abroad, while the lowest-ranked schools sent only 4.2 percent. These data demonstrate that the most highly ranked schools send larger percentages of their students to study abroad.

Similarly, of the top 120 schools, those with SAT admission requirements of 1200 or higher sent on average 27.4 percent of their students abroad. Schools with SAT requirements of 1100 to 1190 sent 24.5 percent; those in the 1000–1090 range, 17.8 percent. The lowest study abroad participation rates showed up in schools that required below a 1000 SAT score for admission; they sent an average of only 9.8 percent of their students abroad.[63] So institutions with the higher SAT requirements have indeed had the greatest proportion of their undergraduates participating in study abroad.

The record of the International 50 offers a discourse describing those leading fifty American private liberal arts colleges that defined themselves by their commitment to internationalization through the latter half of the twentieth century and continuing into the twenty-first.[64] At these schools, academically strong study abroad offerings have represented the very peak of excellence. Faculty at the International 50 have stated their belief that "these colleges attract students because of the strength of their international programs."[65] Graduates of International 50 schools were at least three times more likely to have studied abroad during their undergraduate years than their peers nationally.[66]

In 2004 Harvard University, consistently rated the leading American higher education institution, weighed in, representing the argument that as an institution it should commit to study abroad for all its students. According to an April 2004 article in the *New York Times,* William C. Kirby, dean of the faculty of arts and sciences, wrote a letter to his constituency, saying:

> As a leading American institution, Harvard College has a responsibility to educate its students—who will live and work in all corners of the globe—as citizens not only of their home country, but also of the world, with the capacity not only to understand others, but also to see themselves, and this country, as others see them. . . . And rather than studying, say, Chinese history without leaving Cambridge, students interested in the subject should be spending a semester at Qinhua University in Beijing.[67]

Indeed, the goal expressed in the curricular review conducted by Harvard faculty is that "all Harvard College students pursue a significant international experience during their time in the College, and that completion of such an experience be noted on the transcript."[68]

Perhaps when Harvard voices join in the alternative discourse, they will help change the dominant discourse about study abroad. The same *New York Times* article noted that Harvard's curricular reviews are seen as establishing models for discourse on development throughout U.S. higher education institutions. Called "groundbreaking," they evoke responses in kind. "I think it is an excellent idea to have every American student have some international experience," said Nancy Dye, president of Oberlin College. "I think Harvard is doing an excellent thing."[69]

Yet faculty and administrators at the most highly ranked academic institutions in the United States have long and regularly supported study abroad for their students, an alternative vision of the overseas educational experience that posits that study abroad is for academically able students. This vision is a dominant theme in the alternative discourse of program sponsors. Some components of their discourse and practice are in danger of reinforcing the episteme, a process that Foucault recognizes as inevitable, given the power of the episteme to determine what is validated. But adapting the concept of genealogical analysis to identify the beliefs of the excluded community, alternative conceptions emerge. Analysis of the discourse going back to the earliest study abroad program beginnings in the twentieth century reveals alternative voices consistently describing study abroad as an opportunity for academically strong undergraduates that offers a unique academic alternative to domestic education. Study abroad programs are expected to be academically challenging. Liberal arts programs are designed to offer strong academic experiences, not trivialized cultural acquisition. And women are expected to be as academically strong as men. The vision expressed by these marginalized voices stands in stark contrast to the dominant diminishing vision of study abroad.

ALTERNATIVE VOICES ON THE FUNCTIONAL WORTH OF STUDY ABROAD

The episteme that devalues the academic quality of foreign education developed despite the existence of these alternative discourses. The episteme also devalues the function of foreign education, identifying no purpose for which study abroad should be respected. Alternative voices meanwhile have claimed that study abroad performs important functions in students' educations, functions directly connected to the purposes of American higher education.

Social purpose has always played a prominent role in American discourse about education: "From the very first, the nation's colleges and universities have been considered 'useful' not only to individual students but also to the larger community that granted them recognition and support," stated Boyer and Hechinger in their book, *Higher Learning in the Nation's Service*.[70] The United States' more than three thousand institutions, they wrote, have "essential overarching missions . . . that have become intertwined with higher learning's traditional functions of teaching and research."[71] Institutions of higher education function in service to the nation to train an educated citizenry for a professional life, providing education that "would be useful, not *merely* in the classical sense of preparing gentlemen, but for the practical demands of a changing world [italics added]."[72] From the first allocation of public funds to support higher education (Harvard, 1651) through the nineteenth-century establishment of land-grant institutions (funded by the sale of federal lands) and the rise of the university, American education has been grounded in practicality and designed to solve the problems of society.[73]

These functions were originally vested in the liberal curriculum, but as education was adapted to meet the needs of the emerging nation, liberal education gave way to new disciplines and new research.[74] By the early twentieth century, Lincoln Steffens could write, "the university is as close to the intelligent farmer as his pig-pen or his tool-house; the university laboratories are part of the alert manufacturer's plant."[75] Land-grant institutions with their new curricula were demeaningly referred to as "cow colleges"[76] by those who would keep the liberal curriculum with its humanistic training for the professions.[77] Nonetheless, students often saw practical training as their road to success. This was exemplified, even at Harvard, by the student who told Henry

Adams he studied there because a Harvard degree "is worth money to me in Chicago."[78] At the time that study abroad programs were developing in the early twentieth century, "pragmatic concerns seemed to be conquering higher education not only at the graduate but at the undergraduate level as well."[79]

This discourse of practical functions has dominated in American education, yet the academy has not ascribed functional worth to study abroad. In this book, the term "functional worth" describes education with a purpose that is grounded in practicality, designed to train students to work professionally, and constructed to develop their skills as competent good citizens so they might contribute to the nation's development. The citizenship function of study abroad, as used here, encompasses the goals established by study abroad programs to provide international understanding and enable students to contribute to world peace and security.

Because study abroad is broadly perceived as a Grand Tour by wealthy women who study in the liberal arts to acquire culture, it is demeaned in the discourse for offering no professional preparation. Nor has the dominant discourse assigned value to any alternative functions of overseas education. The international exposure offered through study abroad has not been well recognized in the dominant discourse for helping prepare students for "a changing world." Neither does the dominant discourse recognize a role for overseas education in training effective citizens. Once again, though, a genealogical approach to the discourse of faculty and administrators who have supported study abroad reveals alternative beliefs. From the start, study abroad programs in the liberal arts have been created with oft-stated peace goals and expressly stated professional training goals in mind.

Professional education is defined more broadly in the United States than in the European tradition, where the universities "had four great faculties—law, medicine, theology, and arts."[80] In the United States, the university movement was propelled by democracy "toward reality and practicality," wrote Stanford University President D. S. Jordan in "The Voice of the Scholar."[81] Harvard President James B. Conant observed that "the forces of democracy had taken the European idea of a university and transformed it."[82] As John Brubacher and Willis Rudy put it:

> The rationale under which this uniquely American venture in higher education went forward involved not only equalization of educational opportunity but another closely related and enormously significant principle, respect for all occupational groups. Needless to say, belief in egalitarianism was a helpful factor in inducing this respect. Thus the idea of an intellectual elite never took root in the United States because

it defied deep-seated American traditions of the dignity of all work as well as the worth of each person. American democracy was willing to recognize that some individuals might be better at certain types of work than others. It was even ready "to respect the methods and honor the achievements of specially trained people."[83]

Brubacher and Rudy cited Conant, saying that he "has summed up the significance of this basic outlook" which thus "almost unconsciously" shaped the growth of the modern American university as "none other than a philosophy hostile to the supremacy of a few vocations . . . a philosophy moving toward the social equality of all useful labor."[84] Within this milieu, argued Brubacher and Rudy, the word "profession" had a "much more elastic meaning" than in Europe,[85] indicating many occupations beyond the classical four.[86] This conception of professional education both focused and propelled the vision of study abroad program sponsors.

DISCOURSES OF PROFESSIONAL TRAINING AND COMPETENT CITIZENS: THE UNIVERSITY OF DELAWARE EXAMPLE

Important professional training and citizenship preparation goals were prominent among the aims of the very first Sorbonne-model U.S. study abroad program. Professional training was a central feature in planning discussions among University of Delaware faculty. When Professor Kirkbride of Delaware's Modern Languages department approached President Walter Hullihen to establish the program in 1921, Hullihen was very supportive. He believed that study abroad was an appropriate response to the economic, commercial, and political growth the United States was experiencing. Hullihen felt that the nation and the world needed more college graduates prepared to work internationally. As the University of Delaware archivist summarized:

> He anticipated that a large number of college graduates would be needed, especially men and women with foreign training and experience who would be valuable for positions in business and governmental agencies. There was already a need for well-qualified language teachers in the schools. Not only would a large reservoir of college-trained men and women—each possessing a knowledge of the language, ideas, and culture of a country—be created, but the way might be paved toward international understanding and good will.[87]

While the focus of discourse was on professional training, the concept also emerged that study abroad fulfilled a citizenship goal by creating able citizens who could help America by contributing to international peace through enhanced international understanding. John A. Munroe, writing a commemorative history of the University of Delaware, identifies Hullihen as a "Wilsonian"—a follower of U.S. President Woodrow Wilson and, like him, a proponent of world peace and cooperation.[88] This vision further prompted Hullihen's interest.[89]

When Kirkbride and Hullihen worked together to plan the Delaware program, according to Munroe, they consulted with leading educators, bankers, businessmen, and government officials. Among those with whom they spoke was Herbert Hoover, then Secretary of Commerce and later President of the United States, who had worked abroad as an engineer and had been instrumental in international war relief. Hoover was enthusiastic about training graduates to serve American businesses abroad.[90] Hullihen reported that Hoover supported study abroad because it would prepare a new generation to compete globally:

> He said . . . that there is nothing the United States needs more at this time than 5000 young men trained in the way indicated in our plan; that the United States can not gain the markets of the world through its commercial organizations and methods alone. The men for the undertaking at present are lacking.[91]

When the *Christian Science Monitor* interviewed President Hullihen about the new study abroad program, he explained that he wanted to reach the student who would be going into the business world and that he wanted to train men who could support the efforts of business, industry, commerce, and trade or the work of government and be knowledgeable about work abroad.[92] Clearly, from the inception of modern study abroad in the United States, the discourse among founding supporters assumed that programs would provide professional training. And although Hullihen alludes to "young men," the Delaware program from its second year on admitted women—indeed, as noted earlier, often more women than men—and offered them exactly the same professional training.

The early Delaware program contained courses in the liberal arts and social sciences alongside courses related to business and politics.[93] From the start, courses in the liberal arts curriculum were part of a package designed for professional preparation purposes. Except for size and a few other minor details, the ongoing academic structure of the program followed Kirkbride's ideas, laid out in a memorandum to President Hullihen in January 1921.[94] Hullihen, equally committed, sought program funding from Delaware industrial magnate DuPont and others, all of whom made "substantial contributions to the Delaware program's operating and scholarship funds."[95] Apparently Delaware businessmen saw the program as a sound investment in the professional future of their companies and the nation.

Historian John Munroe confirmed that both Kirkbride and Hullihen wanted to train students to be professionals destined for business, economics, and diplomacy.[96] From the start, then, the purposes for educating students abroad articulated by these alternative voices included educational functions valued in the mainstream of American educational discourse. Study abroad, just as much as education at home, was designed to train an educated and competent professional citizenry who would help America grow.

DISCOURSES OF TEACHER EDUCATION AND SOCIAL FEMINISM: EXAMPLES FROM SMITH COLLEGE AND REID HALL

Other early study abroad programs developed, their sponsors clearly conscious that study abroad fulfilled rather than negated values attached to function in education. For the programs established by Smith College in 1925 and designed specifically for women, founding goals reflected the career paths accessible to women at the time.

One of the purposes of Smith's new program was to train women to teach, for example. The majority of women in the United States who went to work in the 1920s belonged to the teaching profession,[97] but teacher education did not enjoy full professional status in the academic community. College women often chose teaching as a "vehicle for upward social mobility," "an improvement over what their mothers could do to earn a living, a welcome alternative to working in other women's kitchens and laundries or in mills and factories."[98] In this historical context, associations of study abroad with teacher preparation contributed to the image that study abroad was a female pursuit that did not lead to a professional career.

Nonetheless, sponsors of study abroad saw teacher training as an important feature of their academic mission. Twenty years later, Rosary College was still describing the advantages of study abroad to graduates bound for teaching, stating that "For teachers of French, the Foreign Study Plan is an invaluable asset."[99] Sweet Briar College researcher Francis M. Rogers also noted, when examining admissions into the Harvard-Radcliffe Romance Languages graduate program in 1958, that close to one-third of applying students had already studied abroad. He saw these applicants as future teachers and predicted that "the impact of study abroad on our language teaching is inevitably going to increase."[100]

In the early years, some saw study abroad specifically as a career training program for future teachers.[101] By 1923, only 16 percent of Smith alumnae were teaching, but study abroad was still considered an "opportunity for a greater proficiency in a foreign language, with the assumption that most would subsequently go on to secondary or private school teaching."[102] In her paper, "Sixty Years of Study Abroad," Patricia Olmsted recognized that the type of career supported by study abroad at Smith might have been different had the students been men, and over time the limited opportunities available to American women shaped study abroad, both in program design and in reputation. "Thus, for women, the junior year abroad was certainly considered a positive step toward a career, in academe especially," wrote Olmsted, "while men who studied abroad at that time were more likely to be in the professions of law, medicine or academe—such opportunities for women to study in universities abroad were limited as very few universities on the continent were open to women at that time."[103]

Professor Hélène Cattanès, then a new member of the French Department, designed the Smith program at College President Neilson's request. As an "imported Scot," Neilson was an internationalist,[104] so committed to the concept of study abroad that he persisted in establishing the program even in the face of faculty opposition.[105]

Smith College housed its program at Reid Hall in Paris, a building that came to be owned by Columbia University. A Reid Hall Committee of American University Women developed. Its chair, Virginia Gildersleeve,[106] exemplified the sort of academic woman who supported international education in that period. Gildersleeve was a pivotal figure in the development of the International Federation of University Women.[107] She felt that the Federation and similar organizations might train people internationally and help prevent another war,[108] and she wanted to support female teaching professionals by providing them with an international experience. She worked with the American Association of University Women to fund fellowships to help women go abroad to pursue their academic interests.[109]

Gildersleeve belonged to one of the three generations of American women described by Barbara Solomon: Educated after the Civil War but before women's suffrage, they expressed a strong commitment to education and opportunities for women.[110] It was to Mrs. Gildersleeve that Mrs. Whitewall Reid, wife of the American ambassador in Paris, had entrusted the building, to support the artistic interests of American women.[111] After World War I, the building was dedicated to professional and university women. Gildersleeve advocated uses for Reid Hall such as Smith's study abroad program, and she ultimately contributed to the re-establishment of Reid Hall after World War II.[112]

Gildersleeve represents the discourse of social feminism. She was one of a group who advocated women's issues in the 1920s, women described by J. Stanley Lemons as "social feminists," who worked within organizational structures to reform the American socioeconomic and political structure. As they "worked for progressive reform," says Lemons, "they advanced the status of American women. And as they fought for women's rights, they pushed progressivism along in a decade of waning reformist impact."[113] Even Gildersleeve's book's title, *Many a Good Crusade*, reflected this discourse; in practice, so did her active participation in the American Association of University Women and in the formation of the International Federation of University Women. Her support for Reid Hall and for women studying abroad echoed the vision of the Smith College founders. She and they typified a discourse among American sponsors of study abroad in the early twentieth century—a discourse that respected traditional women's occupations, including the teaching profession; advocated women's professional development; and conceived of study abroad as education designed to train competent citizens sure to contribute to the nation's growth.

DISCOURSES OF INTERNATIONAL TRAINING AND PEACE: THE SWEET BRIAR AND BEAVER COLLEGE EXAMPLES

Professional competence and peace interests, central to the discourse of early study abroad development, continued to be manifest in the discourse as programs were re-established after World War II. Two colleges provide examples: Sweet Briar College, carrying on the Delaware program, and Beaver College (today Arcadia University), newly entering the field of international education.

In the 1930s Sweet Briar President Meta Glass, interested in international understanding and therefore international education, organized an exchange between Sweet Briar and Scotland's St. Andrews University.[114] Glass worked closely with Virginia Gildersleeve. She served as president of the American Association of University Women and, like Gildersleeve, contributed to the formation of the International Federation of University Women.[115] She established a strong foundation of international interest at Sweet Briar College.

Succeeding Meta Glass in 1946, Martha B. Lucas continued Sweet Briar's international focus by supporting its program in France. Lucas believed that American college students needed to be educated about international issues in order to understand the complexities of other cultures and be capable of working realistically and competently for world peace. Like Glass before her, Lucas was intimately involved in the campaigns for both peace and social feminism. She had studied in numerous European countries and earned a Ph.D. from the University of London. Her international interests came through clearly even in her inaugural address, delivered in 1946 as she became the fourth president of the forty-year-old Sweet Briar College.[116] For her, engagement in other cultures was not trivial but, instead, urgently needed in the modern world. She encouraged international faculty to teach and international students to study at Sweet Briar College. Supportive of the Institute of International Education, she invited its director, Laurence Duggan, to speak at Sweet Briar in 1947 as part of a peace program.

Of her own growing awareness of the importance of study abroad, Lucas wrote:

> Returning to the U.S. with a British Ph.D. in Philosophy, I became increasingly aware, in my university teaching which followed, that I had brought from my studies overseas far more than a Ph.D. degree. I had gained new perspectives on my American culture and problems, the advantage of understanding, from experience, how students from Europe, Asia, South America and Africa looked upon us and upon each other.[117]

Emile Langlois, director emeritus of the Sweet Briar Junior Year in France program, noted Lucas's extensive international background. In addition to studying in the United Kingdom, she studied in France at the Alliance Française and the Sorbonne, and she studied on her own in Spain, Italy, and Germany. Very active in international issues, she eventually worked on the State Department's Advisory Commission on International Education and Cultural Affairs.[118] Her conception of training for international peace was grounded in her own career preparation and practice.[119]

In 1948 Joseph Barker, professor of French at Sweet Briar College and resident director of the University of Delaware program in France prior to World War II, told Lucas that the University of Delaware was no longer willing to undertake the program's management. Lucas responded that Sweet Briar might adopt it. It was a project Lucas supported because of her own international interests, her commitment to peace, and her belief that American students needed to be exposed to other nations to work effectively to make peace possible. Barker and Lucas negotiated with IIE officials to adopt the program.[120] All-female Sweet Briar agreed to continue to admit male students into the program, although establishing it there also endowed this coeducational program with a private, female, liberal arts college identification, contributing to perceptions about the types of institutions and populations that support study abroad.[121]

Perceptions aside, the Sweet Briar faculty was motivated to support President Lucas's interest in international education, in part because of the growing sense of the catastrophic nature of world events. "There was at that time a strong current of international concern on campus, mostly due to the fear of a nuclear conflict," says Emile Langlois. "This was the beginning of the New Atomic Age, and everyone had the feeling that preserving peace was an urgent task."[122] Sweet Briar College supported a variety of peace-oriented activities, hosting ten foreign scholars between 1946 and 1948, among them visitors from Vietnam and China; holding a major conference called "The Role of Colleges in Promoting Peace Through Understanding"; hosting international education specialists from around the nation; and bringing attention to the college's international interests.[123] Under the leadership of Dr. Lucas and Professor Barker, commitment to foreign study meshed with Sweet Briar's other domestic and international efforts to educate its female student population.

In the first bulletin of the program, President Lucas described the reason for Sweet Briar's interest abroad:

> It is our conviction that the colleges have the essential and all-important responsibility to help bring the peoples of the world together in mutual understanding and lasting peace. A fundamental part of UNESCO's program for promoting understanding among the peoples of the world is an exchange of students and teachers between the schools, colleges, and universities of all nations. We are confident that the Junior Year in France can do so much to implement this purpose by enabling American students to know and work with students of other national backgrounds in a center which has been for so many centuries, and continues to be, the meeting place of scholars from all parts of the world.[124]

Emile Langlois, citing this statement, noted that Sweet Briar's goal was to train its own women students and students from other schools of both genders to function capably in the international arena: "The first purpose of the Junior Year in France was therefore to advance the cause of peace and international citizenship."[125]

Training students with international capability also motivated administrators and faculty at Beaver College (now Arcadia University) in Pennsylvania. There, sponsors embarked on developing the study abroad programs that would soon earn Beaver its reputation as the leading U.S. college offering assisted admission into British universities.[126] In 1948 Beaver initiated the first of many programs, offering directed travel and study in Western

Europe. The first session attracted twenty-three of the college's six hundred currently enrolled women. In his extensive description of the steps taken to develop this program, John A. Wallace, later president of the International Institute for Education, documented that sponsors perceived a need among Beaver students for training in international economics.[127]

Beaver College articulated a commitment to serious professional training for all of its students, at the time all women. The college's goals, wrote Wallace, could be summed up in the words of Raymond Kistler, president of Beaver College, addressing incoming students in 1948: "Our basic purpose is two fold—to help you learn how to live and how to make a living."[128] Statements from Beaver's Department of Commerce and Economics likewise expressed the importance of "the social and economic aspect of life, through finding the abundance in living by participating fully and intelligently in the social and economic activities of the community, state, and world." The Department supported the philosophy "that young women must be trained to help maintain an enduring peace."[129]

Stating the goal to educate internationally—and aware that it did not offer international economics at a time when the need for such a program was growing—Beaver College's Department of Commerce and Economics devised a course along such lines abroad to fill in the gap and contribute to the college's larger aims.[130] General courses were supplemented with professional training, key goals among the several articulated for the college and its female students.[131] Thus faculty organizing Beaver College's initial foray into international education conceived its core to be a commitment to developing female students for a professional life. College sponsors expressed this concern by establishing programs of professional training aimed at contributing effectively to peace efforts.[132]

While dominant beliefs ascribed a lack of serious academic intent or professional function to the education pursued by women through study abroad, the alternative discourses expressed by faculty from women's institutions like Sweet Briar and Beaver College continued after World War II the theme established after World War I: Study abroad was an educational experience with important citizenship and career training functions.

PERSISTENT DISCOURSES OF PEACE AND PROFESSIONAL PREPARATION: INTERNATIONAL UNDERSTANDING, GLOBAL COMPETENCE, AND THE GLOBAL SOCIETY TO THE PRESENT DAY

Discourse validating study abroad as preparation for work and citizenship has continued through to the present, although it has been marginalized and in general unheeded. After World War II, the federal government established the Fulbright Program to support international educational exchange in the new peacetime climate,[133] resulting in the promotion on U.S. campuses of all components of international education, including study abroad.[134] Federal education legislation, described in chapter 3, nurtured this emerging interest.[135] As this growth gained momentum, study abroad in the liberal tradition was lauded for its potential to contribute to international understanding: "As our world shrinks, our understanding must expand," stated Paul Weaver in 1962. "This new dimension in liberal education is to be applauded because the objective is sound."[136] Weaver's statement reflects the self-defining power of the episteme, as identified by Foucault. Voicing the value of study abroad in international efforts, he also suggested that it was a new goal not present in past programs.

This alternative belief in the importance of study abroad had prompted a small group of exchange-oriented organizations to create the Council on International Educational Exchange in 1947. The original impulse, described by the organization's president and executive director, Jack Egle, was:

> as an organization to bring about understanding and cooperation amongst the peoples of the world by men and women who had just lived through the devastation of the Second World War. These people had been brought up under the yet fresh horror of the First World War, and were searching for ways to begin the process of creating a new world, better able to deal with the complex problems of change.[137]

CIEE established a wide variety of programs in support of international exchange for both men and women, beginning in the late 1950s with shorter-term exchanges.[138] By the late 1960s, it was sponsoring its own study abroad programs. Initial programs in Western Europe had a professional focus, with teacher education as the foundation.[139] Subsequently, CIEE developed a wide variety of summer, semester, and year-long academic programs worldwide, with forty individual study centers in fulfillment of these same goals.[140]

Statements published by the International 50 also reflected ongoing discourse that assumed that study abroad offered professional and citizenship preparation. "The world is an interesting, and challenging, and often dangerous place," noted Engerman and Marden in their study of America's international liberal arts colleges, and so these schools trained their students to evaluate world politics in the international interest, producing "scholars, diplomats, linguists and commentators—all professionals needed in the international arena," and, generally, "citizens who understand issues and conditions that underlie them and then vote or otherwise act accordingly."[141] Within this ambitious set of goals, the International 50 articulated a critical mission for undergraduate institutions: "It falls to the nation's undergraduate institutions, supported by the federal government and philanthropic organizations, to motivate and prepare persons to serve the international interest and to meet the United States responsibilities within it."[142]

In the last quarter century, terms such as "global competence" and "global society" have emerged to describe the need to prepare students to work in the international arena and function effectively as world citizens.[143] The language of global interdependence and economic competitiveness has entered the discourse. Leading international education researchers such as Hans de Wit, in his recent *Internationalization of Higher Education in the United States of America and Europe: A Historical, Comparative, and Conceptual Analysis* and in his earlier works, have identified this language as part of the rationale for internationalizing education.[144] Nancy Ruther, author of *Barely There, Powerfully Present: Thirty Years of U.S. Policy on International Higher Education*, observed that economic security, "especially as global competition increased," and national security as well had become important components of the discourse, conveying the most frequently cited motive in the late twentieth century for support of Title VI legislation.[145] All these terms were often voiced as specific motivations for supporting study abroad, reflected most effectively in the very titles of both the first study abroad policy report, *Educating for Global Competence*, and the most recent statement, *Securing America's Future: Global Education for a Global Age*.[146]

NAFSA and the Alliance for International Educational and Cultural Exchange argued in their 2000 white paper that "Americans need enhanced international skills and knowledge to guarantee our national security and economic competitiveness."[147] And in their research paper for the 2003 Duke University conference on Global Challenges and U.S. Higher Education Title VI Reauthorization, titled "U.S. Business Needs for Employees with International Expertise," Ben L. Kedia and Shirley J. Daniel argued that "The main concern of educators is not the transmission of knowledge for its own sake, but the production of highly skilled and educated graduates who can go into the corporate world and perform to the best of their abilities to create more prosperous work environments, firms, industries and nations."[148]

Despite the power of the episteme that devalues study abroad as functionally irrelevant, the predominant discourse among its sponsors has manifested the belief that study abroad—and, for many, its liberal curriculum—train globally proficient men and women. The American ideal to create an educated citizenry, able to act knowledgeably and competently in the national interest, has been reconstituted as an alternative belief in the discourse of study abroad sponsors.

A genealogical study of the alternative voices of study abroad sponsors reveals that the motives articulated for founding or supporting programs have included: providing foreign language training and teacher education; training in international business, politics, and other forms of professional preparation; creating an educated citizenry capable of contributing to international peace, increasingly again since 9/11; and, in sum, for female as well as male students, promoting global competency in an interdependent world.[149] These motives complement the strongly held beliefs that study abroad is a unique experience for the strongest students, including the academically able female constituencies served by the faculty and administrative sponsors of study abroad.

All these beliefs attach significant functional and academic worth to study abroad. More broadly, they offer a line of discourse that, despite being marginalized, presents a strong alternative to the dominant voices of the academy. Dominant voices have portrayed study abroad as a pursuit of culture and have trivialized it under the assumption that its participants are wealthy women, uninterested in public or professional life and pursuing an unchallenging, insignificant liberal arts curriculum though a European-style Grand Tour. To the contrary, from the first Junior Year Abroad model programs, just after World War I, to those of the present day, study abroad in U.S. undergraduate institutions has been founded upon an alternative set of beliefs, displayed in discourse among the faculty and administrative sponsors of foreign study. These alternative voices constituted study abroad as a functionally worthwhile, professionally valid, and academically strong model of education for capable undergraduate women and men.

Chapter Six

Alternative Voices: Discourse and Belief among Students Abroad

Like the faculty whose voices have not been granted respect in the American academy, the students who have pursued study abroad also remain devalued. Those in the higher education community swayed by the prevailing episteme have frequently expressed their suspicions about the competence and purpose of program participants and their downright disdain for the programs they pursue. Again by adapting Foucault's method of genealogical inquiry to listen to the voices and look at the practices of these very students who have participated in modern study abroad programs, it is possible to illuminate the beliefs of these students—including and especially the women upon whose experiences and reputation so much of the devaluing episteme has been built. These participants believe that study abroad offers them a unique opportunity, not always available domestically, for high-quality academic study and professional preparation. This alternative discourse emerges from participants who also reveal themselves to have been and remain today willing, when required, to take risks and undergo hardships to be educated overseas.

ALTERNATIVE VOICES ON RISKS AND HARDSHIPS IN STUDY ABROAD

The Grand Tour paradigm has long presumed that study abroad involves luxury and entertainment,[1] well summed up in the *New York Times* headline, "La Dolce Semester." Academic or professional intentions are not assumed to be part of the paradigm. The mode of travel is presumed to be luxuriant and comfortable, as befits the upper-class student presumed to undertake this experience, a "luxury made possible by the accumulation of excess capital" and "a quest for social superiority," as Thorstein Veblen described the attributes of those who went abroad from America in the 19th century.[2]

At the same time, though, a prevailing thread in the discourse within the study abroad community describes the sense of adventure and self-discovery motivating many students. This line of thought builds on the tradition of travel abroad as an act of independence for women, as Mary Morris and Larry O'Connor observed in *Maiden Voyages: Writings of Women Travelers*.[3] In 1959, John Garraty and Walter Adams found students' primary motives to be "the thirst for travel, adventure, and new ways of looking at life."[4] In 1988, *Educating for Global Competence* described students who went abroad as "risk takers."[5] The 2003 study abroad task force report applauded students who go to nontraditional sites as "adventurous,"[6] and surveys like that done by the Institute of International Education of Students in 2000 report that students see study abroad as benefiting them in personal ways, expressed in statements such as: "Enabled me to learn something new about myself."[7]

Those in the academic community who hold fast to the devaluing episteme of study abroad may associate expressions of this sort with the frivolous excitements attached to a Grand Tour. Such associations likely underlie the comments noted earlier from Ben Feinberg's 2002 *Chronicle of Higher Education* piece, "What Students Don't Learn Abroad," which cited student comments like "I learned I am a risk taker" to characterize study abroad as a dubious voyage of self-discovery.[8] Yet the discourse and practices of program participants reveal an alternative set of beliefs about the risks and circumstances under which they consider study abroad worthwhile.

PARTICIPANT DISCOURSE, PRACTICE, AND BELIEF IN SITUATIONS OF POLITICAL UNREST

The Grand Tour conception of study abroad does not encompass study in politically threatening circumstances. Those presumed to travel for pleasure and cultural acquisition would never take on such risks. Yet the record shows that foreign study amidst political unrest has occurred frequently: prior to World War II, in its aftermath, and during contemporary periods, including the present era of terrorism. Throughout, U.S. students—and at times women students especially—have demonstrated their commitment to pursue education abroad, regardless of difficulties or discomforts.

This courage in women participants was visible even before the advent of modern study abroad. Education historian Sandra Singer observed that when World War I began and European universities began to lose enrollments because of the war, American women enrolled at German universities continued their studies.[9] After a momentary peace, the world returned to political chaos. In Europe, the years between the two world wars were tumultuous, with the rise of Fascism in Germany and elsewhere, the revolution and social upheavals in Spain, and the unrest associated with newly emerging powers. Within this political climate, U.S. study abroad was born. When women set sail in 1925 from Smith College to Paris, they traveled on an ocean liner "complete with the champagne, roses, and confetti send-off as it left apprehensive family and friends weeping and waving at the New York pier."[10] This luxurious departure supported the image of wealthy women embarking on a Grand Tour. It belied their serious academic intentions and could not possibly foretell some of the experiences they would encounter while abroad.

The first major challenge was the unstable political situation in Spain in the 1930s. Smith's President Neilson established the college's second Junior Year Abroad programs there, "undaunted by the brooding and unhappy conditions in Spain."[11] As Olmsted notes, the women studying in Spain ventured from the first day into a politically tumultuous environment. After the collapse of the monarchy, the stage was set for the country to face the social and political issues of the time: women's suffrage, divorce, the formation of the republic, elections, and ongoing political disagreements. Political turmoil discouraged neither the Smith students nor President Neilson himself, who shortly thereafter established study abroad programs in Italy and Germany, scenes of equally turbulent politics.

Aware of escalating political and economic troubles in Europe, Neilson wrote to parents of participants in 1934, calling study abroad "in practically every case much the most valuable year spent in college" and indicating that "as to the political conditions I do not think the risks are such as need give us any concern. We passed through the revolution (in Spain) which overthrew the monarchy and several disturbed periods since but no danger was incurred by any of our students."[12] The directors of the program in Spain, Helen Peirce (in 1933–34) and Katherine Redding Whitmore (in 1935), each commented on how turmoil affected the student experience. Peirce reported "periods of alarm," "periods of danger," and "periods of defense."[13] Whitmore wrote that "the revolution is over and we are none the worse for war."[14] By 1935–36, amid the dissolution of Spanish society, the program was not able to proceed. Rather than return to the United States, students relocated to other Smith programs and remained abroad, undaunted by the difficult conditions they had already witnessed.[15] University of Delaware students persisted as well during the 1930s, eager to set sail for France despite political turmoil. Delaware's

German program was closed in 1934 because of the political changes there,[16] but other programs continued. Students chose to study in Europe as late as 1939, the year when political tensions in Europe forced all programs to be cancelled.[17]

Testimony from the secretary of the University of Delaware Foreign Study Committee, Madeleine Forwood, about her experience abroad reveals a discourse of persistence in the face of political upheaval. Forwood accompanied students abroad in 1932 and 1939 and stated that the most exciting year, bar none, was the last, when "the war was rather imminent, yet we got in touch with Washington and everything was go ahead."[18] Throughout these periods of turmoil just before World War II, the majority of study abroad participants remained overwhelmingly female.

Study abroad programs in Europe came to a halt at the onset of World War II but were quickly reestablished at war's end, with women's institutions once again leading the way. This time students set off "in true troop-ship style,"[19] as Olmsted put it, arriving in 1946 to encounter a Europe destroyed by war. Olmsted shared one student's recorded first impressions: "As we entered the harbor we saw not only the shattered hull, but parts of half-sunken ships protruding from the water, their hulls dark against the water, pink in the early sunrise, a grim reminder of the horror that has only so recently ended."[20] Virginia Bowman, going abroad in 1947 with the Brethren Committee, accompanied by her husband John (later executive director of CIEE), commented that the devastation was everywhere.[21] But post-war upheaval did not daunt women from returning overseas. In the first year of the reestablished Sweet Briar program, thirty-four women and thirty-three men participated, a near-equal proportion due to the G.I. Bill. By year two (1949–50), the balance had shifted to fifty-three women and twenty men; by year three, to sixty women and nineteen men. (See Appendix, Table 3–1, Summary of Sweet Briar Junior Year in France Groups, 1948–49 to 2003–04.)

Firmly reestablished in Paris, the Sweet Briar program underwent several subsequent international crises. "The Berlin Blockade, the Korean War, the Indo-Chinese and Vietnam War, the Algerian War, the taking of the Suez Canal by the French and the British, May 1968, and, closer to us, the bombing of Libya, the growing number of terrorist acts, and now the threat of the war with Iraq," enumerated then–Junior Year Abroad Director Emile Langlois. "Each time it has required plans of actions, and sometimes acts to protect the students."[22] Despite these challenges, every year the substantial majority of participants in the Sweet Briar program remained women. Langlois noted that unrest in the late 1960s in France had "a profound effect on the program," in large part because French universities closed down.[23] In 1967–68, 68 women and 33 men registered in the Paris program; in 1968–69, 62 women and 40 men; in 1969–70, 65 women and 34 men. For those committed to participating, study abroad was worth pursuing even in threatening circumstances.

Olmsted observed that Smith College students and programs did not run away from political trouble either, but rather followed it:

> Just as the 60's made us explore, discover, uncover opportunities for study in Africa, the 70's and the Vietnam War occasioned our return again to the Far East and the Pacific Rim. For eight years, from 1966–1972, Smith operated a program at the University of Manila in the Philippines. Now the stress and political climate of the 80's centers more attention on Central and South America and the Caribbean.[24]

Smith programs established in the Pacific Rim and elsewhere, Olmsted argued, reflected the attraction to both sponsors and participants of areas emerging as politically and economically important, even when they might be experiencing unrest.

In another example, CIEE numbers representing participation in programs in Spain from 1973 to 1984—a period of time coinciding with the anti-Franco movement, the end of Franco's dictatorship, and a sustained period of Basque terrorism—show erratic but continued participation in programs in Spain. (See Appendix, Figure 6–1, CIEE Study Abroad Programs in Spain and France: Participation by Gender.) While no terrorist acts were directed against Americans, they did deter American interest in travel to Spain, according to Jerry Johnson, CIEE program director.[25] Yet a consistent female majority among students remained there throughout these troubled years.[26] Just after the hijacking of an American jet from the Trans World Airlines fleet in Beirut, Lebanon, in the spring of 1985—and during an aftermath marked by turmoil abroad and fear about overseas travel in the U.S.—women still predominated in number, despite a drop in female participation and a rise in male.[27] Indeed, from the time of computerized records in 1990 to the present, through multiple political upheavals, CIEE enrollments in all their programs have remained 66 percent female.[28]

A female majority has persisted throughout the contemporary history of U.S. study abroad, so much so that it has sometimes been only thanks to female participants that overseas enrollments remained steady. With that in mind, it is interesting to relate Sweet Briar Junior Year in France enrollment trends to more recent remarkable world events of the sort that might impact a student's desire—or a parent's willingness for her or him—to study overseas. In December 1988, the terrorist bombing of a Pan American jetliner over Lockerbie, Scotland, resulted in the deaths of U.S. students returning home from studying abroad with Syracuse University. The attack shook America, yet it did not discourage students from choosing to enroll in Sweet Briar's study abroad program the next year. Sweet Briar enrollments in the academic year immediately following the Lockerbie bombing, 1989–90, decreased insignificantly, and female enrollment vastly outnumbered male enrollment, as usual (see Appendix, Table 3–1).

In January and February 1991, American troops launched Desert Storm, initiating air and ground attacks in Iraq and Kuwait. In the 1991–92 academic year, female enrollment in Sweet Briar's study abroad program equaled that of the previous year, while male enrollment in study abroad dropped slightly. Even after the terrorist attacks on the U.S. in September 2001, the Sweet Briar program remained stable. In 2002–03, the academic year after 9/11, the program lost eleven student enrollments, six of them women, but strong female enrollment kept the program stable, with that enrollment leaping by over 25 percent—especially remarkable considering that across the entire U.S. undergraduate population, among students surveyed after 9/11 by ACE, women more than men expressed increased concern about overseas safety.[29]

In 2004, according to StudyAbroad.com, a leading Internet source of information about international education, students' first concern about study abroad was whether they will have enough money, not whether they will be safe (although they believed their parents' first concern was safety).[30] While many say that world politics have become more threatening, especially to Americans overseas, enrollment in study abroad has more than doubled from 1993 to now, with numbers increasing annually.[31] Furthermore, women consistently represent close to two-thirds of that enrollment.[32]

After the March 11, 2004, terrorist train bombings in Madrid, Spain, Ashley Mills, an American studying abroad through IES, commented that despite rising anti-American political beliefs—she had "not always felt comfortable to be an American," she reported—she had no plans to give up study abroad and return to the United States. She follows in a long tradition of study abroad students, including and in the majority women, who have confronted issues of political disarray and safety and still chose to continue their study abroad experiences. Ms. Mills reported, indeed, that three days after the bombings, she traveled by train to Valencia, boarding from the Atocha station where the Madrid bombings occurred. "I was a little freaked out," she told a *Chronicle* reporter, but "I already had my ticket."[33]

PARTICIPANT DISCOURSE, PRACTICE, AND BELIEF IN PHYSICALLY DIFFICULT SETTINGS

Student willingness—and especially that of women—to study abroad in difficult circumstances goes unheralded in the face of the powerful beliefs that dismiss the experience of participants as a comfortable, non-threatening Grand Tour. Other strands of discourse among students who have gone abroad reveal their willingness from the start to study in situations that are not only politically risky but also physically difficult—far from the luxurious environments suggested by the dominant episteme. Smith College President Neilson was aware, for instance, that when in France students would live like the French, which might mean some unfamiliar physical discomforts.[34] Even tougher discomforts were encountered two decades later by Americans returning to study abroad in Europe after World War II. In his history of American study abroad, John Bowman cited a 1949 report:

> In the years immediately following World War II, life in Western Europe was disorganized and difficult. Travel was slow and frequently disrupted. Food was rationed, even in Switzerland. University facilities were frequently not yet restored. Housing was scarce and in poor condition. Americans, including students, were encouraged to stay at home because of conditions in Europe. When the Salzburg Seminar—a summer conference for European and American students—convened for the first time in the summer of 1948, "all food, with the exception of fresh vegetables, was shipped from the United States."[35]

Sweet Briar students suffered similar discomforts. Yet Dorothy Leet, president of Reid Hall, which reopened in September 1947, wrote to Joseph Barker at Sweet Briar to describe the lives of the small number of American students in Paris in 1947–48:

> I cannot remember a winter more interesting for the students studying in Paris. The French people have been wonderful to them, and the intellectual life in the theatre, music and art exhibits has filled all of their hours with the most stimulating programs. In Reid Hall they have not had any hardships at all, and while I may worry from time to time as to whether the next allotment of coal from the Embassy will arrive on time, we have never been short up to this time. We are having excellent food, we are having hot water each week-end, and I have rarely seen a group more content or in better health.[36]

For Leet, post-war trials made studying abroad "more interesting." According to Sweet Briar Foreign Study Director Emile Langlois, conditions at Reid

Hall were actually worse than Leet described. She could have added, he said, "that there was no electricity on Fridays and until Saturday noon, that most apartments had not been repaired since 1939, that elevators did not work, that plumbing needed fixing."[37] France was still, according to the *New York Herald Tribune* of 25 January 1948, "a country of limited economy, where milk, flour and eggs were precious commodities."[38] Nevertheless, American students chose to study there.

In the summer of 1948, Dr. Barker reported:

> Good cuts of meat are unknown and the average Frenchman never even thinks of buying a steak. If you are invited for dinner and have kidneys you are being royally entertained, and that probably means your host will go meatless for days to make amends with the budget.[39]

Before their departure, the first group was advised "to bring or have sent to you: powdered milk, instant coffee, bouillon cubes, instant sweet cocoa, jams, butter, sugar, crackers, candy," none of which were available in Paris.[40] Professor Theodore Andersson remembered that "In the leaky, unheated houses and buildings of Paris we were all cold despite sweaters, overcoats, scarves, gloves, and often overshoes"; yet, as Professor Langlois noted, none of this deterred faculty or students.[41]

The rebirth of study abroad after World War II occurred neither in the lap of luxury nor in an environment that encouraged or even allowed frivolous travel. Yet participants, including again the women, consistently expressed their willingness to endure physical hardships as part of their overseas educational experience.

PARTICIPANT DISCOURSE, PRACTICE, AND BELIEF IN NON-WESTERN EUROPEAN SETTINGS

This willingness among participants is likewise displayed when one analyzes enrollments in the gradually expanding program opportunities in less developed nations. While U.S. study abroad programs originally were founded successfully in European sites and remain largely located there—thus propelling the dominant belief in the Eurocentrism of study abroad—policy makers have advocated site diversification. They have acted on a belief in the inherent worth of studying in new regions[42] and in the hope that programs elsewhere might attract a more diverse population, even increase male participation.[43]

Data available from 2004 show that almost two-thirds (62.9%) of students who study abroad go to Europe (both Eastern and Western)[44]—a proportion that appears high but is in fact low compared to earlier numbers published in the IIE survey history dating back to 1985, when nearly four out of five students abroad (79.6%) went to Europe.[45] The change signifies that a growing number of students are choosing non-European sites for study abroad.[46]

Prevailing beliefs, as suggested above, hold that non-European sites might especially interest male students, yet nationwide gender data indicates that this has not been the case during the period when nontraditional site options have been increasing. For example, data collated by the Council on International Educational Exchange from summer 1987 through spring 1993 indicated that among U.S. students choosing Third World study sites, 61.4 percent were women,[47] a proportion approximating the same two-to-one gender ratio that has long characterized U.S. study abroad enrollment overall. In CIEE programs alone, from 1992 through the end of summer 2004, the same trend held true. Of its enrollments, 34 percent occurred in nontraditional world regions; of that enrollment, 62 percent was female.[48]

Women's interest in non-conventional sites is also reflected in the applications submitted to the National Security Education Program, a federally funded program to promote study in Third World nations.[49] A stated NSEP policy objective is to encourage "gender-balanced participation"—in other words, to increase male participation. This objective led to acceptance of an initial pool of finalists of which 54 percent were female, although more (57%) had applied. [50] Data available from 2000 through 2004 shows a somewhat similar balance in applicants and recipients, with female applicants always exceeding male in number.[51] Finally, data from the Benjamin A. Gilman International Scholarship program, a congressionally funded program dedicated to broadening study abroad in nontraditional sites and disciplines, suggested a similar finding, with women even more predominant than in NSEP in both application and enrollment.[52] In the Fall 2004 list of Gilman recipients, for example, 80 percent of the participants studied outside of traditional Western European sites and 67 percent of the awardees were female.[53] In data provided by Gilman from its founding in 2001–02 to the present, women have outnumbered men in the program each year, representing from 64 percent to 70 percent of Gilman International Scholars. In the two years for which applicant data is available, women have applied to the Gilman program in roughly similar percentages, so women's interest as well as award status is demonstrated. In no year have more than 43.3 percent of Gilman students joined Western European programs.[54] These data all indicate a substantial female interest in nontraditionally located programs, despite prevailing assumptions to the contrary.

Women have clearly evinced an interest in studying abroad in locations even where living conditions are less than comfortable and nowhere near luxurious. Usually in numbers greater than those of men, they have willingly chosen settings that reflect an alternative discourse, validating study abroad as sufficiently worthwhile to experience discomfort and take risks, personal and political, to pursue it. Meanwhile, the episteme continues to frame study abroad as a Grand Tour, and these voices validating study abroad remain obscured within the academy.

ALTERNATIVE VOICES ON ACADEMIC MOTIVES FOR STUDY ABROAD

That study abroad is without academic significance is an idea central to the episteme prevailing in higher education circles. A Foucault-inspired genealogical investigation into alternative discourses reveals that, once again in contrast to the prevailing episteme, participants perceive an important academic role for study abroad in their lives.

First, observing the persistence of the belief that study abroad is academically weak, it is interesting to see how such perception has found voice—and still finds voice today—in a variety of descriptions evoked when study abroad educators report on what they hear from students. For example, study abroad educators collected "mythologies of going abroad" for the American education abroad magazine, *Transitions Abroad*. Students who had chosen not to study abroad were asked why. Some common beliefs offered as reasons were: study abroad benefited only those interested in studying foreign cultures; study abroad hindered rather than advanced academic progress; study abroad would not contribute to professional development; and study abroad might amount to a frivolous experience. In the students' words:

> I'm not a foreign language major, so your programs have nothing to offer me.
>
> I'll fall behind academically.
>
> Going abroad will never do anything for my career!
>
> It will jeopardize my chances of getting into graduate/medical/law schools.
>
> My parents think I'll waste my time when I should be studying.[55]

Other students specifically echoed the dominant belief that study abroad offered weaker academic education than domestic education:

Science isn't as developed in other countries.

Science students have no reason to go abroad.

There are no opportunities for students in the sciences and engineering.

They won't have computers there.[56]

A current strategy of leading program and directory websites is to articulate typical opinions such as these and address them directly. For example, the Council on International Education's study abroad website includes a section headlined "Study Abroad Facts and Myths," which identifies the following:

Myth: I can't afford to study abroad.

Myth: I can't study abroad if I don't speak a foreign language.

Myth: I won't be able to graduate when I am supposed to if I study abroad.

Myth: My GPA is not high enough to study abroad.

Myth: I won't be able to take courses in my major while I study abroad.

Myth: I won't get credit for courses I take while studying abroad.

Myth: Studying abroad is a luxury that won't help me find a job.

Myth: I can't study abroad because I'm on financial aid.

Myth: Only language majors can study abroad.

Myth: Only juniors can study abroad.[57]

This list is interesting because it recognizes so many of the beliefs found to be held by the broader academic community, primarily that study abroad is for wealthier students but is not an important or relevant academic activity. One aberration is of special note, however: the perceived concern among some students that study abroad might be just for those with the strongest GPAs, a perception addressed later in this chapter.

Students often manifest the full range of dominant beliefs in their judgments and choices. While the ACE surveys reported in *Mapping Internationalization* did reflect positive signs of interest in international education,[58] still two-thirds of students said, as noted earlier, they either considered it a waste of time to study international topics or, at best, they considered it useful but still unnecessary for their study focus.[59] Nor did they perceive strong employer interest in overseas education.[60] Survey results at the University of Minnesota reported that from 44 to 50 percent of seniors worried that study abroad would delay their graduation, although fewer sophomores (from 38% to 45%) shared that worry. Close to 60 percent of the Minnesota seniors did not think study abroad was important for their future employment; about one-third of students were certain study abroad was not possible in their majors; but half of all groups surveyed thought study abroad would "enhance their ability to think critically and solve problems"—another interesting aberration in which students report that they perceive academic value in study abroad.[61]

Despite some positive indicators in this data, however, students still do not go abroad. Students are themselves members of the higher education discourse community, so it comes as no surprise that many hold the same devaluing beliefs as faculty and administrators. By identifying the alternative discourse of those who have chosen to go abroad, a genealogical inquiry can focus instead on the motives and perceptions of these students, especially the women, whose voices have been marginalized. These voices can illuminate participant beliefs about the academic worth of study abroad from the earliest years up to the present day, identifying its value to so many participants.

PARTICIPANT DISCOURSE, PRACTICE, AND BELIEF: ACADEMIC EXPECTATIONS OF EARLY PARTICIPANTS

Study abroad sponsors established programs in the United States after World War I with the view that they were academically rigorous and valuable and that they would serve students, women as well as men, with strong academic records. The Delaware program was created for high achievers; the Smith program in Paris was an honors program.[62] The discourse of participants reveals parallel beliefs. These students saw themselves as academically capable students seeking a demanding educational experience. Letters and surveys from the early years of the Delaware program, 1923–36, demonstrate that both male and female participants chose to study abroad in order to develop academic skills and abilities. Neither male nor female students described the experience as preprofessional, but that nomenclature was alien in a culture where male study was presumed to be professional while female was presumed to be cultural.

In 1933 the University of Delaware Committee on Foreign Study conducted a survey of all members of the Delforean Society, the alumni association for participants in its Foreign Study Plan programs, 64 percent of whom were women.[63] Edwin C. Byam, committee secretary, conducted the survey when the program had reached its tenth year, sending out to all 485 program alumni a questionnaire designed to help plan for the program's future "growth and serviceability."[64] Responses came from 127 women, revealing that 29.13 percent had attended graduate school since study abroad; 88.19 percent considered that study abroad had provided scholastic benefits; and 62.99 percent felt that foreign study had helped them develop professional skills.

Of the women responding, 33.86 percent were students, most of them graduate students, since the survey harked back to their junior year experience abroad. The next largest portion of respondents (12.6%) was in business. A smaller proportion (11.02%) considered themselves homemakers, and the smallest number (0.79%) were involved in the arts. In this small vanguard of women who had studied abroad during the first decade of the Delaware program, almost half went on to graduate study or professional work, manifesting a conception of themselves and their education as both academically strong and professionally oriented.[65]

Some individuals wrote comments to this effect. Fredrica Harriman thought her study abroad years in France, in 1923–24 and 1926–27, became "major factors" in her effort to secure a professional position. Ms. Harriman valued the academic quality of her years abroad: "I consider it the most beneficial year in my education—more so than any of the other three years."[66] Helen Fisher, who studied abroad in 1931–32, called the scholastic benefit of her experience "tremendous."[67] Edith Lucas, also a participant in 1931–32, said that her experience abroad produced "discipline in writing and in studying generally."[68] Kathryn A. Rauh (Mrs. R. T. Krogh), abroad in 1930–31, said that the experience taught her how to study so well that her academic average rose from 82–83 in her first two years of college to 91–93 in her senior semesters.[69]

Information from the Delfor Alumni Directories reveals the interests of many early participants, especially the women. Helen Fisher, mentioned above, went on to complete an M.A. degree at the Fletcher School and enter the magazine publishing industry. Susanna Edmondson, a member of the foreign study class of 1927–28, became an economics professor at Columbia University. The Record Book on Delforeans from 1923 to 1936 identified the occupations of as many women as possible:

74 were listed as married

7 of those 74 listed an additional occupation

37 were listed as instructors or teachers

35 were listed as being part of the business world

21 were earning an M.A. or a Ph.D. degree

5 were listed as social workers

In other words, numerous women among those 174 early foreign study alumnae undertook professional or graduate activities following their studies abroad.[70] These women appear to have chosen study abroad as part of larger career intentions, which included academic achievement and professional involvement.

Mrs. Beatrice F. Davis (née Beatrice Hume Farr) said in an interview conducted by Myron L. Lazarus for the Oral History Program of the University of Delaware that her graduate school and career goals were sidetracked when she turned down a fellowship at the Fletcher School of Law and Diplomacy, forced to do so by a serious illness in her family. She was not able to resume graduate study and pursue a fulfilling profession until mid-life. Even then, after her child was grown, she considered that her commitment to advanced study and professionalism arose from her early foreign study experience. "I got a Master's Degree in library science and from then on I just have had an increasingly interesting and active professional life," said Mrs. Davis. "And I know that part of the success of that life has been the fact that I have had this [study abroad] experience. I use it a good bit now."[71]

From the beginning, participants engaged in an alternative discourse that validated study abroad programs and their academic worth. Robert Pace's examination of Delaware and Sweet Briar alumni, conducted in the 1950s (when many of Delaware alumni were still living), confirmed that students reflected serious academic goals in both discourse and practice. Of the Delaware alumni, 302 responded to Dr. Pace's questionnaire; of the Sweet Briar alumni, 144 responded. Of the Delaware alumni responding, 75 percent of whom were women, two-thirds had studied beyond the bachelor's degree level. His findings suggested that all students, male and female, in Delaware's early programs were motivated academically.[72]

In his book, *American Juniors on the Left Bank: An Appreciation of the Junior Year in France*, Francis M. Rogers talked about the academic quality of study abroad just before and after World War II. He spoke as both a participant and a sponsor, since he attended the University of Delaware's program in Paris, then went on to become a professor of Romance languages and literatures and dean of the Graduate School of Arts and Sciences at Harvard University. Remembering the Delaware program, Rogers wrote that: "In my day the famed 'Cours de Civilisation Française' were excellent."[73]

Further evidence shows the high expectations that drew post-war students into study abroad. Based on a project conducted at Oregon State University, a Carnegie Commission study on international programs at American institutions of higher education questioned what students valued in a study abroad program.[74] Responses included:

> The program should encourage the students to think. It should not simply be composed of lecture courses, but, to the extent possible, should be conducted in the manner of a seminar.

> The program should lead to mastery of the language of the host country.

> The program should have flexibility. It should provide for independent study where courses are not offered regularly. Even in the formal course areas there should be options to suit individual interests, such as art, business, or entomology.[75]

Participants who requested program features such as these were engaging in a discourse of academic worth, an alternative discourse that existed from the start of Sorbonne-model study abroad programs after World War I. That alternative discourse continues to this day, defining study abroad as an academically valuable pursuit.

PARTICIPANT DISCOURSE, PRACTICE, AND BELIEF: RECENT ACADEMIC MOTIVES AND EXPERIENCES ARTICULATED FOR STUDYING ABROAD

Statements expressing serious academic motives for seeking study abroad were reported in the late twentieth century when the Council on International Educational Exchange published a profile of students abroad, produced through the survey conducted in 1985 by Jolene Koester—one of relatively few surveys at the time focusing on students' motives for studying abroad rather than the consequences of their participation. The Koester study, previously described, investigated student motives for studying abroad by analyzing their participation modes: students in programs sponsored by U.S. institutions; students enrolled in foreign universities; students developing their own agenda for academic credit; and students choosing study-travel opportunities (programs with the strongest holiday component). In all cases, the majority of participants were female.[76] The survey offered students a list of choices by which they could rank-order the following motives for overseas study:

academic performance, improving education, improving foreign language, gaining knowledge of the country, having fun, meeting people, and improving self-confidence.[77]

Few students, even those electing the more holiday-oriented study tours, stated as their major reason for going overseas "personal development" or "leisure travel." Fully 75 percent of those on study tours and more than 80 percent in every other study mode identified more serious motives for going abroad.[78] Improving academic performance and improving education, both clearly stated academic motives, ranked high in three of the four program modes—a finding that describes an alternative to the dominant discourse about student motives.[79] Two responses are more difficult to characterize in light of dominant beliefs, however: improving foreign language and gaining knowledge of a country. Improving foreign language is part of the diminished liberal arts tradition of study abroad; gaining knowledge of a country could be understood as cultural acquisition. Yet these statements indicate academic motivations as well. Indeed, in every mode, no less than 75 percent of all participants identified an academic over a personal motive for pursuing study abroad.[80]

The CIEE/Darden market study in the mid-1990s, like Koester's, examined students' motivations for going abroad and revealed discourse that could be heard both to sustain dominant beliefs and to express alternatives.[81] In this study, only 7.1 percent of all students going abroad identified recreation as a primary motive. Instead they ranked learning a language (37.7%), learning about another culture (31.2%), and gaining expertise in a specific discipline (11.9%) higher.[82] Students did, however, recognize the pleasures of international travel, naming recreation as the third of their top three reasons for going abroad; the first and second were interest in international culture and improved language skills.[83]

In the Institute for the International Education of Students (IES) survey of its alumni from 1959 to 1999—an outcomes, not motives, survey presumed to be the largest of its type—students also reported benefits other than academic. Among the 23 percent of alumni who replied to the survey, many reported important experiences including personal growth, though they cast it not in the disparaging language reported by Feinberg in his *Chronicle* article but instead as increased awareness "of their own cultural values and biases."[84] Nonetheless, these reported personal motives or benefits do reinforce the episteme. Challenging this, Amy Ruhter McMillan and Gayly Opem, in a report of their IES findings in *Abroad View Magazine*, describe the impact of study abroad on their responding alumni:

After studying abroad, most students never view their education in the same way again. A powerful experience, it often influences subsequent educational endeavors, including the decision to pursue higher degrees. More than 52 percent of respondents indicated that they had achieved a post-graduate degree, compared to the 9 percent of U.S. Americans obtaining graduate degrees as reported by the U.S. Census Bureau*. More than 80 percent of respondents agreed that studying abroad had enhanced their interest in academic study.[85] (*U.S. Census Bureau, Educational Attainment in the United States: March 2002, detailed tables [PPL-169].)

Taken together, findings such as Koester's, the CIEE/Darden market study results, and the IES alumni survey describe an alternative discourse of serious academic intent among latter-twentieth-century participants, although some components of the discourse can reinforce the dominant beliefs comprising the episteme. Investigation of the early programs—the programs that resulted in the development of these dominant beliefs—reveals clear evidence of strong academic interests and high academic expectations among many program participants, even as the dominant beliefs about study abroad have the power to spin comments such as "learning a foreign language," "gaining knowledge of a foreign country," or, most especially, "learning about another culture" or "learning about myself" into statements describing an interest in a Grand Tour for genial cultural acquisition.

Nonetheless, as Koester concluded in her study, most students are motivated to study overseas by a strong interest in academics:

> These students also overwhelmingly associated their proposed trip with *a strong emphasis on knowledge and academic experiences as source and goal for international travel.* When asked to indicate source of interest and major personal goal, these students consistently selected knowledge related choices. Although the self-report nature of the information may exaggerate students' claims, the fact that so many are so predisposed to identify learning as important for their overall experience is significant [italics in original].[86]

Similarly Dickinson College recently conducted a research project about study abroad's impact on its alumni, comparing experiences with Dickinson students who had not gone overseas. According to overseas program participants, "study abroad continues to make a difference in their lives to a much higher degree than campus alumni report that their campus-based experience does"; "they continue to use the foreign language that they studied or used at their study abroad destination more than alumni who did not study abroad do"; and they appeared to "continue to learn from reflecting upon and remembering their experience more than campus-based students do."[87]

In sum, many students have expressed academic motives for attending study abroad programs (and for choosing study abroad over other travel options). They have clearly indicated beneficial academic outcomes. Indeed, this may well be a message heard by their peers who do not choose study abroad, helping to explain why the at-home peer group sometimes sees study abroad as an opportunity to enhance critical thinking capacity and sometimes fears they are not academically strong enough to study overseas. Program participants' views parallel those of their academic mentors, who articulated serious motives for establishing, operating, and supporting these programs. Students' decisions to go overseas reflect an alternative set of beliefs, manifesting a conception of study abroad as a worthy academic endeavor, pursued even in difficult times and challenging settings. More broadly, the discourse of this community presents an alternative to the vision that study abroad is chosen by women uninterested in academic pursuits and instead seeking a Grand Tour and the presumed frivolous pursuit of cultural acquisition attained through its form of liberal education.

ALTERNATIVE VOICES ON PROFESSIONAL TRAINING, THE LIBERAL CURRICULUM, AND STUDY ABROAD

The alternative discourse of sponsors and participants has manifested the belief that the liberal curriculum is a valid field for study. Dominant beliefs casting study abroad participants as women who attend weak programs, usually in the liberal arts, define them at best as cultural guardians and at worst as social dilettantes. These beliefs describe the academic programs for these women as lacking in serious professional training purposes. Men, who study abroad in far fewer numbers, are assumed to be planning a professional life regardless of their sojourn abroad, and the belief has historically been expressed that most men remain "in the United States to build their careers."[88] Once again, overlooked or dismissed participant discourse displays alternative beliefs about the value of preparing overseas for professional, vocational, or other job-related skills.

AMERICAN DISCOURSE AND PRACTICE ABOUT WOMEN, PROFESSIONAL EDUCATION, AND THE WORLD OF WORK: THE IMPLICATIONS FOR STUDY ABROAD

Women had little access to professional education in the United States until the latter twentieth century.[89] Female students contributed in large numbers to the great modernization that swept through American universities prior to and just after World War I,[90] but they found themselves largely excluded from the newly developing professional disciplines. Margaret Rossiter called the attempts from 1870 to 1900 by women to gain higher university degrees, both in the U.S. and in Germany, "a process of quiet infiltration, a kind of educational 'guerrilla warfare' or slow 'war of attrition' against the universities."[91]

A small number of women did pursue their studies abroad successfully in these early decades.[92] In the U.S., when women were accepted into graduate schools, they sometimes found that professors did not hold the same expectations for them as they held for their male counterparts.[93] "While for men the pattern of extending educational years for professional training after college became conventional after 1910, for women the decision to attend a liberal arts college and to continue with further education involving long years of expense and commitment usually meant having to delay or renounce the option of marriage," wrote Barbara Solomon. "As going to college became the acceptable way to spend late adolescent years for the middle-class girl, so the notion of continuing in professional training became the nonconforming act of a few women."[94]

New career paths depended upon a foundation of professional education. These careers garnered greater respect, as did the theoretically based training for them.[95] Women played a part in these trends, but they did not always fully partake of them. Women gained no more than 10 percent of the degrees offered in the new disciplines and no more than 10 percent of the employment in these fields by mid-century.[96] Women neither gained access nor participated in early professional training programs in the universities. Professional education was a male bastion.

Unable to prepare academically, women were similarly denied access to the professional work world. Yet they worked, although society maintained the illusion that they did not—one of those situations, as Foucault describes, in which an episteme imposes its powers on perception. In the 1920s, when America's first study abroad programs were taking shape, women also represented a large proportion of the professional work force: 45 percent.[97] Within this category, women more often filled the semi-professions, including social work and librarianship, as well as older female-dominated occupations such as teaching and nursing.[98] The label "semi-profession" was a denigrating term, describing fields considered "less demanding, less permanent, and more appropriate for women than the prestigious ones reserved for men"—fields that were "perceived as continuing and updating the female tradition of service to society," wrote Barbara Solomon.[99]

In higher education in the twenty-first century, women have continued to gravitate toward and dominate enrollment in the humanities and social sciences and in nurturing fields like education and nursing.[100] And while female access to careers has continued to grow, gender differences have persisted.[101] Women have remained severely underrepresented in those occupations traditionally not held by women, even though they have paid 20 to 30 percent more than traditionally female jobs.[102] This underrepresentation has persisted even as—according to the last full census, conducted in 2000—73 percent of women with a college degree participated in the U.S. civilian labor force.[103]

From 1920 to the present, women have held jobs, no matter whether they were single, married, or with children. Historically, as Mabel Newcomer wrote, "whether or not the college authorities intend to prepare them, the [female] students themselves use their education" for professional gains[104]—a pattern women followed throughout the twentieth century. Yet they have often done so without recognition, certainly through the first two-thirds of the twentieth century—a striking example of the power of an episteme to render a practice ignored. The work of many educated women, whether vocational, professional, or otherwise, has long been grounded in the liberal education tradition, a tradition that continues to the present despite remarkable increases in women's access to professional training.[105] Any aspect of that education, including study abroad, has carried the potential for professional development and career preparation. These characteristics of women's experience through much of the twentieth century in America are neither validated nor recognized within the framework of the prevailing beliefs.[106]

PARTICPANT DISCOURSE, PRACTICE, AND BELIEF: PROFESSIONAL PURPOSE AND THE LIBERAL CURRICULUM

Dominant beliefs did not validate the motives of students who pursued education overseas, but vocational intentions and a concern for career preparation surface persistently in the discourse of participants pursuing the liberal curriculum abroad. When early Smith College participants were asked what they would do with their knowledge and appreciation of another language and culture, participants gave voice to their aspirations. "What we are doing with our lives after June, people seem to think will prove something conclusive about the benefits derived from the year of years when we were juniors in France," Olmsted quoted one participant as saying. The comment continued:

Ten of us are to teach French in secondary schools, . . . ten more are going to do graduate work, not all in French; one will work in philosophy, another in Italian, a third enters Oxford, a fourth has won a fellowship to the University of Bonn, still another is to study sculpture at the Ecole de Beaux Arts in Paris, and a sixth is planning to take an M.A. in music at Yale. Four, for the glory of the major, are continuing French either at Columbia, Johns Hopkins, or the University of Chicago. Of the rest, one is entering the training squad at Macy's in the fall, . . . two with secure positions in bookstores and one has a reporting job on a Boston newspaper. The rest are either engaged or have fathers who consider trips around the world the only aftermath of a college education.[107]

A few of these students were describing their vision of the Grand Tour, but the majority (24 out of 37) from that first year of Smith's program in France articulated future professional and educational plans, stating goals for either graduate study or jobs. The few who did not were the ones recognized by the emerging normative perception, and their discourse contributed to the empowerment of the episteme.

Smith students were not alone in conceiving themselves as destined for a professional life. In the Pace study of the first modern program and its heir, Delaware and Sweet Briar alumni identified improved language skills and improved study methods as values of their year abroad. Both groups named vocational or career results of their experiences. While the Pace study examined the consequences of—not the motivations for—program participation, the results reflected a discourse of career-oriented education planning. Two-thirds of the Delaware alumni and half of the Sweet Briar group studied beyond the bachelor's degree level, suggesting not only academic but also professional intentions.[108] In his study of the first quarter-century of the Sweet Briar Junior Year in France program, R. John Matthew found that "there is hardly a field of human endeavor which the Junior Year in France participants have not entered. They are actors, actresses, architects, artists, doctors, lawyers, editors, writers, diplomats, social service workers, librarians, foreign correspondents, museum directors, farmers, businessmen, musicians, as well as secretaries and professors."[109]

The oral histories, letters, and documents available from Delaware participants reveal their articulation of career-oriented motives even in the earliest years of undergraduate study abroad programming. In Aureta E. Lewis's letter back to the University of Delaware, reflecting her experience among study abroad students in 1937–38, she recalled that "other French majors with secondary interest in economics intend to take business courses after graduating from college and hope in the future to obtain positions in which they can make use of their French as well as of their business train-ing."[110] "I feel that my experience in the University of Delaware foreign study group has been most remunerative—socially, academically, finan-cially," wrote Mary Leet, who participated in the program in 1927–28. Amanda Macy, another teacher, who studied abroad in 1933–34, consid-ered her Delfor experience a "business investment."[111] For these pioneer students, the Junior Year Abroad was, according to Patricia Olmsted, a "positive step toward a career, in academia especially,"[112] and especially for women, who had limited access to professional studies at home and even less access abroad. Nonetheless, they could still ground their professional interests in a liberal education.

This sense of the function of overseas study in higher education persisted through the reestablishment of foreign education after World War II. Although reports in the Sweet Briar Junior Year in France alumni newsletter were anecdotal, they reflected the self-reported professional engagement of some of the post-war participants. Alumni notes came from women who were college professors, a manager in a major New York accounting firm, a market researcher, a public interest attorney, an estate and tax lawyer, the founder of a preschool in South Africa, the assistant treasurer at a New York bank, a polit-ical consultant, a published author, a sales assistant at a stock brokerage, an industrial development analyst, a congressional researcher, a computer soft-ware marketer, an architect, and a systems engineer. One woman did report that "I devote most of my time to cleaning, cooking, diapers, and pleasing a husband," but her case was distinctly in the minority.[113]

"Significant numbers of study-abroad participants expect to have international dimensions in their future careers and hope that time abroad will enhance their marketability," stated Stephen Cooper and Mary Anne Grant in their work on the demographics of education abroad. "U.S. stu-dents in higher education show marked career orientations, and those going abroad more often than not link their vocational goals in some way to their international academic experiences."[114] The majority of these stu-dents were, of course, women, and most of them were pursuing a liberal arts curriculum. The authors of *Study Abroad: The Experience of Ameri-can Undergraduates in Western Europe and in the United States* reported that "between 87 and 95 percent of the study abroad students felt that they would be able to utilize the international experience in their later profes-sional life."[115] The earlier Koester study also demonstrated a discourse manifesting professional preparation, indicating that at least half of study abroad participants expected their overseas experience to play a role in their professional development.[116] And, for example, the recent IES alumni survey reported that 60 percent of alumni with a Ph.D. or Ed.D. degree deemed study abroad as an important influence on their career development.[117]

The professional interests of many participants are substantiated by the alumni survey of Sweet Briar students. The survey results reveal strongly stated intentions to work professionally. Asked reasons why they chose to study overseas, almost an equal percentage of men and women responded that they wanted to enhance their career skills. (See Appendix, Table 2–3.) In answer to career interest questions asked in the survey, 89 percent of male respondents and 81 percent of female said they hoped to pursue graduate or professional work after graduation. (See Appendix, Table 6–1.) Sixty-eight percent of female participants felt that study abroad was significant preparation for their subsequent professional training. (See Appendix, Table 6–2.)

Since women as well as men entered the study abroad experience with strong professional motivations, it is not surprising that they reported that their overseas experience did not change those goals; rather, half the women and almost the same proportion of the men viewed their study abroad experience as directly connected to their later work (as shown in Appendix, Table 6–3). Of the women who responded to the survey, 70 percent replied to the question about their after-college activity. Almost 80 percent of this group said they went to graduate school; 74 percent reported holding a professional or full-time job. Among the men responding to the survey, 82 percent answered the post-college activities question, with 90 percent reporting attendance at graduate school and almost exactly the same percentage as women holding a full time or professional job (as shown in Appendix, Table 6–4). Women also indicated more frequently than men that they worked nonprofessionally, part-time professionally, part-time nonprofessionally, or as volunteers.

Both motivations and experiences articulated by students abroad reveal their professional and career-oriented goals. For these students, study overseas was not a frivolous Grand Tour, as the dominant belief defined it, nor did they choose the liberal arts only to broaden their cultural horizons. Students, including females, conceived of study abroad and its liberal curriculum as a way to gain skills and knowledge with direct application to their future careers.

AN EMERGENT DISCOURSE OF PROFESSIONAL TRAINING

Opportunities for and interest in overseas study in the professional disciplines themselves are relatively new. IIE statistics show that as late as 1985, only 19.3 percent of students abroad came from discipline-specific professional majors such as business, education, health, engineering and agriculture. Another 5.1 percent in mathematics, computer science, and physical science made for a total of 24.4 percent of students majoring outside the humanities and social sciences who chose to study abroad. In 2003, 29.3 percent of students abroad were in discipline-specific professional majors and 9.5 percent in math and science, a total of 38.8 percent of students abroad outside the liberal arts tradition.[118] None of this data shows, however, in what types of programs these students actually registered overseas.

Study abroad advocates have hoped to increase male participation in their programs, linking these hopes to diversified options including opportunities in the professions.[119] "Gender and discipline are still intimately connected," stated Barbara Burn in a progress report on the 1990s. "I think that male students in such fields as law, business, engineering, and in other professional fields are getting the message and are studying abroad in slowly growing numbers."[120] In fact, the gender ratio in study abroad enrollment has remained steady.

Do the professional program offerings display newly evolving beliefs about study abroad? Are they attracting new audiences—more students and more men—to study abroad? The data suggests that math/science and professional program options in some areas, like business, are attracting new audiences, since enrollment from students with these majors has grown almost 14 percent since 1985—and certainly there are men among these new participants. However, just as the number of students going abroad from these disciplines has not impacted the gender ratio in study abroad, neither have new foreign study programs in these areas necessarily introduced new motives for pursuing study abroad to either male participants or, particularly, female participants, who have long been pursuing study overseas for career development, even when professional program options have been few.

Many speculate that the reason business majors have taken the lead among professional students abroad is that there may be a "willing awareness that business means *international* business. As interest in international trade expands and the federal government continues its support of program development, this may be the fastest-growing group of students in study-abroad programs."[121] Growing interest from students in domestic professional programs helps increase study abroad enrollments, but there is insufficient data to verify the long-term effect on participant numbers with the creation of new professional study abroad programs. Some have linked fluctuations in students' overseas program choices to domestic enrollment trends rather than changing interest in new overseas options.[122]

It is difficult to evaluate how men or women conceive of these relatively new programs and whether they see them as opportunities different from those offered in the past. IIE statistics do not provide the gender of nontraditional majors. Two organizations that collect national study abroad data, IIE and Peterson's, do not have accurate counts of students registered in professionally oriented overseas programs, nor do they have gender information about the registrants.[123] Therefore sample program statistics and other data can only hint at a profile of which students are choosing these programs.

One such sample is the work abroad program sponsored by the British University's North America Club (BUNAC). Different from study abroad, this program attracts students for many reasons, including the need to earn money to fund their international experiences as well as a desire for work experience in an international setting. Based on studies of enrollment from 1991 to 2004, BUNAC reported that work abroad experiences in Britain—the top location chosen by U.S. students—have consistently attracted women in the majority, and in proportions at or near those in traditional study abroad programs.[124] Internship abroad programs—those placing students in credit-bearing worksite placements as part of their study abroad sojourn so they can develop international competence—can provide another indicator. Boston University International Programs offers ten sites worldwide that specialize in these placements.[125] Boston program sponsors too, reported that women have dominated enrollments, with a typical minimum of 65 percent women across all the Boston University placements.[126]

Few science and technology majors—male or female—are going abroad,[127] and gender breakdowns of enrollments are scarce. Low numbers may reflect that technical curricula often require strict sequences of courses, making it difficult for students to break that sequence by going overseas and less likely for faculty to recommend that they do so.[128] Goodwin and Nacht further noted that, amidst the suspicion with which the American scientific community has frequently regarded international education, the presumption has been that science education in particular is best pursued in the United States.[129] Professor Peter Fong of Gettysburg College reported that faculty skepticism persists today as a significant barrier to study abroad among science majors. "Some faculty think that they are the best science teachers," said Fong, "or that American education is better than overseas counterparts."[130] The episteme still dominates the discussion.

In one effort counter to such attitudes, Massachusetts's Worcester Polytechnic Institute developed overseas programs to prepare professionals for international work in science, engineering, and management. Paul W. Davis, dean of the school's interdisciplinary and global studies division, reported that women composed only 25 percent of enrollments at the institution but

40 percent of study abroad enrollments in their technical programs, far exceeding male participation rates.[131]

Al Balkcum, director of the Learning Abroad Center at the University of Minnesota, offered a similar report on gender in engineering study overseas. Balkcum stated that his university initiated its extensive curriculum integration project with engineering students first for two reasons: first, to generate interest within a discipline not traditionally involved in overseas education, and second, to increase male participation. At the same time Minnesota was recruiting women into its engineering programs heavily and experiencing an increase in female undergraduate enrollments. The two efforts merged. Study abroad enrollment increased among Minnesota engineering students—and the majority of engineering students going abroad were female.[132]

Statistics from Denmark's International Studies program (DIS), which offers a number of discipline-specific as well as traditional humanities and social science programs, have offered checkered though inconclusive information on women's participation in professional programs. DIS reported that historically, U.S. women predominated in Danish humanities and social science programs, while U.S. men predominated in their international business and architecture programs. This balance has gradually shifted. In 2003–04 DIS offerings spanned ten professional or science-based programs (two of them the female-dominated fields of education and nursing, the others architecture and design, medicine, business, and the sciences) and two humanities and social science programs. That year women outnumbered men by nearly a two-to-one ratio, similar to that in U.S. study abroad enrollment figures overall.[133] In a CIEE study of enrollment in nontraditional disciplines, Martin Hogan reported that 60 percent of students enrolled in business programs, 84 percent in health-related programs, and 68 percent in science programs were women. Only in engineering did men outnumber women, and here the statistics were not helpful because only eight students studied engineering program in this period, five of them male.[134]

Since data are insufficient, it is not possible to identify a clear discourse describing how participants perceive these emerging programs. But examples suggest women may dominate enrollment in many professional overseas programs. Women certainly choose traditional liberal arts courses over professional programs, according to the data from all sources, and far more women than men continue to go abroad regardless of the variety of study options offered. Some of these gender patterns may be influenced by domestic degree program enrollments. Women outnumber men in undergraduate programs at U.S. institutions, 128 female undergraduates for every 100 male undergraduates.[135] More women than men enroll in the humanities and social sciences; yet more men than women enroll in mathematics, sciences, and pre-professional fields. In most business disciplines, women actually outnumber men.[136]

All of these data are inconclusive. Women do predominate in liberal arts programs—humanities and social sciences—domestically and internationally. Women may participate in professional study abroad programs, like engineering, at a rate exceeding that of women pursuing degrees in those fields.[137] More women than men receive degrees in international business (with only slightly more than three thousand degrees awarded, fewer than 10 percent of all business degrees).[138] Women do study business abroad, although there is no explanation why so few women in U.S. undergraduate business programs go overseas for part of their undergraduate education. More significantly, since women continue to pursue liberal arts studies domestically and overseas with career goals in mind, there is no discourse demonstrating that professional programs introduce new motivations for pursuing overseas study, nor is there any clear discourse manifesting new beliefs about these emergent programs. One explanation for this silence may be that the discourse of motivation for study abroad among sponsors and participants has always included professional development goals.

While the evidence is inconclusive, it does not support the expectation that professionally oriented programs will significantly increase study abroad enrollments or male participants. The number of professional program majors studying abroad has increased, to be sure, but female-male ratios in study abroad remain at two to one. Some new programs are grounded in fields where women are rarely in the majority domestically, yet even in those fields women still often outnumber men overseas. It is possible that the less than enthusiastic participation in some professional study abroad programs reflects the influence of the devaluing episteme. It is also possible that as women's access to the professions increases, their need to use the liberal arts as a career pathway will decline, potentially impacting study abroad enrollments.

Many still hold the dominant belief that women's interest in the liberal arts shows their lack of professional intent. Because these valuations prevail in the American academy, the professional potential of study abroad, along with any career-related reasons why women might choose it, have been ignored. Until more men participate, thus presenting an insoluble challenge to dominant beliefs, many in the American academic community will continue to regard study abroad as insignificant.[139] As men have participated in professional programs overseas, the discourse has used their presence to validate this new direction in study abroad. Encouraging greater male participation and calling for more professional programs to accomplish this goal has been one of the ways that policy makers have attempted to break out of the holding pattern that keeps study abroad on the periphery of American higher education. Meanwhile, the academic and professional value of study abroad in women's lives—past and present—continues to be ignored.

RISKS AND HARDSHIPS, ACADEMIC MOTIVES, PROFESSIONAL TRAINING, AND THE CONFLUENCE OF ALTERNATIVE BELIEFS IN DISCOURSE ON STUDY ABROAD

There exists a consistently articulated discourse from study abroad participants, conceiving the experience as an academically strong and important avenue for professional development by way of the liberal curriculum, especially for females. Especially since September 11, 2001, student discourse has emerged describing international education as a means to contribute to world peace and security. Women who have been willing to experience risk and discomfort in order to pursue their intended educational programs do not themselves manifest belief that study abroad is a Grand Tour, an academically lightweight alternative, or a choice they have made only to acquire culture. Their motivations, experiences, and memories form an alternative discourse—and yet, like those of the sponsors who encouraged them, their voices remain unheard.

Their study abroad sponsors have believed that an overseas educational setting provides capable academic students, including the disenfranchised female majority, with a valuable educational opportunity not to be found domestically. Through the liberal curriculum offered in study abroad, they recognized, these students obtain training that enables them to function professionally. Sponsors have believed that these students, educated through study abroad, will become effective citizens able to contribute to the nation's development and the world's peace efforts, having enhanced their own international knowledge. Since study abroad participants have by and large been women, these hopes and expectations have applied particularly to female students all along.

Yet within the higher education community from the earliest years of study abroad on, women participants have been regarded as marginal, their studies frivolous. Beliefs held in the American culture about women and their educational goals have devalued females' reasons for seeking higher education. This discourse about women became associated with study abroad itself. All these beliefs joined together in discourse of the academic community, with the effect of devaluing women's educational and professional choices on the one hand and study abroad on the other. Today the ongoing primacy of women as participants in study abroad serves to sustain the broadly held American episteme that study abroad is academically weak and lacks functional, especially professional, purposes. As domestic education continues to be validated over that available abroad, all these beliefs accumulate, blocking out the alternative voices.

The power of discourse is to constitute reality. "It produces domains of objects and rituals of truth," according to Michel Foucault.[140] This power "gives gold stars for good behaviour . . . and the tendency is for that which transgresses its dictates to be defined not only as bad but as abnormal."[141] Universities and their constituencies are among those institutions that, according to Foucault, exert and sustain the power of the norm.[142] Within American higher education, the norm is the prevailing episteme, marginalizing study abroad and empowering domestic education. Sponsors and participants of study abroad have been seen as "transgressors" in the academy. But only the alternative discourses clearly define study abroad to be academically and professionally beneficial.

For Foucault, a genealogical inquiry such as this one can serve as a call to action, bringing alternative versions of reality into view.[143] Accepting his argument that discourse produces belief and directs change, one may argue that by bringing the discourse of study abroad's sponsors and participants to the fore within the American community, advocates of study abroad may have the best chance of improving its future acceptance and growth. Indeed, Foucault believed that the purpose of any inquiry is transformation.[144]

If this inquiry into dominant beliefs and alternative voices in study abroad effects any sort of transformation, it can only begin with the reconsideration of the prevailing episteme. Therefore, in its final chapter, this book considers the implications of a reshaped episteme in future study abroad policy development.

Part Four
The Future of Study Abroad

Chapter Seven
Policy Implications

For the past quarter century and more, policy statements have announced the need to enhance the role and reputation of study abroad in the American academy. Study abroad advocates have stressed the goal to educate globally competent citizens capable of functioning in an interdependent world. They have called for 10 percent of U.S. undergraduate students to study overseas by the year 2000, yet statistical reports since then reveal that the goal has not been reached. The numbers continue to convey how marginal a role study abroad plays within American higher education. Only 2.71 percent of all full-time undergraduates at American two- and four-year institutions study overseas. Indeed, whether commenting about study abroad or the broader issues of campus internationalization, authors such as Philip Altbach have explicitly recognized that "reality lags considerably behind rhetoric."[1] Sheila Biddle titled her 2002 book *Internationalization: Rhetoric or Reality.*[2] There have been plenty of calls to recognize the significance of international education in American higher education, plenty to include study abroad as part of new academic initiatives. Still, study abroad remains at the periphery.

Michel Foucault's theory of the power of discourse has proved useful in analyzing this relative failure of policy; likewise, it will prove useful in evaluating the role of educational policy in the current failure. For Foucault, the purpose of any inquiry is to expose the foundations of belief, with the potential outcome of undermining their power to define.[3] With the full exposure of the episteme comes the potential for its transformation and a subsequent redistribution of its power.[4]

In Foucault's vision, transformation cannot occur through calls for change in strategy or action. Transformation is possible only when the episteme that controls the fundamental perception of an activity changes. These fundamental codes "do not perish in response to a compelling independent body of contrary evidence and argument, but rather . . . in response to cultural sea changes."[5] While these changes are most often discontinuous[6]—that is, they emerge suddenly and without historical referent—it is also possible to create the potential for a "sea change" by introducing new voices into the discourse, voices that challenge the episteme.[7] Inquiry into the foundations of the existing episteme can expose how and in whose interest powerful beliefs developed, framing an opportunity for alternative discourses to be heard.[8] Foucault argues that those best suited to create the conditions for transformation are members of the group affected by an episteme, because they speak the language, understand the issues, and therefore have the greatest opportunity to influence other group members with their dialogue. They also have the most to gain from the transformation, for it is their experience that is limited by the prevailing episteme.[9]

The advocates of overseas education must find a different way to effect the change they are seeking. It is from this group that so many policy makers have emerged. As members of the academy—albeit marginalized members—they know the academy's terminology and understand its concerns. They are members of the higher education community themselves, nonetheless their calls to action have not succeeded in transforming the dominant beliefs about study abroad. Indeed, the current episteme imposes constraints on their ability to gain recognition for the worth they perceive in this educational activity. It is their work, their reputations, their futures, and their students who suffer. Clearly there is a relationship between the power of the episteme and the effectiveness of policy, and in this case, policy discourse has tended to be driven by an episteme that marginalizes the work and ideas of those supporting study abroad.

The argument of this book provides a framework within which to analyze the difficulties policy makers continue to encounter in their efforts to change how study abroad programs are perceived in the United States. Central to this framework is the role that dominant beliefs have played in the formation and reception of policy statements over the course of the last fifty years. This final chapter will return to policy discourse, observing it through the lens of the devaluing episteme about study abroad, which derides the experience as academically weak and functionally worthless. It will assess possible new avenues for policy development. All told, the chapter will consider how alternative voices might be less marginalized and more influential in future discourse on study abroad in the American higher education community—a necessary step toward strengthening the role of overseas education within the U.S. undergraduate curriculum.

DOMINANT BELIEFS AND LIMITS TO POLICY SUCCESS

In Spring 2002, Jaclyn Rosebrook-Collignon, director of Albion College's study abroad program in Grenoble, France, sent an e-mail message to subscribers of the NAFSA online discussion list, essentially supporting Ben Feinberg's opinions expressed in his *Chronicle of Higher Education* editorial:

> "What Students Don't Learn Abroad" points to one of our greatest weaknesses as international educators. In our efforts to ensure a "safe" and "fun" study abroad experience (safety, excursions and "fun" group activities, and positive evaluation forms—"Did you have a good time?"), we forget the true pedagogical objectives of our students . . . it is our job to confront, counsel, and guide our students before, during and after their study abroad experience. Pushing them, prodding them, asking them how the overseas experiences they are having or plan to have enter into to their educational objectives (usually, it should be linguistic and/or cultural understanding and proficiency). And often we forget to remind them why they are abroad—to experience and learn about another culture. And that only through the prism of another culture will they truly learn something new about themselves. Bungee jumping and swimming with the sharks will do nothing to further their immersion in and understanding of another culture. We aren't supposed to be like their parents and say: "Well, as long as it's fun and exciting for you, then it must be good." Study abroad experiences should be difficult and challenging to our students' identities, certitudes and value systems. Students should be expected to come back with solid linguistic skills and a more profound understanding of the target culture and its history. Sadly, too many of them come back waving stamped-up passports and wearing t-shirts from the Haufbrauhaus or various Hard Rock cafés. They've merely transplanted their lives for a period of time in a new exotic decor.
>
> This perhaps is a relatively new problem in study abroad due to a broader based student public. On the one hand, study abroad is not only for the "elite" classes and this is good. (Not to say that the "elite" classes did much better while studying abroad, there were just fewer of them.) On the other hand, we are encountering a student public whose understanding of the world is too often "superficial" . . . Students can't break free of their own cultural chains (relating to time, productivity and consumption) to be able to truly carry, feel and understand the cultural chains of others.[10]

This statement encompasses so many of the dominant beliefs—those that have existed in both past and present, those that speak of both past and present, and those that are part of the discourse even among some who support the growth of study abroad. Certainly not every advocate of study abroad shares Rosebrook-Collignon's vision of the experience. Still, most of us lack a history to inform ourselves of alternative conceptions. Belief constrains perception, says Foucault, and it constrains our own perceptions as professionals in the field of study abroad. These perceptions can be manifest even in the policy we write or support.

Policy discourse about study abroad is formulated by policy makers who come to their role from a variety of directions. Some come from the community of faculty and administrators who sponsor study abroad for their students. Others are trained in academic disciplines, such as foreign languages, and their interests lead them into the area of study abroad. Some represent groups affiliated with the academy, the non-governmental agencies, or the governmental agencies whose charges encompass study abroad activities and issues. Some are from the private sector, seeking through an academic venue training they perceive missing in their employee pool.[11] The members of this group—especially those rooted in the academy—are among those who can say most clearly, "I know that knowledge can transform us."[12]

While members of a community may hold a vision that is not entirely circumscribed by the predominating episteme, nonetheless the power of any episteme is so pervasive that it is impossible to escape its influence.[13] In the case of study abroad, policy makers, while they may not agree with the description of the experience provided by Feinberg or Rosebrook-Collignon, cannot fully escape the power of the episteme prevailing within their larger academic community. An analysis of policy discourse reveals that even as policy advocates ask the higher education community to recognize the value of study abroad, they sometimes repeat the dominant devaluing beliefs about it. If the potential for transformation lies in the introduction of new discourse, policy that prescribes change without challenging beliefs will be ineffectual. The discourse simply perpetuates the episteme that marginalizes it. Even if inadvertently, policy makers can contribute to reinforcing the episteme by repeating dominant beliefs, by stating evidence that sustains the belief without countering it with evidence from alternative discourse, or by making assertions contrary to dominant belief without introducing new discourse to establish alternative conceptions.[14]

Chapter 1 established three reports as representative of the discourse within the academic community: *Educating for Global Competence: The Report of the Advisory Council for International Educational Exchange*, published by the Council for International Educational Exchange in 1988; *A National Mandate for Education Abroad: Getting on with the Task*, a report of the National Task Force on Undergraduate Education Abroad published by NAFSA: Association for International Educators in 1990; and *Securing America's Future: Global Education for a Global Age,* a NAFSA task force policy statement in 2003. The statements in these reports, as well as beliefs conveyed elsewhere by report contributors, constitute a discourse field in which to seek the presence of dominant beliefs. If Foucault's theory of the episteme applies in this instance, then the authors of these reports— even though advocates of study abroad—were constrained by the prevailing episteme, which confined their vision and obscured from their view much alternative discourse and practice.

For example, comments by policy advocates about the Grand Tour suggested how dominant beliefs were intermingled and perpetuated, while alternative discourses were ignored. Both the CIEE and the first NAFSA reports at times reflected the dominant belief that study abroad is a Grand Tour, thus echoing negative definitions, providing no context for how the definitions developed, and illuminating no alternative discourse. *Educating for Global Competence* specifically linked the Junior Year Abroad to the Grand Tour: "The traditional grand tour, part of the education of a small segment of young Americans in the past, and the more recent 'Junior Year Abroad,' focused on the European cultural heritage and was most applicable to the liberal arts and humanities students," the report read. From this association, it proceeded to a recommendation: "Now global competence for our citizens requires us to expand study abroad into other areas."[15] Implying that study abroad has not helped students develop global competence, such statements reinforce the perception of a Grand Tour and sustain the episteme that foreign education does not offer serious academic study or professional preparation.

Policy authors also emphasized the European focus of study abroad so closely connected to the Grand Tour conception. Authors of the first NAFSA report, observing that the majority of U.S. students continue to go to Western Europe, commented, "This is neither good public policy nor good education."[16] The newest NAFSA task force report, *Securing America's Future,* did recognize the worth of European study, but it also criticized Europe as the primary location for study abroad[17] and called for "increased study in nontraditional locations outside the United Kingdom and the rest of western Europe."[18] Statements such as this, well intended to support diversified locations for study, can, when heard outside the context of study abroad history and experience to frame them, inadvertently reassert the link, at least for suspicious listeners, between Europe as a location and study abroad as a devalued cultural pursuit.

Other links might have the same effect. For example, the 1990 NAFSA report also associated the predominant study abroad programs with the humanities and social sciences, saying that they provided "essential insight into our own culture and history,"[19] a statement that risks reinforcing the dominant belief that study abroad in Europe results in genial cultural acquisition and that its liberal curriculum does not enhance global competence. The 2003 NAFSA report stated that, among students encouraged to study overseas, "We also need to look beyond the usual suspects—the language majors and the rest of those in the humanities. We don't teach science and math only to those who plan to become scientists or mathematicians. Likewise, international education should be an integral part of education for all students in the United States."[20] The very phrase "the usual suspects," with its derogatory connotations, could be easily heard by those holding the dominant beliefs about study abroad as confirmation of all their devaluing suspicions that liberal education abroad is guilty of being a frivolous endeavor, not serious enough to qualify as preparation for a public and productive life in American society.

Dominant beliefs about the Grand Tour in European locations pursued for cultural exposure systematized with conceptions about women and the role of their education, building toward the episteme about study abroad. These themes have emerged in policy discourse as well. One example is found in statements by Richard Lambert, then director of the National Foreign Language Center at the Johns Hopkins University, contributor to *Educating for Global Competence* and a resource consultant for *A National Mandate*. Lambert has described the typical study abroad participant as a prosperous white woman studying foreign languages, the humanities, or social sciences.[21] Such a statement feeds the cliché, associating study abroad with well-to-do women who go overseas to pursue the liberal arts or to undertake the language study so frequently devalued in the American academy. Inadvertent negative associations arise in Lambert's discourse, even though he is a vigorous advocate of foreign study.

The late Barbara Burn, also a frequent contributor to policy discourse through much of the last half of the twentieth century, recognized the power of dominant beliefs when she argued that education for women had been perceived as less serious than that for men.[22] She tried to challenge beliefs that denigrate study abroad as insignificant because it has been an experience primarily for women.[23] Nonetheless, when her statements conveyed the idea that current study abroad programs are different from earlier ones in that they no longer send women abroad to train them as "cultural guardians,"[24] the resulting discourse, despite her intentions, reflected and reaffirmed dominant beliefs.

Suspicions about women and wealth are inadvertently reinforced in the newest NAFSA policy statement with the report's general call for "ethnic, socioeconomic, and gender diversity."[25] These links were reasserted, implicitly connecting to the historical devaluation of women's liberal arts colleges, when the authors wrote, again with the best of intentions:

> We believe that campuses and other study abroad program providers should make every effort to keep study abroad as affordable, accessible, and enticing as possible, especially for those who now consider it beyond their reach. We must go beyond the models and incentives that applied to a time when study abroad was the province of elite, liberal arts colleges. Higher education will never be truly democratized until all students can access the opportunity to build necessary skills through study abroad.[26]

This statement explicitly reinforces the belief that study abroad was owned by the wealthy and may well imply to many a derogatory connection to the liberal institutions that so often supported it.

These intermingled themes persist in the advocacy. Both the CIEE report and the first NAFSA report recommended that programs be broadened and strengthened. NAFSA authors in particular bemoaned "the narrow scope of undergraduate education abroad," which "limits opportunities to a select few."[27] The second NAFSA report urgently encouraged a diversification of disciplines studied and audiences served.[28] The CIEE report stated that the population of U.S. college students studying abroad represented "a narrow spectrum of the population"—"predominantly white females from highly educated professional families."[29] The cited demographics suggested wealth, or at least prosperity. The first NAFSA report concluded that study abroad serves "a small fraction of American undergraduates, mainly upper middle class."[30] These statements, without contextualization or expression of an alternative discourse that describes the career preparation motives articulated for overseas study, again reinforce the Grand Tour perception that associates wealthy females with liberal arts study abroad.

The first NAFSA report directly assailed the belief that study abroad is expensive: "There is also the perception, *often not accurate,* that study abroad adds materially to educational costs, thus preventing some who would otherwise be interested from considering it seriously [emphasis added]."[31] This is a stand-alone statement, however, with no reflection about further implications that cast valuation on study abroad. The report did not explore why, even with financial aid, women continued to be the primary users of study abroad, nor did it reflect a recognition that when some administrators discouraged the use of financial aid for overseas education, they contributed to the empowerment of the devaluing episteme. The newest NAFSA report, too, argued against the belief that study abroad is the sole province of the wealthy, emphasizing that "it sometimes costs less to spend a semester on the other side of the world including air travel than it does to stay in the dorms, eat in the cafeteria, and attend classes at home."[32] But just as the new report tried strenuously to increase awareness that study abroad is more financially accessible than many assume, at the same time it reinforced the belief, certainly inadvertently, that study abroad is not accessible, with comments like, "We underscore the importance of making study abroad a reality for all college students, not just the white and the wealthy."[33]

Policy statements continue to sustain the belief that study abroad is the domain of wealthy women. In the emergence of the episteme, beliefs about women and wealth also systematize with beliefs about the role and function of liberal education to reaffirm the perception that participants have no serious career intentions. The very same beliefs reappear in the discourse generated by the advocates of study abroad. Archer Brown, former deputy director of NAFSA, has written that U.S. students abroad have historically focused on language and culture rather than on career skills, noting that only recently has professional preparation become significant.[34] Without hearing alternative discourses, those already under the influence of the prevailing episteme could receive this statement as confirmation of their belief that the liberal curriculum does not further professional development.

Indeed, the authors of all the policy reports seemed to assume that since study abroad is primarily a liberal arts experience, with professional disciplines underrepresented, it is unconnected to professional training. In the CIEE report, study abroad is described as having been "most applicable to the liberal arts and humanities students," and therefore it needs to expand "into other areas: mathematics, science, medicine, business and industry, technology, international affairs, economics and education."[35] Likewise the first NAFSA report stated that study abroad opportunities focus primarily on humanities and social science studies and "largely neglect . . . internationally important professional fields."[36] The newest report argued that change must occur in programming content to include the opportunity to develop career skills, applauding efforts at Duke University to include study abroad in its mathematics, sciences, and professional school undergraduate programs,[37] urging accreditation agencies to support study abroad as an appropriate step in fulfilling new global competencies for which the NAFSA authors hoped the agencies would call,[38] and reinforcing previous calls to "Promote the diversification of the study abroad experience, including . . . underrepresented subjects such as mathematical and physical sciences and business."[39]

In these worthy calls to include professional disciplines, the reports again inadvertently reinforced the episteme without introducing the alternative discourses. Lacking an accessible history to inform them, the authors excluded the perceived tradition in the alternative discourses that foreign education, and, for most, a liberal curriculum of foreign study, offers a unique avenue for developing skills relevant to career goals and global capability.

The NAFSA reports argued for increased corporate support; statements within all these reports built on the assumption that early programs had no professional foundation. The authors overlooked the discourse of sponsors like the University of Delaware program founders, who articulated goals to train globally competent citizens to operate professionally throughout the world and who instituted, from the start, practices to draw the corporate world into program sponsorship.[40] Both NAFSA reports indicated that corporate concern for international competence was a new phenomenon,[41] directly reflecting the dominant beliefs that degrade the functional value of study abroad. Increasing state and federal government support have been important policy calls in these documents as well, given special emphasis in the newest of the task force reports.[42]

Of course not all policy discourse has reflected perceptions constrained by the episteme. Just as the NAFSA reports suggested the inaccuracy of beliefs about the high cost of study abroad, so too the advocacy discourse about the academic quality of study abroad has not always reflected the dominant belief that overseas education is academically unchallenging. This was certainly the case in the newest NAFSA policy statement, which did not address as a significant issue the question of quality in overseas programs. Nevertheless, these examples of advocacy discourse have still sometimes inadvertently reinforced beliefs about academic weakness. The first NAFSA report, for instance, stated that "Although in the past undergraduate study abroad may have in some instances been deficient in academic substance and lacked institutional and national support, its importance is now beginning to be more widely recognized in the United States."[43] The language reinforced suspicions about academic worth.

The report did recognize that the growth of study abroad has been inhibited by "inadequate information about education abroad opportunities and their relative quality."[44] Yet that statement stood without further discussion and without any reference to alternative discourses that affirmed the quality of programs and their students. The new NAFSA document complains that language immersion "is the exception, not the rule" and comments that most students study in shorter-term programs and in English.[45] Expressing his vision of the impact of the task force's work, chair Carl Herrin argued that "it's time to bend the ears of the people who can make improved, increased U.S. education [abroad] a reality."[46] Despite this strong assertion, those perceiving through the cloud of the episteme may hear simply that study abroad must get better because it has not been good.

The first NAFSA report did try to combat these long and deeply held perceptions directly. "Unfortunately, there are some programs in existence which deserve criticism; but these are the great exception," it read. "They are easily offset by examples of learning experience abroad which surpass the experience of those who study only on campus."[47] The report criticized faculty for "selectively" focusing on student reports that study abroad was not as rigorous as study at home and for ignoring the "academic legitimacy" of many student experiences,[48] but it did not describe those higher-quality practices they believed existed.

While the report's assertions challenged dominant beliefs, they were presented without contextual evaluation and without any newly introduced discourse. Since they did not conform to the normalized view of the episteme, these challenges are likely to be dismissed. The CIEE report did identify study abroad participants as high-achieving, risk-taking women, although the statement occurred in the same paragraph as a phrase describing the majority of study abroad participants as wealthy white women studying the liberal arts[49]—a statement almost literally repeated, as observed earlier, in the newest NAFSA policy statement. While intended to express admiration, terms like "risk-taker" and, in the newest NAFSA report, "adventurous,"[50] when applied to students going abroad but heard within the context of the episteme, often link to conceptions of the Grand Tour, not to perceptions of intellectual or personal courage.

All three reports recognized the detrimental effect of the common belief that education abroad is inferior to education at home. The CIEE report cited that "Foreign academic systems and facilities may be perceived as inadequate, inhospitable or not matching up with their own structure, and therefore not conducive to an effective learning environment for American students."[51] All the reports tried to counter that belief. The first NAFSA report also reported the extent to which study abroad is held suspect within the higher education community and recommended institutional strategies to encourage faculty support.[52]

The most recent report was explicit in describing the marginalization of study abroad, at the same time implicitly recognizing the validation with which domestic education has so long been endowed. In a section titled "Barriers to Be Overcome," task force members concluded:

> The fault, as Cassius tells Brutus in Act I of *Julius Caesar,* is not in our stars, but in ourselves. College policies, albeit often unconsciously, discourage study abroad more than they encourage it. Colleges must take a hard look at the possible institutional barriers that stand in the way of study abroad, which may include: a lack of leadership on the part of senior campus officials, faculty indifference, rigidities in the curriculum, anachronistic rules, ineffective enrollment management, program designs that are inaccessible for nontraditional students, and a lack of predeparture preparation and reentry assistance. Furthermore, colleges and universities need to emphasize to their students and faculty the importance of study abroad. Internationalizing learning is a mission that every college and university—two- and four-year institutions alike—should undertake. While many colleges make a nod in this direction, too few make it happen. Indeed, colleges often unwittingly erect roadblocks that discourage students from pursuing education abroad. Instead of actively building on student enthusiasm, they unconsciously stifle it.[53]

In these policy statements, advocates did present their views of the worth of study abroad and the enhanced role it should play in higher education. Given the dominant beliefs of their audience, this was a discourse received with skepticism. It was a discourse directed to the domestic educators, whose vision of the superiority of their institutions over those abroad derived from the episteme they were challenged to abandon. The policy reports asserted the value of study abroad, but, as Foucault argues, change does not come by claiming its need; it comes by exposing the foundations of the episteme that inhibit change and by introducing new discourses instead. These steps are missing in contemporary policy discourse. Contextualization—investigating the origins and emergence of the devaluing beliefs about study abroad—was entirely absent from the reports, as was an articulation of whose vision is empowered by these beliefs. There was no inquiry of the type Foucault described as necessary for the transformation of belief.

Because such inquiry was absent, so is the new discourse that it could have produced. A Foucault-inspired archaeological investigation would have exposed the foundations of dominant beliefs and revealed them to be the products of historical confluence, not absolute truth. Alternative discourses would have been illuminated through a genealogical investigation, which could have revealed historical practices that confirmed the worth of study abroad. Instead, assertions of worth—statements claiming that overseas education is academically strong; that participants, including female participants, are very capable; that the functional purposes of study abroad are sound and significant; and that not all programs are costly—stood unsupported.

According to Foucault, what is heard in discourse is that which is synonymous with normalized views. What is likely to be heard in policy discourse, then, are those statements that appear to confirm the suspicions embedded in the dominant beliefs. Statements describing study abroad participants as wealthy women, statements criticizing programs based in Europe, statements describing some programs as academically weak and criticizing some curricula as cultural—all contain language that mirrors and reinforces the normalized view. Regardless of why such statements may have been articulated, they can delay, perhaps even inhibit, any process of real change.

Members of a discursive community are incapable of divesting themselves completely of the beliefs that form the fundamental view held by their group. Policy makers in U.S. study abroad have been unable to pull free of the powerful prevailing episteme. In some cases study abroad advocates have overtly sustained the dominant beliefs by presenting them as truths. They have offered prescriptive statements that confirm dominant beliefs, either by commission or by omission, rather than contextualizing beliefs or descriptively introducing alternative discourses into the discussion.

For policy goals to succeed, the American higher education community needs to be persuaded that study abroad is worthy of support. The episteme devaluing study abroad as academically weak and functionally irrelevant empowers the domestic academic community and perpetuates its prevailing negative valuation of study abroad. Calls to give up this power and share respect and resources with foreign education programs threaten to undermine the benefits the episteme confers upon the larger community. Advocacy discourse, as well-intentioned as it is, sometimes inadvertently or overtly reinforces the community's dominant beliefs without introducing new discourse that might evoke epistemic change.

Policy makers, committed to the growth of study abroad in higher education, need to calculate new strategies to effect such change. By viewing recent discourse about the status and future of study abroad along the lines of thought proposed by Michel Foucault, advocates may discover new approaches. There may well be opportunities to introduce new discourse and contribute beneficially to changing the widely held beliefs in the American academy that disparage overseas education.

NEW DISCOURSES, NEW POLICY IN U.S. STUDY ABROAD

Carl Herrin, chair of NAFSA's Strategic Task Force on Education Abroad, which authored *Securing America's Future*, wishes to be heard in order to effect such change. He was motivated to chair the task force by his recognition that previous calls had failed.[54] As task force members stated, "the time for lip service" had ended.[55] "Those who read these lines need to do more than nod in agreement," wrote the late Senator Paul Simon in the preface to the report. "This is a battle for understanding that you must help wage."[56]

How are battles for understanding waged? According to Foucault, transformation of belief is accomplished by viewing inquiry as a call to action. "Inquiry acts upon reality . . . the inquirer must aim to change the ensemble of rules that determine what is true and what is false, and that thereby govern action."[57] As discourse changes, belief changes. With beliefs, definitions of normal and abnormal change as well.[58] American educational policy makers can help generate conditions for transformation—not transformation of policy by fiat, but transformation of the very episteme that has marginalized study abroad. It is true that policy makers are unlikely to turn to a theory like Foucault's to explore how to build policy. They come from diverse backgrounds where such theories are not necessarily prominent. Nevertheless, Foucault's theory of the power of discourse and the episteme it produces, and his vision of how an episteme might change, suggest possible practical approaches.

Policy makers might engage in research to uncover the foundations of beliefs about study abroad and expose the power vested in the prevailing episteme. Exploration of the alternative discourses could make accessible to the policy makers and to their audiences the conceptions and practices of those who have supported modern study abroad since its inception in the United States after World War I. Such approaches to policy formulation could introduce new discourse into the national and international dialogue about study abroad. This approach also suggests that as they explore the temporal events that formed the discourse, created the episteme, and excluded alternative discourses from the conversation about study abroad, the policy makers might divest themselves of the powerful forces that may be constraining their own views. By introducing new discourse, they will find a new way to empower themselves.[59]

Among study abroad supporters, and certainly among policy makers, there are already advocates affected but not fully controlled by the episteme, and they do urge research to increase understanding about the quality and function of study abroad. *Educating for Global Competence* (1988) called for such inquiry, for example: "Deliberate evaluation and further research must be carried out on study abroad, with regard to actual numbers and categories of students, where they go, what they do and how they do it, and the extent to which their programs meet the objectives of their institutions."[60] Research also continues to be encouraged by study abroad leadership, through organizations like the Forum on Education Abroad, on whose board NAFSA's policy chair, Carl Herrin, serves.[61]

According to Foucault, an inquiry that ignores the existence and power of discourse to produce beliefs and that ignores the roots of those beliefs cannot transform the episteme. Successful inquiry "flushes out" the past and tries to change it.[62] If transformation is to occur, the investigator introduces the new discourse that must be heard as part of the process of inquiry. Indeed Hans de Wit, international education researcher and practitioner and a member of the CIEE Board of Directors, called for research across the landscape of internationalization, arguing that "research on the internationalization of higher education by schools of education and other disciplines is needed to make this area more accepted by the community of higher education researchers and beyond."[63]

In this statement, de Wit recognized that discursive power is not exerted by an authority from above or outside a community. Rather, power is exercised by everyone in the community as their shared discourse creates and sustains an episteme.[64] Together the members of a group define what is believed and normalized and what is suspect and marginal.[65] The entire higher education community needs to participate in any new dialogue about study abroad, becoming recipients of policy dissemination and even partners in policy formulation. Such a model of inclusion cannot guarantee faculty support, but it can enhance the possibility for a new set of beliefs to emerge. Carl Herrin has addressed this need. "It is virtually axiomatic for an international educator to advocate that more U.S. citizens" go abroad, he observed, and he noted that the effectiveness of this advocacy "depends on the ability of international educators to work with these other decision makers," namely campus decision makers, the business community, and government leaders.[66]

The need for full community participation in the transformation of the episteme is all the more compelling given the democratic structure of American higher education, with no central authority, either national, regional, or local, able to mandate a change in study abroad activity. Indeed, public policy is often viewed in the United States "as an intrusion into institutional autonomy and an impediment to positive institutional change."[67] There exists in the United States an "historic mistrust of centralized national policy," and so there is no centralized U.S. public policy about international education.[68] The system is decentralized not only at the federal and state levels but also within the institutions themselves.[69] The power of curricular development usually rests with the faculty.[70] These traditions are comprehended by study abroad policy makers, as Carl Herrin reflected: "Unlike the central role the U.S. government has with regard to foreign student and scholar flows, in education abroad the government responsibility is secondary. . . . If anyone is waiting for Uncle Sam to make this happen, they're in for a long wait and a great deal of disappointment."[71]

In other words, transformation of policy cannot occur by dictum in the American system. Change emerges from within the system itself. Nor does any centralized mechanism exist to ensure that faculty and administrators become part of a dialogue expressing new discourse which might change policy. Policy reports do mention this need to make sure that key discourse is heard. The 1990 NAFSA report identified steps which must occur for policy recommendations to be implemented: "We urge that at each level the community concerned with undergraduate study abroad work through existing organizations to move strategically on these goals. Where organizations do not exist they must be created or the task absorbed within some other entity."[72] The report urged action on the national, state, and institutional levels. *"The goal is to create a grassroots mandate for study abroad* [emphasis original]."[73] The CIEE report also articulated the need to involve the broader community if study abroad opportunities are to be respected and study abroad programming to grow. "Expansion of study abroad, as an essential part of the strategy, will require initiative and support from campus leadership as well as from leadership outside higher education institutions. Our report is intended to reinforce the understanding of such leadership about how to get on with the job," read the introduction.[74] "This report encourages college and university presidents, senior officers and boards, as well as legislators to act to expand international activities in higher education," the report later stated.[75]

While the CIEE and NAFSA reports call for inclusion of many constituencies in the dialogue about study abroad, rarely is such discourse about foreign education widely disseminated. For example, the most recent of the NAFSA policy statements, *Securing America's Future,* was posted on the NAFSA website, accompanied by e-mail, newsletter, and magazine announcements of its online availability. For most, the report was available in hard copy by request only, and printed versions of the report were distributed only to international education policy leaders identified by NAFSA, handed out at a press conference announcing the report, and mailed to each member of Congress.[76] Mailing the task force report to members of Congress did carry the report outside the circle of discourse among those who already support study abroad, although Congress is unlikely to become a savior of study abroad. College presidents may represent a more promising audience, but a hard copy of the report was not sent to them, and indeed even distributing it to them would not guarantee significant discourse change. As it is, these reports do not circulate to the grassroots faculty who make curricular decisions—the individuals who, as recognized in the reports, must support policy in order for it to be implemented. The vast majority of American faculty are completely unaware of the existence of these reports or the arguments they contain.

To build grassroots support, all who hold the power—all members of the academy—need to join in the discussion. Recognition of this responsibility to engage the broader higher education community in dialogue about study abroad is building. "In order to be successful, involvement in internationalization must extend beyond the circle of true believers," argued Madeleine Green and Christa Olson in their 2003 book, *Internationalizing the Campus: A User's Guide.*[77]

At issue is how to extend discourse about international education to larger audiences. Venues sponsoring research that can help produce this discourse about study abroad in particular and international education generally have indeed increased. The Association of International Education Administrators (AIEA), formed in 1982, began publishing the *International Education Forum* and issued "A Research Agenda for the Internationalization of Higher Education in the U.S."[78] AIEA awards grants totaling $10,000 annually in support of research related to all forms of international education.[79] In the fall of 1995, Boston University began publishing its journal, called *Frontiers: The Interdisciplinary Journal of Study Abroad,* designed to have an academic orientation and an appeal to both students and faculty.[80] The Forum on Education Abroad formed in 2001, with its central mission "to promote the greater good of the field of education abroad," including research.[81] While these organizations and others support research and, in some cases, publish research findings, journals on study abroad rarely circulate in the broader education community. CIEE and AIEA reported this problem in their initial journal efforts.[82] Today *Frontiers,* while read by some faculty and intended for many, reaches only libraries and study abroad professionals, with about 500 subscribers and a total circulation of 1,200 per issue.[83] Articles that might engage, inform, or challenge the views of the broader faculty community are not reaching them.

In an effort to strengthen the voice of study abroad advocates, the Council on International Educational Exchange expanded its research agenda in 2000 by planning joint research and publication projects with other international education groups, including AIEA. Their efforts included merging the CIEE and AIEA journals. Ten of "the world's most prestigious international education organizations,"[84] both regional and national, have joined forces with CIEE to stimulate research in international education, an effort out of which a new publication, the *Journal,* is the first concrete product. The resulting new organization, the Association for Studies in International Education (ASIE), stated as its mission "to encourage serious research and publications concerning international education and academic mobility, to stimulate interest in such work, and to develop and promote ways to disseminate this work in cost-effective and accessible format."[85]

Edited by Hans de Wit, the *Journal* sees as its mission "to broaden the discourse on the role of international cooperation and exchange." In January 2001, ASIE partnered with Sage Publications, a decision that expanded the outreach of the *Journal of Studies in International Education* and increased its frequency from biennial to quarterly.[86] This major commitment to supporting emergent discourse and broadcasting it more widely, however, continues to be noticed primarily within the community of true believers.[87] This fate is shared by two other magazines that encourage research: *International Educator,* a quarterly magazine now in its eighth year, published by NAFSA,[88] and *IIENetworker,* published since fall 2001 by the Institute of International Education.[89] In both cases primary subscribers include members of the publishing organizations—already advocates of and for international education.

New publications encouraging research on international education represent venues where articles introducing new and alternative discourses might be published. Panels and committees dedicated to research have begun to appear at national conferences, such as those of NAFSA, the Association of International Education Administrators, the Mexican Association of International Educators, and the European Association for International Education.[90] These efforts project the voices of policy advocates, though again the audience they reach remains largely within the boundaries of the international education community, and no plan is articulated to broaden their reach.

Empirical studies of colleges and universities with successful, broadly supported study abroad programs indicate that one of the most effective methods for change is to "build widespread faculty support," says Ann Kelleher, who conducted such a study.[91] Success is achieved by engaging faculty across the entire curriculum, revising the episteme about study abroad within the institution itself, and thereby building grassroots support of the type called for in the NAFSA reports. Several publications in recent years have offered similar suggestions to promote internationalization, including ACE's *Internationalizing the Campus: A User's Guide*, NAFSA's *Internationalizing the Campus: Profiles of Success at Colleges and Universities*, ACE's *Promising Practices*, ACE's *Reforming the Higher Education Curriculum: Internationalizing the Campus*, and Sheila Biddle's *Internationalization: Rhetoric or Reality*. The University of Minnesota won its Archibald Bush Foundation grant to make just such an investment in curriculum integration of study abroad specifically and reported on their results at their April 2004 conference. These assessments share in the effort to engage new audiences in support of international programs in higher education. They share the strategies used at institutions where this broader engagement has already occurred, offering models of ways to expand the discourse community. What they repeatedly demonstrate is that effective initiatives all move outside the international education community and engage others in the institution in dialogue about study abroad. Their results, as well as the results of research and analysis central to this book, ultimately suggest that foreign education advocates seek wide distribution venues of their policy statements and partnership in discourse with faculty outside international education circles.

Models of this approach are emerging within some of the disciplinary associations in the U.S. One example exists in the American Assembly of Collegiate Schools of Business (AACSB). Together with the Association of American Colleges, AACSB sponsored research and published *Beyond Borders: Profiles in International Education*, by Joseph S. Johnston, Jr., and Richard J. Edelstein in 1993,[92] which Ann Kelleher cited in her work as exemplary. This is a book of case studies showing how business and liberal arts faculties have cooperated to plan innovative international education projects. The two organizations collaborated to undertake, publish, and disseminate all research to their joint constituencies, thereby extending their audiences. Each organization carried to its own constituency the credibility needed to give weight to the message. Today in its magazine and newsletter publications, AACSB has continued to incorporate support for and examples of curriculum internationalization and programs abroad.[93]

Other academic organizations are joining in the endeavor, linking with members of their own organizations, with representatives from disciplines involved in international education, or with those who share an interest in international education goals, in order to work together to identify the global interests within their disciplines. Two emerging examples are the American Chemical Society and the Accreditation Board for Engineering and Technology (ABET), the accrediting agency for college and university programs in applied science, computing, engineering, and technology.[94]

In its 2004–06 report, the American Chemical Society emphasized "global scientific collaboration." A headline on the report cover announces "ACS: Enabling global collaboration."[95] The society's educational division[96] publishes the *Journal of Chemical Education* where, for example, Northeastern University chemistry department faculty member Geoffrey Davies wrote:

> We still offer science education as groundwork of many career alternatives, but provide too few opportunities for students to experience them. With tough times in store for the foreseeable future, it is imperative that more science students have the chance to hone their skills in experiential, cooperative education, and study abroad activities. This needs hard work by faculty and employers to identify student opportunities, monitor progress, and provide program continuity, but the benefits are self-evident.[97]

Scientists who also devote a portion of their professional time to international education at their institutions—for example, Lawrie Davidson, emeritus professor of mineral science and extractive metallurgy and emeritus director of international education, Murdoch University, Western Australia, and Dr. Peter Schiffman, professor of geology and director, Education Abroad Center at the University of California, Davis—voice excitement that an academic association such as ACS has stated interest in international issues and even study abroad. Even with a long way to go before enrollments in study abroad increase dramatically, these science faculty doubling as study abroad advocates say that discourse presented by scientists to scientists has sparked the first serious interest in study abroad in their fields.[98]

ABET has begun to encourage international education among its recommendations for quality programs in engineering and applied science, reports Peter J. Hudleston, professor of geophysics and associate dean at the University of Minnesota's Institute of Technology. Hudleston, speaking at the Minnesota Curriculum Integration Conference in 2004, said that since 2000, ABET has stipulated that graduates in accredited engineering programs must have international knowledge of some type, although not necessarily a study abroad experience. Hudleston is nevertheless enthusiastic over the role study abroad is coming to play in engineering education, since ABET speaks the voice of the profession. If a relationship can be built between study abroad and engineering education professionals, together with practicing engineers, as it is being done in Minnesota, this message might have a positive impact on efforts to internationalize a broader curriculum and to include study abroad among the important options offered to engineering and technology students.[99]

NAFSA recognizes the importance of partnering with academic groups. During the review of its own 1990 policy report, members of some disciplinary associations were invited to provide input.[100] But, like the most recent report, the first NAFSA report was not circulated to faculty in such organizations, nor was it a research report. The approach offered by *Beyond Borders* and more recent efforts includes joint research and communication that reaches an audience beyond those already committed to international education.

If study abroad advocates were to follow these latter models, not only would more faculty members be reached, but their belief systems would be more vigorously challenged, since the message would be coming from within their own ranks.[101] The range of potential links is extensive. They include the professional associations across all the higher education disciplines. These professional societies, their researchers and their members, can speak to colleagues in their own voices and language—generate their own renovated discourse—about study abroad.

An epistemic vision is powerful. It is produced and sustained by everyone within a community. Its foundations are often forgotten, yet discourse perpetuates and empowers it. Foucault himself is never clear about how exactly to effect epistemic change, though that is the fundamental goal of his work and philosophy. Further, Foucault provides no guidelines for how to address a group destined to lose authority were it to accept a change in an episteme. Nevertheless, he is clear that change does not occur through proclamation or prescription. Rather transformation of an episteme is possible only when new discourse challenges old beliefs.

Sources for new discourse can extend well beyond those described in this book. As Josef Mestenhauser has observed, it is important now to institutionalize international education and to make it a bonafide part of higher education's mission and function; and to do so, he argues, requires much more research on what is going on in all aspects of the field.[102]

Identifying and articulating shared interests, concerns, and values within these topics and among all in the academy—domestic educators who distrust study abroad as well as their peers who advocate it—opens up the possibility for new discourse. Action on these fronts will make it all the more likely that recommendations articulated by study abroad policy makers will be more openly and actively received. When the audience is a community that marginalizes study abroad, generating support is difficult. When dominant beliefs unintentionally form part of the content of policy statements, the discourse itself perpetuates the problems it is meant to solve. Study abroad advocates need to do more than prescribe change to the academy if they hope to be successful. To create an audience willing to hear new discourse, ready to engage in policy dialogue, and open to validating the practice of study abroad, policy makers must engage in acts of transformation.

CONCLUSION

Opportunities for new discourse that could produce transformation exist at the same time that study abroad in American education remains marginalized. This book has sought explanations for this phenomenon by adapting the perspective of Michel Foucault's discourse theory as a method for understanding the role of study abroad in American higher education. This technique does facilitate a unique understanding about the existence, evolution, and power of beliefs about study abroad. Adapting Foucault's methodology has helped highlight how clichés about study abroad, far from being trivial, actually coalesce into a coherent and powerful discourse that devalues American undergraduate study abroad, representing it as academically weak and without functional value, especially in training students for professional roles in American society; that marginalizes its advocates; and that validates domestic education over any pursued abroad.

At the same time, Foucault's methodology has facilitated an analysis of alternative discourses, revealing a different valuation of study abroad. Study abroad has been valued and consistently practiced by women more than men—in a ratio of two to one—despite changes in format, duration, location, content, cost, and support from diverse institutions. The discourse of female students has revealed that they pursued a liberal curriculum in study abroad for much the same reasons that they pursued it at home—as an academic avenue for career preparation. They, and the faculty who supported them, have envisioned the education they attain abroad to be unique, unavailable in the United States, and of the highest academic quality. The faculty and administrators who supported this study have consistently identified women as a group worthy of the best education that could be provided by American institutions, advocating for women a form of education perceived as academically challenging, appropriate for career preparation, and valuable as a training ground for citizens capable of contributing to world peace. In these alternative discourses, study abroad is perceived to be at the heart of the United States's educational mission. Finally, these faculty have been willing to express positions deemed marginal and invalid by many of their peers.

Policy statements that prescribe change are likely to be met with continued resistance if the prevailing episteme devaluing study abroad is left unexamined and allowed to dominate thought and value judgments. Within discourse itself—discourse that exposes, confronts, and undermines old beliefs—exists the seedbed of change. Therein lies the possibility that education outside the United States might come to be understood as central and worthwhile in the life of the American undergraduate student, revitalized in the perception of every American professor and administrator in every discipline. With such a change, the potential grows for policy transformation to be considered, appreciated, and implemented within U.S. higher education. Faculty and administrators who support foreign education can become empowered, and student participants—including and perhaps especially the women among them—can gain respect for having chosen to study abroad.

Notes

NOTES TO CHAPTER ONE

1. Laura Siaya and Fred M. Hayward, *Mapping Internationalization on U.S. Campuses: Final Report 2003* (Washington, D.C.: American Council on Education, 2003), viii. Hereafter cited as *Mapping Internationalization.* This report is part of a broader Ford Foundation study called "Mapping the Landscape: A Status Report on the International Dimensions of U.S. Higher Education," online at http://www.acenet.edu/bookstore/. Researcher and international educator Josef A. Mestenhauser observed that "universities lack clear definitions of international education and have failed to institutionalize it" ("In Search of a Comprehensive Approach to International Education: A Systems Perspective," in Walter Grünzweig and Nana Rinehart, eds., *Rockin' in Red Square: Critical Approaches to International Education in the Age of Cyberculture* [Washington, D.C./Münster, Germany: Lit-Verlag, 2002], 165).
2. Sheila Biddle, *Internationalization: Rhetoric or Reality*, ACLS Occasional Paper No. 56 (New York: American Council of Learned Societies, 2002), 1.
3. Fred M. Hayward and Laura M. Siaya, *Public Experience, Attitudes and Knowledge: A Report on Two National Surveys About International Education*, funded by the Ford Foundation (Washington, D.C.: American Council on Education, 2001), 5. Hereafter cited as *Public Experience.* This report contains the results of a national public opinion survey conducted by ACE and KRC Research along with a student survey by studentPOLL (Art & Science Group).
4. *Mapping Internationalization*, viii.
5. Ibid., x.
6. While the events of September 11, 2001, temporarily diminished foreign travel from the United States, American students still want to study abroad. After 9/11 and the ensuing concerns about war and terrorism, available numbers reflect study abroad enrollments continuing to build. "More Americans are studying abroad—55% increase in five years," read the title of the November 18, 2002, press release announcing the results of an informal online survey conducted by the Institute of International Education (IIE) (18 November 2002, http://www.iie.org/). The survey found

that 45 percent of respondents experienced an increased interest in study abroad in 2002. The full study, with statistical details, can be found at http://opendoors.iienetwork.org/. IIE's annual statistical analysis showed that even in 2001–02, the number of students receiving credit for study abroad grew by 7.4 percent from the previous year. The American Council on Education's survey registered some reluctance on the part of parents and students (Center for Institutional and International Initiatives, American Council on Education, "One Year Later: Attitudes about International Education since September 11," *Public Opinion Poll,* September 2002, 5–7, http://www.acenet.edu/bookstore/pdf/2002_one-year-later.pdf/), yet still Allen E. Goodman, IIE president and CEO, asserted that "Despite efforts by terrorists to isolate America from the rest of the world, the response by American students and American campuses is to become more intensely engaged in international affairs, and to seek out more opportunities for first-hand interaction with other cultures and other countries," as quoted in IIE press release cited above.

7. American Council on Education, *Beyond September 11: A Comprehensive National Policy on International Education,* 2002, 8. Hereafter cited as *Beyond September 11.* This document can be downloaded from the ACE Bookstore, http:/www.acenet.edu/bookstore/.

8. *Public Experience,* 1–3.

9. IIE, "More Americans are studying abroad." Full statistics accessible at http://opendoors.iienetwork.org/.

10. Ibid.

11. U.S. Congress, House Report 108–10, *Making Further Continuing Appropriations for the Fiscal Year 2003, and for other purposes, accompanying H.J. Res. 2, Consolidated Appropriations Resolution,* 2003.

12. *Mapping Internationalization,* viii.

13. See enrollment data later in this chapter (section titled "The Current State of Study Abroad"). For a discussion of percentages cited in current literature, see Daniel L. Ritchie [chancellor, University of Denver], "Global Beat Syndicate," 29 September 2003, http://www.nyu.edu/globalbeat/syndicate/ritchie092903.html/.

14. As stated in American Council on Education, "Higher Education Groups Propose National Policy on International Education," *Higher Education and National Affairs* (online edition), Vol. 51, No. 9, 13 May 2002, http://www.acenet.edu/hena/issues/2002/05–13–02/international.ed.cfm/.

15. *Beyond September 11,* 8.

16. Institute of International Education, "Study Abroad Surging Among American Students: After Sept. 11, interest in study abroad continues to grow rapidly," press release, 15 November 2004, http://opendoors.iienetwork.org/?p=50138/. Goodman's comment was part of a press event announcing highlights from *Open Doors 2004,* http://opendoors.iienetwork.org/. Study abroad enrollments increased 8.5 percent from the previous year, while at the same time U.S. higher education undergraduate enrollment was up 4.44 percent (calculated from projections of enrollments in four-year public plus four-year private schools for 2002 and 2003, with 2001–02 enrollments projected

at 9,554,000 and 2002–03 at 9,978,000 [http://www.nces.ed.gov//programs/projections/ tables/table_17.asp]).

17. *A National Mandate for Education Abroad: Getting on with the Task, Report of the National Task Force on Undergraduate Education Abroad* (Washington: NAFSA: Association for International Educators, May 1990), 1. Hereafter cited as *A National Mandate.*

18. *Securing America's Future: Global Education for a Global Age, Report of The Strategic Task Force on Education Abroad* (Washington, D.C.: NAFSA: Association of International Educators, November 2003), 5. Hereafter cited as *Securing America's Future.* The ACE survey confirmed in 2001 that "the overall level of Americans' international knowledge remains low" *(Public Experience,* 3).

19. Bijal V. Trivedi, "Survey Reveals Geographic Illiteracy," *National Geographic Today,* 20 November 2002, http://news.nationalgeographic.com/news/2002/11/1120_021120_GeoRoperSurvey.html/. Full survey results at http://geosurvey.nationalgeographic.com/geosurvey/.

20. *Securing America's Future,* 1.

21. Vic Johnson, "From the Front Lines: International Education as a National Security Issue," *Newsletter, NAFSA: Association of International Educators,* vol. 53, no.4 (May/June 2002), 3.

22. Carl Herrin, "It's Time for Advancing Education Abroad," *International Educator,* vol. XIII, no. 1 (Winter 2004), 3; *Securing America's Future,* 1.

23. *Securing America's Future,* iii.

24. Ibid., 1.

25. "One Year Later," 1. This poll, updating *Public Experience, Attitudes, and Knowledge* (2000), reported that 60 percent of undergraduate students surveyed believed that all students should have a study abroad experience while pursuing their higher education (*Mapping Internationalization,* 3).

26. "One Year Later," 8.

27. The conference was sponsored by four organizations—the Association of American Colleges, the Council on Student Travel (renamed the Council on International Educational Exchange in 1966), the Experiment in International Living, and the Institute of International Education—and supported by the Ford Foundation, the Danforth Foundation, the Hazen Foundation, and the Corning Glass Foundation. It featured speakers from the academic community, including rectors, chancellors, and presidents from institutions like the University of Geneva, Mount Holyoke College, and the University of California. Freeman's report encouraged a strong nationwide commitment to academic quality in the development of study abroad. See John E. Bowman, *Educating American Undergraduates Abroad: The Development of Study Abroad Programs by American Colleges and Universities* (New York: CIEE Occasional Papers, series no. 24, 1987), 17–18.

28. *A National Mandate,* 4.

29. Gary Rhodes, "Exploring the Framework for Entrepreneurial Growth in Study Abroad," in Todd Davis, ed., *Open Doors 1996/977: Report on International Exchange* (New York: Institute of International Education, 1997), 156.

30. Richard W. Riley, "The Growing Importance of International Education," speech presented at La Maison Française, Washington, D.C., 19 April 2000, http://www.ed.gov/Speeches/04–2000/00419.html/.

31. *Securing America's Future*, 2.

32. "A Message from the Honorable Paul Simon, Honorary Co-chair," in *Securing America's Future*, ii.

33. Hey-Kyung Koh Chin, ed., *Open Doors 2003: Report on International Educational Exchange* (New York: Institute of International Education, 2003), 16, 58. Also see IIE, "More Americans are studying abroad." Full statistics can be found at http://www.opendoors.iienetwork.org/.

34. National Center for Education Statistics, *Digest of Education Statistics, 2002*, Table 170, "Enrollment, staff, and degrees conferred in postsecondary institutions. . . Fall 2000, Fall 1997, and 2000–01," http://nces.ed.gov/programs/digest/d02/tables/dt170.asp/.

35. Ibid., Table 177, "Total fall enrollment in degree-granting institutions by level of enrollment, sex, attendance, status . . . : 2000," http://nces.ed.gov/programs/digest/d02/tables/dt177.asp.

36. "American Students Studying Abroad," in Chin, ed., *Open Doors 2003*, http://opendoors.iienetwork.org/?p=36524/.

37. National Center for Education Statistics, *Digest of Education Statistics, 2002*, Table 177.

38. Ibid.

39. For 2001–02 the figure is 12.44 percent: 160,920 study abroad students out of 1,291,900 students who received bachelor's degrees in 2002. For 2002–03 it is 13.22 percent, calculated by dividing the total number of study abroad students in 2002–03 (174,629) by number of degrees conferred in June 2003 (1,311,000), a total provided by the National Center for Educational Statistics, *Projection of Education Statistics to 2013*, Table 27, http://www.nces.ed.gov//programs/projections/tables/table_27.asp/.

40. Foreign Student and Total U.S. Enrollment 2002/2003 in Chin, *Open Doors 2003*, http://opendoors.iienetwork.org. In 2000–01, foreign nations sent 547,867 students to the United States for higher education.

41. See, for example, Table 6.3, Foreign Students by Academic Level, Selected Years, 1954/55—1990/91, *Open Doors 1990/91*, 33, on Institute of International Education, *50 Years of Open Doors* (CD-ROM).

42. For the first forty years of surveys, from 1947–48 to the late 1980s, engineering drew the largest number of foreign students. In 1988–89, for the first time, foreign enrollees in business and management outnumbered those in engineering: 19.5 percent and 19.0 percent of the population total respectively. Mathematics, computer science, and the physical and life sciences also drew large numbers of foreign students in a pattern culminating in 1997–98, when 58.4 percent of all foreign students came to the U.S. to study, in descending order of popularity: business and management, engineering, physical and life sciences, math and computer science, health sciences, and agriculture. Table 6.0, Foreign Student Totals by Field of Study, 1996/97—1997/98, *Open Doors 1997/98*, 64, on *50 Years of Open Doors*.

43. In 2000–01 foreign students represented nearly 4 percent of the entire U.S. higher education enrollment. Of those, 57.1 percent were male, almost half in graduate programs. Foreign students made up 13.3 percent of graduate student enrollments in the academic year 2002–03. Students from abroad continued to major in business and management, engineering, and mathematics and computer sciences in the main. Chin, ed., *Open Doors 2003*, 2, 15, 55.

44. *Open Doors 1986/87*, 80, *50 Years of Open Doors.*

45. "About the Students," *Open Doors 1997/98*, 100, *50 Years of Open Doors.* See also Table 8.f, Study Abroad Enrollments by Sex, 1985/86–1996/97, *Open Doors 1997/98*, 101, on *50 Years of Open Doors.* IIE developed comprehensive analyses of study data from 1985–86 to 1997–98, and the information became increasingly accurate from 1986–87 on, thanks to new survey protocols.

46. Table 8.e, Study Abroad Enrollments by Academic Level, *Open Doors 1997/98*, 101, on *50 Years of Open Doors;* Table 12.6, "Academic Level of U.S. Study Abroad Students, 1988/89," *Open Doors 1988/89*, 82, *50 Years of Open Doors.*

47. Table 8.c, "Business or Philosophy?, 1985/86–1996/97," *Open Doors 1997/98*, *50 Years of Open Doors*, 95.

48. Chin, ed., *Open Doors 2003*, Table 26, "Profile of U.S. Study Abroad students, 1993/94–2001/02," 62.

49. Ibid.

50. Ibid., Table 22, "Host Regions of U.S. Study Abroad Students, Selected Years 1985/86–2001/02," 58.

51. Ibid., Table 24, "Fields of Study of U.S. Study Abroad Students, Selected Years 1985/86–2001/02," 61.

52. Ibid., 19.

53. Ibid., 18–19.

54. William Hoffa, e-mail to SECUSS-L members, 18 April 2002. Study abroad is part of the broader higher education internationalization efforts. Definitions of international education and the concept of "internationalizing the campus" are also often lacking. Useful definitions of these concepts, of which study abroad is a component part, can be found in Hayward and Siaya, *Public Experience, Attitudes, and Knowledge*, and in Philip Altbach, "Resource Review: Perspectives on International Higher Education" in *Change*, Vol. 34, no. 3 (May/June 2002), online at http://pqasb.pqarchiver.com/change/. According to Hayward and Siaya, "International education is the term most commonly used in the United States to describe the international dimensions of education. It generally includes languages, area studies, study abroad, and international relations. It involves an infusion of international perspectives into the curriculum and co-curriculum" (43). According to Altbach, "internationalism" is a major trend but "widely misunderstood." He posits that "Internationalization refers to the specific policies and initiatives of individual academic institutions, systems, or countries that deal with global trends."

55. For example, see Council on International Educational Exchange, *Annual Report 94–95* (New York: CIEE, 1995). Also see Liudmila K. Mikhailova, *The History of CIEE: Council of International Educational Exchange and*

its role in international education development: 1947–2002 (master's thesis, University of Minnesota, 2003; online at http:www.lib.umn.edu/arti-
cles/proquest.phtml). For an online CIEE history based on contributions
from Mikhailova, see "History" at http://www.ciee.org. CIEE has
approximately 500 staff members in 30 countries, 274 member institutions, and 183 academic consortium members. According to CIEE's own
policies, as stated online, students in CIEE programs "are required to
take a full course load as offered by each program (usually the equivalent
of 15 U.S. semester-hour credits)." See "Policies and Procedures" at
http://www.ciee.org/.

56. Marie O'Sullivan, ed., *IIE Passport: Academic Year Abroad, The Most
    Complete Guide to Planning Academic Year Study Abroad,* 33rd edition
    (New York and Chester, Penna.: Institute of Education, 2004), vii.

57. Ibid., x.

58. Beatrice Beach Szekely and Maria Krane, "The Current Demographics of
    Education Abroad," in William Hoffa and John Pearson, eds., *NAFSA's
    Guide to Education Abroad for Advisers and Administrators,* 2nd ed.
    (Washington: NAFSA: Association for Foreign Student Affairs, 1997), 150.
    Hereafter cited as Hoffa and Pearson, eds., *NAFSA's Guide,* 2nd ed. Also
    see *Open Doors 2002/03,* 18.

59. Szekely and Krane, "The Current Demographics," 150–159. For a mid-cen-
    tury review of program types, see Larraine Mathies and William G. Thomas,
    eds., *Overseas Opportunities for American Educators: Perspective and Possi-
    bilities* (New York: CCM Information Corporation, 1971). Also see, in that
    volume, William Allaway, "The American Campus Moves Abroad," 18–19.

60. Frances Haley, *Reforming Education for the International Century* (New
    York: Coalition for the Advancement of Foreign Languages and Interna-
    tional Studies, 1989).

61. Bowman, *Educating American Undergraduates Abroad,* 17–18; Institute of
    International Education, *Transplanted Students: A Report of the National
    Conference on Undergraduate Study Abroad* (New York: IIE, 1961). The
    conference had been preceded and encouraged by a meeting at Mt.
    Holyoke College sponsored by the Council on the Junior Year Abroad of
    the Institute of International Education (whose members are schools with
    long-established study abroad programs), the Association of American Col-
    leges, and the Experiment in International Living. The meeting took place
    in January 1960 with a mission "to provide long-needed guidance in an
    increasingly chaotic field" (Irwin Abrams and W. R. Hatch, *Study Abroad,
    New Dimensions in Higher Education,* No. 6, U.S. Department of Health
    Education and Welfare and Office of Education, Washington, D.C.: U.S.
    Government Printing Office, 1962, 3).

62. A. Lee Zeigler, "History of SECUSSA," panel presentation, NAFSA: Asso-
    ciation of International Educators National Conference, 28 May 1998. The
    discussion of how NAFSA: Association of International Educators should
    best support the development of international education in the United
    States continues to the present, with debates about reorganization. See
    NAFSA: Association of International Educators, Task Force, *Strengthening*

the Association for the 21st Century, March 2004, at http://www.nafsa.org/strengthening/.

63. *Strength Through Wisdom,* n.p. President Carter's commission established the tone of reports in the 1980s. Policy statements issued under Carter described a climate of "economic vulnerability," the "inability of U.S. corporations to be competitive" in the international marketplace, and "American ignorance of the world, leading to deteriorating manpower and management capacity" (Barbara Burn, *Expanding the International Dimensions of Higher Education* [San Francisco: Jossey-Bass, 1980], 6).

64. This report suggested that study abroad was a viable way to address the educational shortcomings cited in the Carter report. National Commission on Excellence in Education, Report to the Nation and the Secretary of Education, *A Nation at Risk: The Imperative for Educational Reform* (Washington: U.S. Department of Education, 1983).

65. Richard D. Lambert, *Points of Leverage: An Agenda for a National Foundation for International Studies* (New York: Social Science Research Council, 1984) and *International Studies and the Undergraduate, A Special Report* (Washington: American Council on Education, 1989).

66. Craufurd Goodwin and Michael Nacht, *Abroad and Beyond: Patterns in American Overseas Education* (Cambridge: Cambridge University Press, 1988).

67. Addressing administrators, this statement proposed higher national standards in foreign language skills and global competencies, seconded by policy makers in government and business. The Higher Education Panel of the American Council on Education, *What We Can't Say Can Hurt Us: A Call for Foreign Language Competence by the Year 2000* (Washington: American Council on Education, 1989).

68. This report emphasized global education as a strategy for economic development. National Governors Association Task Force on International Education, *America in Transition: The International Frontier* (Washington: National Governors Association, 1989).

69. *Reforming Education for the International Century* (Washington: CAFLIS, 1989) articulated a "unanimous conviction that international education must become a higher national priority."

70. *Educating for Global Competence. The Report of the Advisory Council for International Educational Exchange* (New York: Council on International Educational Exchange, August 1988). Hereafter cited as *Educating for Global Competence.*

71. This report stated that educational exchange offered a means for exerting international leadership and was "a proven and remarkably inexpensive policy instrument." Published by the Liaison Group for International Educational Exchange (1990), it was summarized in testimony presented by Richard W. Dye before the Subcommittee on International Operations House Committee on Foreign Affairs, 1 August 1990.

72. Barbara Burn, *The Contribution of International Exchange to the International Education of Americans: Projections for the Year 2000,* a report to the Occasional Paper Series of the Council on International Educational

Exchange (New York: IEE, 1990). Student participation should broaden, Burn argued, in gender and ethnicity and in the range of disciplinary fields pursued abroad; program growth should be targeted by funding agencies.

73. *Educating Americans for a World in Flux: Ten Ground Rules for Internationalizing Higher Education* (Washington, D.C.: American Council on Education, 1995).

74. John N. Hawkins, Carlos Manuel Haro, Miriam A. Kazanjian, Gilbert Merkx and David Wiley, eds., *International Education in the New Global Era: Proceedings of a National Policy Conference on the Higher Education Act, Title VI, and Fulbright-Hays Programs*, accessible at http://www.isop.ucla.edu/pacrim/title6/, proceedings of meetings among more than 250 scholars, practitioners, policy makers, and foundation leaders on the current status and future development of U.S. international education and foreign area studies.

75. See, for example, diverse commentary in sources that include Hans de Wit, *Internationalization of Higher Education in the United States of America and Europe* (Westport, Conn.: Greenwood Press, 2002); Grünzweig and Rinehart, eds., *Rockin' in Red Square* (cited above), and Barbara Burn, "The Contribution of International Educational Exchange to the International Education of Americans: My 1990 Forecasts Revisited," in Martin Tillman, ed., *Study Abroad: A 21st Century Perspective*, Volume I (Washington, D.C.: American Institute for Foreign Study, 2001) and online at http://www.aifs.org/aifsfoundation/burn.htm.

76. Marlene M. Johnson, "Advancing U.S. International Education: Leading by Example," *International Educator*, Vol. XII, no. 1 (Winter 2003), 3.

77. *Beyond September 11: A Comprehensive National Policy on International Education*, was a report signed by the American Council on Education and thirty-three other organizations including NAFSA, AIEA, and the Alliance for International Educational and Cultural Exchange. It called for an "urgently needed comprehensive national policy that identifies international education policy objectives for the U.S., and specific strategies and resources for meeting them" (8).

78. "Strategic Task Force on Education Abroad: Mission and Scope," http://www.nafsa.org. In 2003, this task force produced *Securing America's Future*.

79. Duke University, Conference on Global Challenges & U. S. Higher Education, http://www.duke.edu/web/cis/globalchallenges/. The Ford Foundation and the U.S. Department of Education's Office of International Education and Graduate Programs Service, along with Duke, sponsored the conference. Conference-goers heard calls for better integration of study abroad experiences into the undergraduate curriculum and for better assessment of the impact of study abroad. "Not surprisingly, there was consensus that the U.S. still needs more people with AIFL [a new acronym coined at the conference, standing for 'area, international, and foreign language'] competence," reported Donna Parmelee of the University of Michigan's Center for Russian and East European Studies. "Discussion of ways to address this need went well beyond 'traditional' Title VI programs," Parmelee reported to SECUSS members, citing "a proposal to set up a $100 million fund—

50% from the federal government, the rest in matching funds—to support a goal of having 25% of all U.S. students participate in study or other learning abroad activity by the end of the decade" (Donna Parmelee, e-mail to SECUSS-L list members, 28 January 2003).

80. *Educating for Global Competence,* 5.

81. Ibid.

82. NAFSA Association of International Educators, About NAFSA, http://www.nafsa.org/Template.cfm?Section=InsideNafsa&NavMenuID=4.

83. *A National Mandate,* 7.

84. Ibid., 7–8.

85. "Strategic Task Force on Education Abroad Formed, Begins Work," *NAFSA Newsletter,* vol. 53, no.5 (July/August 2002), 15.

86. http://www.nafsa.org/content/publicpolicy/stf/missionandscope.html/.

87. *Securing America's Future,* iv.

88. Ibid., 2.

89. Ibid. In 2004, NAFSA's stated public policy priorities included the plan to "Increase Global Competency Through Study Abroad" by stimulating a national conversation based on the 2003 Study Abroad Task Force report, *Securing America's Future;* lobbying for the late Senator Simon's Lincoln scholarship proposal; and joining a Michigan State University proposal calling "for a federal government partnership with U.S. higher education to increase undergraduate participation in study abroad"("2004 Public Policy Priorities: International Education and the Search for Security," *NAFSA Newsletter,* vol. 55, no. 2 [March/April 2004], 11–12).

90. *Securing America's Future,* 10.

91. "A Brief History of Rhetoric and Composition," http://www.bedford-books.com/bb/history.html.

92. *Oxford English Dictionary,* 1973 edition.

93. *Dictionary of the History of Ideas: Studies of Selected Pivotal Ideas,* vol. IV (New York: Charles Scribners' Sons, 1973), 167–172.

94. Benjamin Lee Whorf, "Science and Linguistics," in *Basic Concepts of Intercultural Communication: Selected Readings,* ed. Milton J. Bennett (New York: Intercultural Press, 1998), 85–96. Originally published in *Language, Thought, and Reality: The Selected Writings of Benjamin Lee Whorf,* ed. J. B. Carroll. Cambridge, Mass.: MIT Press, 1956.

95. Milton J. Bennett, "Intercultural Communication: A Current Perspective," introduction to *Basic Concepts of Intercultural Communication: Selected Readings,* op cit., 12–35.

96. See Michel Foucault, *The Archaeology of Knowledge,* transl. A. M. Sheridan Smith (New York: Pantheon Books, 1972), 32–33, 117, 138. For a more detailed explanation of Foucault's methodology and its usefulness in the analysis of educational discourse, see chapter 2, "A Conceptual Framework for an Analysis of Discourse and Belief about Study Abroad," in Joan Elias Gore, *Discourse and Traditional Belief: An Analysis of American Undergraduate Study Abroad* (London, U.K.: Doctoral dissertation, Institute of Education, University of London, 2000), 40–77. Foucault describes

statements in discourse that combine to form a dominating vision about a particular activity or event.

97. Foucault, *Archaeology,* 117.
98. Ibid., 186–187. For definitions of "discourse formation" and "discursive formation," see Foucault, *Archaeology,* chapter 2; J. G. Merquior, *Foucault* (London: Fontana/ HarperCollins, 1991), 34; Michel Foucault, *The Birth of the Clinic: An Archaeology of Medical Perception* (New York: Vintage Books, 1978), xix; and Philip Barker, *Michel Foucault, An Introduction* (Edinburgh: Edinburgh University Press, 1998), 7.
99. Michel Foucault, *The Order of Things,* transl. Alan Sheridan (New York: Random House, 1970), xxii.
100. Michel Foucault, *Madness and Civilization: A History of Insanity in the Age of Reason,* transl. Richard Howard (London: Tavistock, 1965), 164.
101. Michel Foucault, *Death and Labyrinth: The World of Raymond Roussel,* trans. Charles Ruas (New York: Doubleday and Co., 1986), 164–165; Foucault, *Archaeology,* 32–33.
102. Foucault, *Archaeology,* 117; Barker, *Michel Foucault,* 66–67.
103. Foucault, *Archaeology,* 64; Ralph Cohen, interview, 1 September 1999.
104. Foucault, *Archaeology,* 138–141, 162, 164, 205; Foucault, *The Order of Things,* xxi. According to Foucault, archaeology seeks to define the structure of discursive practices as they rationalize together into meaning.
105. Foucault, *Archaeology,* 205–206.
106. Michel Foucault, *Language, Counter-Memory, Practice: Selected Essays and Interviews,* edited by Donald F. Bouchard (New York: Cornell University Press, 1977), 146–152. Also see "The Discourse on Language," Appendix to *Archaeology,* 215–237.
107. Foucault's genealogical inquiry is grounded in analysis of the immediate circumstance. It seeks to minimize the intrusion of the values of the historian into the interpretation of discourse. It focuses on the discursive events themselves, exclusive of interpretations through historical precedents or transcendental referents about what the events mean. This allows the historical voice to be heard, on the one hand, and increases awareness of the historian's own beliefs and how they shape his or her investigation. Genealogy is at heart, in Foucault's approach to discourse, a way to identify the struggle of the disenfranchised and establish a basis for change.
108. Barker, *Michel Foucault,* 66–67.
109. Cohen, interview. Also see Foucault, *Archaeology,* 39ff. For a fuller explanation of Foucault's theories and their utility in this study, see Gore, *Discourse and Traditional Belief,* especially chapter 2.

NOTES TO CHAPTER TWO

1. Edward Chancey, *The Grand Tour and the Great Rebellion: Richard Lassels and "The Voyage of Italy" in the Seventeenth Century* (Geneva: Slatkine, 1985).
2. As defined in the *Shorter Oxford English Dictionary on Historical Principles,* 3rd edition (1973).

3. Bruce Redford, *Venice and the Grand Tour* (New Haven: Yale University Press, 1966), 1.

4. R. A. McNeal, *Nicholas Biddle in Greece: The Journals and Letters of 1806* (University Park, Penn.: Pennsylvania State University Press, 1993), 26.

5. Geoffrey Trease, *The Grand Tour* (New York: Holt, Rinehart & Winston, 1967), 3.

6. Ibid., 213.

7. William W. Stowe, *Going Abroad: European Travel in Nineteenth-Century American* (Princeton, N.J.: Princeton University Press, 1994).

8. Foucault, *Archaeology*, 64.

9. Asa Briggs and Barbara Burn, *Study Abroad: A European and an American Perspective, Organization and Impact of Study Abroad* (Paris: European Institute of Education and Social Policy, 1985), 5.

10. Bowman, *Educating Americans Abroad*, 13.

11. Briggs and Burn, *Study Abroad*, 35.

12. Herbert Maza, "Backlash in Education Abroad," in Larraine Mathies and William G. Thomas, eds., *Overseas Opportunities for American Educators: Perspective and Possibilities* (New York: CCM Information Corporation, 1971), 23–24. In that volume, see also William Allaway, "The American Campus Moves Abroad," 17.

13. Goodwin and Nacht, *Abroad and Beyond*, 5.

14. Ibid.

15. Briggs and Burn, *Study Abroad*, 5.

16. Archer M. Brown, "U.S. Students Abroad," in Hugh M. Jenkins and Associates, *Educating Students from Other Nations* (San Francisco, Washington, London: Jossey-Bass, 1983), 72.

17. Lily Von Klemperer, oral history interview by Tom Roberts, sponsored by NAFSA: Association of International Educators, spring 1990.

18. David C. Engerman and Parker G. Marden, *In the International Interest: The Contributions and Needs of America's International Liberal Arts Colleges* (Beloit, Wisc.: The International Liberal Arts Colleges, 1992). While the International 50 is not active except as an online organization today, its website recognizes the role that liberal arts colleges (and one liberal arts university) continue to play in international education. The International 50, according to the site, is composed of small selective institutions "dedicated to liberal education" and supplying "crucial leadership in international scholarship." The statistical profiles kept by these fifty schools comprise useful information about national trends and motivations for the support of foreign study. Research at member institutions continues to focus on international programming and its importance in the larger context of liberal arts education. Information is published online under the title *What Works in International Education*, http://www.beloit.edu/~i50/; http://www.beloit.edu/~i50/whatworks.html/. For a list of member institutions, see http://www.beloit.edu/%7Ei50/i50directory.html/.

19. Engerman and Marden, *In the International Interest*, 41.

20. *Educating for Global Competence*, 9.

21. Richard D. Lambert, *International Studies and the Undergraduate, A Special Report* (Washington: American Council on Education), 3.
22. Elizabeth Bernstein, "Study-Abroad Programs Grow in Uncertain Times," *Wall Street Journal*, 7 February 2003.
23. Ibid.
24. Andrea Petersen, "Sex, Drugs and Junior Year Abroad: Doctors Work to Protect Travelers," *Wall Street Journal*, 31 July 2003. Another report, this time on the effort at Tufts University to maintain quality in study abroad, intimated a fear of creeping Grand Tourism, even in the *Chronicle of Higher Education* headline that announced it: "Keeping the Study in Study Abroad: Tufts tries to make sure that its traveling students are more than tourists" (Megan Rooney, "Keeping the Study in Study Abroad," *Chronicle of Higher Education*, 22 November 2002, http://chronicle.com/prm/weekly/v49/i13/13a06301.htm/).
25. Ben Feinberg, "What Students Don't Learn Abroad," *Chronicle of Higher Education*, 3 May 2002, http://chronicle.com/prm/weekly/v48/i34/34b02001.htm. Feinberg suggested the need to deemphasize individual growth in preparing students for overseas study and instead spur students to pay more attention to their experience.
26. Ibid.
27. At the onset of World War II, the Delaware program was suspended. It reemerged with student placements in Switzerland after the war, but soon thereafter Delaware discontinued its involvement and the program was reestablished at Sweet Briar College, from which it has operated ever since.

   From its earliest years, administrators maintained excellent enrollment records. The Archives of the University of Delaware hold those records, together with other documents and correspondence through the 1940s, including files from the Foreign Study Office and from the University's Paris office. The program has also maintained excellent alumni records over a long period of time. The 902 students who attended the Delaware study abroad program (including 786 in Paris) established an alumni organization, whose publications and documents are also housed in the University archives, together with a directory, some student profiles, the letters and diaries of some participants, oral history interviews with early participants, and a video copy of a 16mm film about the earliest program. Sweet Briar College has continued to maintain and update comprehensive student and alumni records. Alumni publications since 1974 also represent a bank of information.

   In 1995, a survey was designed by this author to canvass perceptions of Sweet Briar study abroad alumni about their motives for participating in the program. This survey was updated in the summer of 2004 to include alumni through the year 2003–04.

   The first survey went out to a statistically significant sample of the 4,844 students (3,571 women and 1,273 men) who attended the Sweet Briar Junior Year in France program between academic years 1948–49 and 1993–94. In this survey, of the total Sweet Briar alumni group, every fifth name thereafter, or 20 percent, were contacted. Of the 969 surveys mailed

out, 206 (21%) were returned—a low response rate by social science standards. For a copy of the original survey, see Appendix B of Gore, *Discourse
and Traditional Belief*. This survey was updated in the summer 2004, using
alumni from 1994–95 through 2003–04. The same survey technique was
used: of the total Sweet Briar alumni group, every fifth name thereafter, or
20 percent, were contacted. Of the 956 total enrollments, 192 were mailed
the survey, of which 45 returned it, for a return rate of 23 percent. This,
too, is a low yield. Foremost among the reasons for these low response
rates is that Sweet Briar Junior Year in France has not proactively sought to
update contact information for its participants and since 1993–94 has not
regularly updated its address profiles for this most recent group of alumni.
Therefore, difficulties in obtaining accurate mailing addresses for the
alumni preclude substantial returns on mailings. No e-mail addresses are
available for Sweet Briar Junior Year in France alumni, according to Margaret Scouten, director of the Sweet Briar Junior Year in France Program,
in an e-mail, 22 July 2004. Nevertheless, the responses received from the
original survey and its update provide a useful and interesting picture of the
study abroad experience through one of America's most venerated programs. Results from this survey can be calculated in various ways. For
example, when respondents can choose more than one answer, data can be
reported as a percent of all responses to a question. In this book, unless
otherwise noted, all Sweet Briar survey data is presented as a percentage,
by gender, of all who answered each question. The number of answers to
each question is noted.

28. These alumni could have chosen alternative answers that reflected foreign
language learning capabilities and educational opportunities for experi-
mentation and growth.

29. Gertrude Stein, *Paris and France* (New York: Charles Scribners' Sons,
1940), 2.

30. Richard D. Lambert, "Study Abroad: Where We Are, Where We Should
Be," in *Proceedings of the 41ˢᵗ Annual Conference on International Educational Exchange* (Cannes, France, November 1988), 13.

31. William Hoffa, John Pearson, and Marvin Slind, *NAFSA's Guide to Educa-
tion Abroad for Advisers and Administrators* (Washington, D.C.: NAFSA:
Association for Foreign Student Affairs, 1993), ix-x. Hereafter cited as
Hoffa, Pearson, and Slind, *NAFSA's Guide* (1993).

32. *Educating for Global Competence*, 13.

33. *A National Mandate*, 6.

34. *Securing America's Future*, 2

35. "Undergraduate Scholarships 1994–1995 Competition Cycle Summary
Report" in the *Report on NSEP Undergraduate Allocations* (Washington:
Institute of International Education, National Security Education Program,
1994). The National Security Education Program (NSEP), established in
1991 as a trust fund in the U.S. Treasury under the National Security Education Act, was designed to fund international education through scholarships, fellowships, and grants, including scholarships for U.S.
undergraduates studying in non-Western European world regions and in

disciplines not frequently studied overseas (*NSEP: Undergraduate Scholar-ships for Study Abroad Preparing for the Future* [New York: Institute of International Education, 1994], opening page). The NSEP goal is to "encourage study of languages and cultures in a wider range of countries outside Western Europe and Canada" (Institute of International Education, "National Security Education Program, Undergraduate Scholarships, 1994–1995," *Competition Cycle Summary Report* [Washington, 1995]).

36. The goals of the CIEE Study Abroad Baseline Survey were threefold: to understand how international educators perceived trends about student study abroad interests through the turn of the century; to create a profile of current college and university administrators involved in study abroad; and to identify the current structure of international education offices. This researcher helped in the construction of the mailing list, to ensure that the survey reached senior international education administrators, and con-tributed to the design of questions, to ensure full coverage of issues perti-nent to international education administrators and to study abroad development. For further information on survey techniques and results, see Gore, *Discourse and Traditional Belief,* 193–194. Also see Council on International Educational Exchange, *Study Abroad Baseline Survey* (New York, 1996), 1–2.

37. Question 13: Areas of Interest for Program Development, CIEE, *Study Abroad Baseline Survey.*

38. *Open Doors 2004: Report on International Educational Exchange* (New York: Institute of International Education, 2004), http://opendoors.iienet-work.org/?p=49941, Host Regions . . . 1985/86–2002/03, 2. The only consis-tent efforts to identify the number and type of U.S. students going abroad can be found in the surveys conducted annually for the past forty years by the Institute of International Education and published in *Open Doors* as reports on foreign student enrollments in higher education institutions. The single most important source of statistical data, annual reports by the Institute of International Education, have had self-identified limitations (Chin, ed., *Open Doors 2003,* 94; William W. Hoffa, "What Are Participation Rates . . . And Why Should Anybody Care?," http://www. iienetwork.org/?p=41566/; Kath-leen Sideli, "When It Comes to U.S. Education Abroad, Everybody Counts," http://www.iienetwork.org/ ?p=41589/), yet since IIE has been the only regu-lar public reporting source about nationwide study abroad activity, its data have been accepted by the higher education community. No other publicly reported data on study abroad activity represent the broad U.S. higher educa-tion community, nor has any available statistical information ever been evalu-ated or interpreted by being coupled with extensive historical analysis. IIE reports have established the standard statistical profile, defining who goes where to study what for the higher education community. As the primary descriptor of study abroad in the United States, IIE has provided an important strand of discourse in the dialogue about study abroad.

39. Charles Homer Haskins, *The Rise of Universities* (Ithaca and London: Cor-nell University Press, 1987, reissue of New York: H. Holt & Co., 1923), 65.

40. Henry Steele Commager, *The American Mind: An Interpretation of American Thought and Character Since the 1880's* (New Haven: Yale University Press, 1950), 3; Frederick Rudolph, *The American College and University, A History* (New York: Vintage Books, 1962), 334.

41. Laurence R. Veysey, *The Emergence of the American University,* 3rd ed. (Chicago and London: University of Chicago Press, 1974), 2–3.

42. Bowman, *Educating,* 13.

43. Veysey, *Emergence,* 125–130.

44. According to Veysey, the peak enrollment year was 1895–96, with 517 American students enrolled in German institutions (ibid., 130).

45. Carol S. Gruber, *Mars and Minerva: World War I and the Uses of Higher Learning in America* (Baton Rouge: Louisiana State University Press, 1976), 17.

46. Ibid., 18–19.

47. Barbara Miller Solomon, *In the Company of Educated Women: A History of Women and Higher Education in America* (New Haven and London: Yale University Press, 1985), 134–135.

48. Veysey, *Emergence,* 131.

49. Bowman, *Educating,* 13.

50. Ibid.

51. Ernest L. Boyer and Fred M. Hechinger, *Higher Learning in the Nation's Service* (Washington: The Carnegie Foundation for the Advancement of Teaching, 1981), 12. Beginning with the passage of the Morrill Act, which provided federal funding to develop institutions to serve the national need and gave access to education to new classes, this democratization of education continued throughout the twentieth century, spurred mid-century by the GI bill, which opened the opportunity to attend college to every World War II veteran and established for their families the tradition of college attendance (Boyer and Hechinger, *Higher Learning,* 10–15).

52. Bowman, *Educating,* 13.

53. Solomon, *In the Company,* 63–64.

54. Bowman, *Educating,* 13–14.

55. John A. Munroe, interview, 7 February 1994.

56. Ibid.

57. Francis M. Rogers, *American Juniors on the Left Bank* (Sweet Briar, Va.: Sweet Briar College, 1958), 10. Other models of study abroad occasionally emerged, though they did not develop as the primary model for educating undergraduates abroad. Short-term programs and educational tours continued. For example, see *The Sixth Annual Floating University World Voyage* (New York: University Travel Association, 1936), 5; "American Assistants in French Lycees," *School and Society* 18 (25 October 1923), 497–498; "Vacation Courses for Foreigners in French Universities," *School and Society* 20 (August 1924), 247–248; "Educational: American Students at Oxford University," *School and Society* 21 (10 June 1925), 40–41. Some non-study activities were practiced, such as volunteer projects abroad offered by institutions like Syracuse University and Princeton before World

War I (William Hoffa, SECUSS-L Discussion List, History Project e-mail network discussion, 14 April 2000).

One of the more interesting alternative models to develop, emulating in some ways the Junior Year Abroad model, was the Shipboard Education model. James Edwin Lough, dean of the Extramural Division of New York University, conceived of a program in which students would travel world-wide, via ship, over the course of an academic semester or year, taking academic courses taught by faculty from American colleges and universities (Paul Liebhardt, "The History of Shipboard Education," *Steamboat Bill,* Number 227, Vol. LV, No. 3 [Fall 1998], 175–178). The first voyage occurred in 1926, with six subsequent voyages occurring, under varying organizational auspices, until 1936 (ibid., 178–180). In some ways, the shipboard model emulated features of the Junior Year Abroad model: courses were offered for undergraduate students ("The College Cruise Around the World," University Travel Association, 1928, 2). Commitment to academic quality was expressed through the appointment of advisory boards composed of leading American educators (*Sixth Annual Floating,* foreword, 4–5). Faculty from American colleges and universities taught liberal arts courses on the ship (Liebhardt, 173–180; Henry J. Allen, *Student Magellan* [New York: Stanley D. Woodard, 1927], 6–7. The *Student Magellan* was the official yearbook for the 1926 voyage, found among uncatalogued documents in the archives of the Institute for Shipboard Education: Semester at Sea, University of Pittsburgh, Pennsylvania, and provided to this researcher by Paul Watson, Director for Enrollment Management, Institute for Shipboard Education, University of Pittsburgh, Pittsburgh, Penna.). Lough expressly stated the goals for the program were not to offer "a mere sightseeing trip but a college year of educational travel and systematic study; to develop an interest in foreign affairs; to train students to think in world terms; and to strengthen international understanding and goodwill" (Allen, *Student Magellan,* 5).

This model diverged in many ways from the Sorbonne model, which established the prototypical structure for the first junior year programs. This was not a program offered by an accredited academic institution. Though initially Lough sought and received sponsorship from New York University (Liebhardt, 178), NYU withdrew its support before the first voyage. Many on the faculty at New York University were suspicious of the idea of a floating university (ibid., 78). Indeed, Lough was fired from New York University when he returned from his first voyage (ibid., 78). While documentary material states the program received a charter from the New York Department of Education to operate a university on ship (ibid., 78), this cannot be confirmed today in the Department of Education's records (Sherry Seyffer, New York State Department of Education, Albany New York, interview, 13 April 2000). Students might apply to their home universities to be awarded credit for the work done onboard ship but the program itself could not award credit (*Sixth Annual Floating,* 9; "The College Cruise Around the World" [n.p.: University Travel Association, 1928], 34). The program was open to any student in preparatory school (pre-college level), any undergraduate, or any graduate student, regardless of academic abilities (ibid., 9). The cruise was open to non-students as well, who were offered "General Lectures" (ibid., 9). Parents and others were invited "to join to see the world in a leisurely manner and listen in on any of the lectures in which they are interested" ("College Cruise Around the World," 6). The cruise was very costly: $2500 to $3700 for the year (ibid., 43), explained as "necessarily somewhat higher than the cost of the average World Cruise, but very considerably less than the combined costs for attending land universities and an extensive world tour" (*Sixth Annual Floating*, 5). The cruise was advertised in popular literature, sometimes in conjunction with vacation travel advertising ("College Cruise Round the World" [magazine advertisement], *Time* 9:20 [16 May 1927], 35). In its first few years, at least, the cruise was advertised for men only (*Time* advertisement; Watson, correspondence, 13 April 2000), but when an insufficient number of men signed up, it was opened to women (Watson, correspondence, 13 April 2000). Thus, of the 504 students onboard the first cruise in 1926, this program experienced a very different ratio from that typically seen in modern study abroad programs: 4:1, with males in the majority (Paul Watson, correspondence, 12 April 2000, reporting archival material developed from a reunion of alumni from the 1926 voyage, 18 September 1976, Queen Mary Hotel, Long Beach, Calif.). Documents confirming gender ratios on other cruises are not included in the archival material; the organization sponsoring the trips no longer exists; and searches are ongoing currently to supplement existing records.

Some traits of this program did reflect the emergence of the modern study abroad Sorbonne model. Many traits reflected the concept of the Grand Tour described in this chapter, however, including the cruise's association with wealth, leisure, culture, and extensive travel. Its structure reflected the description John Bowman gave to the remnants of the male Grand Tour tradition, carried on by the sons of wealthy men, referred to earlier in this chapter (Bowman, *Educating*, 13–14). The cruise was advertised in popular journalistic publications and stories about it were reported in the popular press (Liebhardt, "History," 178), so its existence was part of the broader public discourse contributing to the image of education overseas.

Nonetheless, the cruise did not fit the academic model of modern study abroad that emerged after World War I. It was rejected as a model for credit-bearing sponsorship by an American higher education institution. And this model did not enter the discourse about study abroad that evolved within the higher education community after World War II. William Hoffa, author of the SECUSS-L history project, reported only passing reference to the program in materials collected for the project (Hoffa, e-mail network discussion, 11–14 April 2000). This model did reemerge in the 1960s and eventually became "Semester at Sea" (Liebhardt, "History," 173). In its contemporary form, however, the program has followed the modern study abroad format, seeking affiliation with an accredited academic institution (Liebhardt, "History," 180–186) and imposing academic requirements for admission to the program, designed for college-level undergraduates (see program website at URL http://www.semesteratsea.com). Enrollment Manager Paul Watson confirms that the gender ratio among participants in the Semester at Sea Program now consistently reflects the gender ratio in modern study abroad programs, with women routinely two-thirds of the enrollment annually (Watson, correspondence, 13 April 2000).

58.   As part of the history project sponsored by NAFSA: Association of International Educators project, author William Hoffa compiled the most thorough list to date of all education-related activities abroad. Dr. Hoffa's effort is to gather a broad range of data describing activities extending beyond study abroad: "the broader scope of my work is 'education abroad' in all of its manifestations, so I am also trying to learn about American student participation in experiential programs—e.g., volunteerism, work projects, internships, etc.—which are organized in the U.S. or overseas but do not necessarily result in the award of credit." The majority of these efforts do not include the junior year abroad model that entered the discourse about study abroad. They do include non-credit-bearing activities such as volunteer programs, non-accredited programs, and study travel tours. This list includes, as well, American and other national efforts to establish special programs, not necessarily as sites for American students, and describes the other study abroad models discussed in this endnote.

Dr. Hoffa's list is as follows:

Academic Activities prior to World War II:

1866: American University in Beirut (dates at which American students first entered unknown)

1882: Indiana University sponsors "Tramp Cruise" for students (credit award status unknown)

1898: "Princeton in Asia" (volunteer program)

1905: Center for Study Abroad-Fudan University program in Chinese language and culture begins

1910: London School of Economics begins the "General Course" (one year, for non-degree graduate students from other countries); American-Scandinavian Foundation founded

1917: Mozarteum International Summer Academy, Salzburg, Austria begins; Siena University per Stranieri, Italy, begins; "Workcamps" in Europe started

1918: University of Paris (Sorbonne) begins special courses for foreigners ("Cours de civilization")

1919: American University in Cairo founded (date of American enrollment as yet unidentified)

1920 or 1931, date unconfirmed: College International de Cannes, France

1921–22: University of Vienna begins Summer and Academic Year courses ("Wiener International Hochschulkurse")

1922–23: Cambridge University begins Summer Term (for foreigners)

1923–24: University of Delaware program in Paris begins (JUNIOR YEAR ABROAD INSTITUTION)

1924–25: Marymount program in Paris begins (JUNIOR YEAR ABROAD INSTITUTION, seven female students in initial enrollment)

1925–26: Smith program in Paris begins (JUNIOR YEAR ABROAD INSTITUTION); Rosary College program in Fribourg, Switzerland begins (JUNIOR YEAR ABROAD INSTITUTION, four students); University of Heidelberg begins summer courses for foreigners; American School of Classical Studies at Athens founded

1926–27: "World University Cruise" (see above, endnote 57)

1927–28: Committee on the Junior Year Abroad founded by the Institute of International Education, led by Stephen Duggan and including the presidents of the University of Delaware and Smith College

1930–31: Marymount program in Italy (Rome) begins (JUNIOR YEAR ABROAD INSTITUTION); Smith program in Spain (Madrid) begins (suspended 1936; JUNIOR YEAR ABROAD INSTITUTION)

1931–32: Smith program in Florence begins; Courtauld Institute of Art (London, for postgraduates)

1932–33: Experiment in International Living founded by Donald Watt (summer program, family stay); University of Delaware begins Germany program (in Munich, discontinued as a Delaware-sponsored program in 1934, JUNIOR YEAR ABROAD INSTITUTION); Banff Centre for the Arts, Canada, summer program begins; Marymount program in Rome begins (JUNIOR YEAR ABROAD INSTITUTION)

1934–35: "Delaware" program in Munich continues under sponsorship of an independent committee until 1938–39, when it operated for a year in Switzerland before being discontinued until after the war.

1936–37: Smith founds program in Mexico as alternative to Madrid (JUNIOR YEAR ABROAD INSTITUTION); suspended the next year.

1938–39: University of Delaware begins program in Switzerland (JUNIOR YEAR ABROAD INSTITUTION)

1939–40: All Europe programs canceled; Indiana University offers an alternative program in education studies in Mexico

(William W. Hoffa, SECUSS-L Discussion List, History Project e-mail network discussion, 9 August 2000.)

59. Delfor Alumni Association, Foreign Study Plan Records, 1922–48. Box 52 (AR 52) (AR 96) Folder 1631, 33/0/8, University of Delaware Archives. Delfor Alumni Address list from Group I, 1923–24, through Group XVII, 1939–40.

60. Bowman, *Educating,* 13.

61. Briggs and Burn, *Study Abroad,* 35.

62. Rosary College, *The Rosary College Foreign Study Plan*, River Forest, Ill., March 1947, no. 1. In the Archives of the University of Delaware: Rosary College General, Folder 418, AR64, 33/0/3 General Correspondence, Box 20.

63. Junior Year Abroad study destinations before the onset of World War II in 1939 in Europe were all European, with the brief exception of a Smith University effort in Mexico (see note 58 above):

    University of Delaware: France, Germany, then Switzerland

    Marymount: France, Italy

    Smith: France, Spain, Italy

    Rosary: Switzerland

    See Bowman, *Educating*, 14. See also Patricia Olmsted, "Sixty Years of Study Abroad: A Backward Glance at the Profession," paper prepared for NAFSA Conference, Long Beach, Calif., May 1987.

64. Bowman, *Educating*, 14.

65. Barbara Burn, *Expanding the International Dimensions of Higher Education* (San Francisco: Jossey-Bass, 1980), 1.

66. Ibid.

67. Gilbert Roy, University of Virginia faculty member and a CIEE China Consortium member active in the development and administration of undergraduate programs in China, notes his serendipitous introduction to the Chinese language. As a young member of the military, Roy was told that he had a choice of two or three different institutions to attend, with different languages taught at each. Yale appealed to him because it was near his home and girlfriend and offered Chinese. Thus Roy began on a path toward an academic career that has included the establishment of U.S. study abroad programs in China. Roy's is a very personal example of how the U.S. political agenda, in this case the institutional support of Chinese studies at a college he had chosen for other reasons, bears an impact on the shape of U.S. study abroad (Gilbert Roy, interview, 23 July 1994).

68. *Open Doors 2004*. Students pursued programs in Africa, Asia, Latin America, the Middle East, and Oceania. Approximately 31 percent of students enrolled in non–Western European locations. This report did not distinguish undergraduate from graduate students, so the percentage of undergraduates at non-Western European sites is likely to be slightly less (though not significantly, since over 90 percent of the population reported is undergraduate).

69. Lawrence Levine and Margaret Byrne, *The Opening of the American Mind: Canons, Culture, and History* (Boston: Beacon Press, 1996), 86.

NOTES TO CHAPTER THREE

1. Glenn C. Altschuler, "College Prep: La Dolce Semester," *New York Times*, 8 April 2001, 4a, 17, col. 1; http://www.nytimes.com.

2. Profile of U. S. Study Abroad Students, 1993/94–2002/03, *Open Doors 2004*.

3. Lambert, "Study Abroad: Where We Are, Where We Should Be," 14.

4. *Securing America's Future*, 3.

5. Meredith Stoffel, in *The Heights*, Boston College, 3 February 2004, page 1, online at http://www.bcheights.com/news/2004/02/03/Features/Gender.Difference.In.Study.Abroad-594562.shtml?page=1.

6. Emile Langlois, interview, Sweet Briar, Va., 17 February 1993; Jennings L. Wagoner, Jr., and Wayne J. Urban, *American Education: A History* (New York: McGraw-Hill, 1996), 268, 280.

7. Jolene Koester, *A Profile of U.S. Students Abroad—1984 and 1985* (New York: Council on International Educational Exchange, 1987), 114.

8. This data is calculated in two ways. Gender identification has been included in CIEE records since computerized enrollment began, in 1991. For records before that, the study depended on a first-name analysis of records to identify gender when possible. The paper-copy analysis was conducted in 1991 at CIEE offices in New York by this researcher, using records maintained by Cindy Sittler, then Director of Campus Relations for CIEE. Computerized data was provided in 2004 by Martin Hogan, Vice President, External Relations and Programming, CIEE International Study Programs, in an e-mail dated 9 August 2004. Study results determined that between 1973 and 1992, students participating in CIEE study abroad programs amounted to 5,161 females and 2,359 males, or 68.5 percent female and 31.2 percent male, with the balance of 32 unidentifiable by gender. From 1992 to 2004, 17,116 women studied abroad and 8,821 men studied abroad, 66.0 percent female and 34.0 percent male.

9. Courtney Peters, personal e-mail, 6 May 2004. Responses were collected from more than 3,700 IES alumni, representing all IES programs, regions of the U.S., and more than 500 U.S. colleges and universities. Also see Joan Gillespie and Carla Slawson, *IES Outcomes Assessment Project*, online at http://www.iesabroad.org/info/alumnioutcomes.pdf. Additional information on documented enrollments by gender through three decades provided by Michael Steinberg, Director, Institute for the International Education of Students, personal e-mail, 5 August 2004.

10. "Plenary Resources" in *Internationalizing the Curriculum*, conference program and resource notebook, International Conference on Study Abroad Curriculum Integration, April 15–17, 2004, Minneapolis, Minnesota, 2.

11. Ibid., 5–8. At the fourth campus, Crookston, study abroad is negligible, rising from 0 to 11 students from 2000 to 2003, with 7 males altogether.

12. Briggs and Burn, *Study Abroad*, 52.

13. Bowman, *Educating*, 13.

14. Briggs and Burn, *Study Abroad*, 39.

15. Stephen Cooper and Mary Anne Grant, "The Demographics of Education Abroad," in Hoffa, Pearson, and Slind, eds., *NAFSA's Guide* (1993), 90.

16. SECUSS-L, ongoing e-mail discussion, 27 February through 4 March 1997, initiated by William Hoffa of Academic Consultants International and hosted by SECUSS-L, the U.S. study abroad adviser online discussion list.

17. Ibid.

18. Ibid.

19. Ibid.
20. Ibid.
21. Ibid.
22. The Forum on Education Abroad (http://www.forumea.org), formed in 2001, is a new organization whose "exclusive purpose is to serve the field of education abroad. Its members are educational institutions, consortia, agencies, organizations, and individuals that provide, direct, or manage educational opportunities in the field of education abroad." Numbering 146 at the time of this writing, the Forum membership represents more than 40 percent of all study abroad enrollments from U.S. institutions, as indicated in its Annual Report 2002–2003, online at http://www.forumea.org/annualreport03.html.
23. Posted by William Hoffa, 22 July 2004, Subject: Study Abroad: not a Guy Thing? ForumEA.org, The Forum on Education Abroad Message Boards, The Forum on Education Abroad, http://forum.forumea.org, accessed 15 August 2004.
24. Indeed, a recent faculty survey demonstrated that only 30 percent of faculty may strongly encourage either gender to participate in study abroad (Study Abroad Curriculum Integration Team and the University of Minnesota's Office of Measurement Services, "Evaluation of Initiative," *Study Abroad Curriculum Integration Initiative Surveys, March 2001,* reported in "Plenary Resources," *Internationalizing the Curriculum,* 71).
25. Solomon, *In the Company,* 11–12.
26. Rudolph, *American College,* 309.
27. Helen Lefkowitz Horowitz, *Alma Mater: Design and Experience in the Women's Colleges from their Nineteenth-Century Beginnings to the 1930s* (New York: Alfred A. Knopf, 1984), 63–68.
28. Rudolph, *American College,* 328, quoting from Thomas Woody, *A History of Women's Education in the United States* (New York: The Science Press, 1929), vol. 2, 150.
29. Horowitz, *Alma Mater,* 147.
30. Solomon, *In the Company,* 83.
31. Horowitz, *Alma Mater,* 97 n10. Horowitz also refers to M. Carey Thomas's famous rejoinder, "The Bryn Mawr Woman," reprinted in Barbara M. Cross, *The Educated Woman in America* (New York: Teachers College Press, 1965), 139–144.
32. Solomon, *In the Company,* 95. While the culture did not approve of education for women, the presumption about those attending school was that they were hard working and academically serious (Solomon, 68; Horowitz, 37).
33. Solomon, *In the Company,* 95–97.
34. Ibid., 157–159.
35. Ibid., 159.
36. Ibid., 170.
37. Briggs and Burn, *Study Abroad,* 39.
38. Altschuler, "College Prep: La Dolce Semester."
39. *A National Mandate,* 2.
40. *Securing America's Future,* 10.

41. See chapter 1, "The Current State of Study Abroad," for earlier discussion of this conference.
42. Bowman, *Educating*, 18.
43. Goodwin and Nacht, *Abroad and Beyond*, 10, 75–77.
44. As quoted in Sara Grimes, "World Class: The Leading Personality in International Exchange Pulls No Punches," *Massachusetts*, Winter 1994, 13.
45. Nancy Stubbs, "Financial Aid," in Hoffa and Pearson, *NAFSA's Guide*, 2nd ed., 75.
46. Question 21, Students consider many factors in deciding to study abroad, CIEE, *Study Abroad Baseline Survey*, 1996. Advisors rated financial aid availability and study abroad program cost the top two factors students consider when deciding about study abroad.
47. Ayres, H. Fairfax III, et al., *CIEE Market Study: Motivations for Study Abroad*, Charlottesville, Va.: Darden School of Graduate Business Studies, University of Virginia, May 1996. In 1995 this researcher, on behalf of the Council on International Educational Exchange, commissioned this survey, which was conducted by a group of students at the Darden Graduate School of Business of the University of Virginia. The intent was to profile students who had chosen to study abroad as well as those who had chosen not to (i-ii, 31).
48. Ibid.
49. At about the same time that the Darden survey was conducted, a request went out by e-mail to a nationwide group of study abroad advisers, asking them to recall "Mythologies of Going Abroad" that they had encountered among students they were advising. "Money Issues" was one of the primary categories among advisers' answers. Students were reported to believe that "It's too expensive," "I will loose *[sic]* my institutional scholarships," and "I can't use my financial aid/scholarships to go abroad" (Ruth Sylte, e-mail correspondence, 5 April 1996).
50. "Evaluation of Initiative," *Internationalizing the Curriculum*, 63.
51. Ibid., 71.
52. Bowman, *Educating*, 13.
53. Briggs and Burn, *Study Abroad*, 35.
54. Goodwin and Nacht, *Abroad and Beyond*, 14.
55. Altschuler, "College Prep: La Dolce Semester."
56. Thorstein Veblen, *The Theory of the Leisure Class: An Economic Study of Institutions* (New York: Modern Library, 1934); see especially chapter 2.
57. William W. Stowe, *Going Abroad: European Travel in Nineteenth-Century American Culture* (Princeton, N.J.: Princeton University Press, 1994), 161–162.
58. Robert C. Pace, *The Junior Year in France: An Evaluation of the University of Delaware-Sweet Briar College Program* (Syracuse, N.Y.: Syracuse University Press, 1959), 14–15.
59. John A. Munroe, *The University of Delaware: A History* (Newark, Del.: University of Delaware, 1986), 264.
60. Ibid., 264.
61. Jean F. Brown (Director, University of Delaware Archives), interview, 7 February 1994.

62. Munroe, *University of Delaware*, 266–267.
63. *Bulletin of the University of Delaware*, vol. XXVI, new series, no. 6 (November 1931).
64. R. John Matthew, *Twenty-Five Years on the Left Bank* (Sweet Briar, Va.: Sweet Briar College, 1973), 33.
65. Ibid.
66. Emile Langlois, unpublished financial aid records, Sweet Briar, Va., spring 1996.
67. Margaret Scouten, e-mail correspondence, 22 July 2004.
68. The CIEE Study Abroad Baseline Survey demonstrated that advisers found a variety of aid sources for students, including federal financial aid, state financial aid, and institutional aid most frequently provided and scholarship aid less frequently provided (Question 16, *Study Abroad Baseline Survey*, 1996).
69. Chin, *Open Doors 2003*, 63.
70. Gail A. Hochhauser, "Demographic Factors Redefining Education Abroad," in Martin Tillman, ed., *Study Abroad: A 21ˢᵗ Century Perspective*, vol. II (Stamford, CT: American Institute for Foreign Study Foundation, n.d.), 12–13.
71. *Mapping*, 19.
72. See, for example, scholarship programs at the Council on International Educational Exchange, listed online at http://ciee.org; at Denmark's International Study Program, http://www.discopenhagen.dk; or at the Institute for the International Education of Students, http:/www.iesabroad.org.
73. Langlois, unpublished financial aid records, Sweet Briar, Va.
74. Scouten, e-mail correspondence, 22 July 2004.
75. Hogan, e-mail correspondence, 9 August 2004. Recent years have seen efforts to develop and publicize lower-cost program options for students. Jon O. Heise, former study abroad adviser at Loyola University, developed an informal list, which he made available nationally, of "rock bottom" study abroad programs: programs costing under $5000 a term, including tuition, fees, room, board, and transportation (now at http://www.istc.umn.edu, under the supervision of Richard Warzecha). Heise originated it because he believed study abroad should be made accessible to students lacking wealth (Jon Heise, interview, 25 March 2000). A major effort proposed by the newest task force on study abroad and supported by NAFSA is the development of a massive Lincoln Fellowship fund to encourage students to pursue overseas study (*Securing America's Future*, ii). These efforts, inherently important, also reinforce existing perceptions about the relationships between wealth and study abroad.
76. Students and their advisers sometimes presume that financial aid at their home college will not support study abroad—a perception held at many institutions despite federal actions and communications of the past decade. Federal financial aid has since 1965 been governed by Chapter IV of the Higher Education Act, reviewed every five years by Congress. During reauthorization discussions in 1990, a group of study abroad professionals requested new language to specify that students could use federal aid for

study abroad. Such has been the case since the act was passed into law, but beliefs to the contrary remain, even after Congress reauthorized the application in July 1992 (Stubbs, "Financial Aid," in Hoffa, Pearson, and Slind, NAFSA's Guide [1993], 39–40).

77. Abrams and Hatch, *Study Abroad, New Dimensions in Higher Education,* No. 6, 2.

78. Ibid., citing the Institute of International Education, *Foreign Study for U.S. Undergraduates* (New York: IIE, 1958), 6–7, 26–31.

79. Bowman, *Educating*, 19.

80. Allaway, "The American Campus Moves Abroad," 17.

81. Bowman, *Educating*, 23.

82. William H. Allaway and Hallam C. Shorrock, *Dimensions of International Higher Education, The California Symposium on International Education Abroad* (Boulder and London: Westview Special Studies in Education, 1985), xiv.

83. John A. Wallace, "Characteristics of Programs for Study Abroad," *Journal of General Education* 13, no. 4 (January 1962), 254. Also see Mary Elizabeth Conway Gwin, *Study Abroad Advising: Information Delivery and Quality Assessment in Computer-Assisted Advising on Study Abroad Opportunities* (doctoral dissertation, University of Mississippi, 1985), 25; Barbara Burn, *Expanding the International Dimensions of Higher Education* (San Francisco: Jossey-Bass, 1980), 1; Bowman, *Educating*, 23. Among international educators, some limited discourse did begin to emerge in American education reflecting inherent value simply in living in another culture (W. F. Hull, W. H. Lemke, and R. T. Houang, *The American Undergraduate, Off Campus and Overseas: A Study of the Educational Validity of Such Programs* [New York: CIEE Occasional Papers Series, no. 20, 1977], introduction; Wallace, "Characteristics of Programs," 255.)

84. David Arnold, interview, 15 October 1990; *Beyond 9/11*, 22.

85. *Beyond 9/11*, 22.

86. Goodwin and Nacht, *Abroad and Beyond*, 3, 4, 60–61.

87. Clark Kerr, "Introduction" in Allaway and Shorrock, *Dimensions*, xiii; President's Commision, *Strength Through Wisdom*, 1–2.

88. *Educating for Global Competence*, 1.

89. *Securing America's Future*, 3.

90. Marie O'Sullivan, ed., *IIEPassport: Academic Year Abroad*, 33rd Edition (Chester, Pennsylvania: Study Abroad Directories, 2004), xi and back cover.

91. Marie O'Sullivan, ed., *IIEPassport: Short-Term Study Abroad*, 54th Edition, (New York: Institute of International Education, 2004), xi and back cover.

92. Brown, "U.S. Students Abroad," 69.

93. Goodwin and Nacht, *Abroad and Beyond*, 14. See also *Open Doors, 2003*, 63–68, for information by Carnegie classification on types of institutions supporting student participation in study abroad.

94. *Mapping*, 68.

95. Ibid., 57, 46, 37.

96. Ibid., 47.

97. Engerman and Marden, *In the International Interest,* 7.
98. Ibid., 43–44
99. Ibid.
100. This wealthy image is sustained in study abroad regardless of financial aid support for students. See financial aid policies at these colleges, http://www.beloit.edu/~i50/i50directory.html.
101. Chin, *Open Doors 2003,* 63.
102. *Mapping,* 69. A late-twentieth-century survey of its member institutions by the American Association of State Colleges and Universities (AASCU) reported "a breadth of international activity as diverse as the many public institutions across the United States, Guam, Puerto Rico and the Virgin Islands that comprise AASCU's membership" (Harold Vaughn, "International Activity on State College and University Campuses," news server message, 7 May 1996). The Council on International Educational Exchange's study abroad programs show an increased diversity of supporting institutions, with 205 Academic Consortium member institutions sponsoring them. CIEE Academic Consortium Membership is listed on the website, http://www.ciee.org. One-fourth of this membership is from public institutions. In addition, CIEE reports more than 1,000 feeder institutions sending students to CIEE study programs (Council on International Educational Exchange, *CIEE A World of Opportunity,* 2003 Annual Report [New York: CIEE, 2003], n.p.).
103. The 2003 *Open Doors* report included 1,286 public and private institutions, received responses from 1,120, and reported that 73.1 percent of institutions sponsored solely their own institutional programs (Chin, *Open Doors 2003,* 94, 63). But statistics about institutions do not match those about students attending. An examination of feeder or sponsor schools can help portray the growing diversity of institutions supporting international education.

The University of Delaware programs in France at the onset of World War II drew students from a number of other institutions. Of the 128 institutions supplying students, only 20 percent can be confirmed as public institutions. Sweet Briar College continued to recruit nationally, and by 1957, Sweet Briar had enrolled over 600 students from 104 American colleges and universities (Martha Lou Lemmon Stohlman, *The Story of Sweet Briar College* [Sweet Briar, Va.: Alumnae Association of Sweet Briar College, 1956], 205), with many from small liberal arts colleges. Denmark's International Study Program reports that in recent years, almost half of its top feeder institutions (11 out of 25) are public (Deborah Kaplan, IT Consultant, Denmark's International Study Program, e-mail correspondence, 29 August 2002). A study across time of sending institutions can reinforce the traditional belief about the role of liberal arts colleges, but it also reflects the increasing diversity of institutional types supporting study abroad.
104. Foucault, *Archaeology,* 216; Michel Foucault, "The Eye of Power," in Colin Gordon, ed., *Power/Knowledge: Selected Interviews and Other Writings 1972–1977* (New York: Random House, 1980), 61.

105. Roger P. Mourad, Jr., *Postmodern Philosophical Critique and the Pursuit of Knowledge in Higher Education* (Westport, Conn., and London: Bergin and Garvey, 1997), 60–61.
106. Cohen, interview.

NOTES TO CHAPTER FOUR

1. O'Sullivan, ed., *IEPassport*, 54th ed., xi.
2. Quoted by John Coatsworth (director, Harvard's David Rockefeller Center for Latin American Studies), *Christian Science Monitor,* 15 March 2005, http://www.csmonitor.com/2005/0315/p14s01-legn.html/. Coatsworth cited this tradition in an article describing new and supportive study abroad policies adopted at Harvard.
3. Thomas Bartlett, "Academics Discuss How to Explain the Value of the Liberal Arts to Those Who Pay the Bills," *Chronicle of Higher Education,* 26 January 2004, http://chronicle.com/daily/2004/01/2004012605n.html/.
4. Marshall Gregory, "A Liberal Education Is Not a Luxury," *Chronicle of Higher Education* , 12 September 2003, B16.
5. Kathleen M. Reilly, unpublished paper (1995), 1.
6. Ibid.
7. Barbara Burn reflected this same strand of thought within discourse, stating that women have enrolled in liberal arts colleges' study overseas programs in order to broaden their cultural horizons, selecting humanities first and social sciences second: "Humanities and arts fields . . . still predominate as the focus of college-sponsored study abroad programs, close to one-third in 1979–80 and over one-third in 1980–81," wrote Burn. She continued: "This is undoubtedly because so many of the college-sponsored programs are in the language and culture fields in which it is much easier for students to study abroad for a year or semester than in professional fields. Foreign language departments have more incentives to set up study abroad programs because they can greatly improve students' language proficiency, help attract students to major or minor in foreign languages, and often offer to foreign language faculty at American colleges the opportunity to spend time in their foreign language country as foreign program director. Few professional fields offer comparable incentives for faculty to organize overseas study programs (Briggs and Burn, *Study Abroad*, 39).
8. Karen Jenkins and James Skelly, "Education Abroad Is Not Enough," *International Educator* , Vol. 13, no. 2 (Winter 2004), 8.
9. John Engle and Lilli Engle, "Neither International Nor Educative: Study Abroad in the Time of Globalization," in *Rockin' in Red Square*, 29. See also in that volume James L. Citron, "U.S. Students Abroad: Host Culture Integration or Third Culture Formation?," 41–42.
10. Mabel Newcomer, *A Century of Higher Education for American Women* (Washington: Zenger Publishing Co., 1959), 240–244.
11. Ibid., 241.
12. Catherine Stimpson, "Colleges in the U.S. Beginning to Ask, 'Where Have All the Men Gone?'" *New York Times* , 6 December 1998, A38.

13. These perceptions link with ideas articulated by Stephen Freeman, author of the report on the 1960 Study Abroad conference mentioned in Chapter 1. Freeman's comments appeared in "Undergraduate Study Abroad," published in *International Education: Past, Present, Problems, and Prospects: Selected Reading to Supplement H.R. 14643*, prepared by the Task Force on International Education, Committee on Education and Labor, U.S. House of Representatives (Washington, D.C.: U.S. Government Printing Office, 1966), 387–392; cited in Gilbert W. Merkx, "The Two Waves of Internationalization in U.S. Higher Education," *International Educator*, Vol. XII, no. 1 (Winter 2003), 8–12.

14. M. Archer Brown, "U.S. Students Abroad," in Hugh M. Jenkins and Associates, *Educating Students from Other Nations* (San Francisco, Washington, London: Jossey-Bass Publishers, 1983), 74.

15. Engle and Engle in *Rockin' in Red Square*, 29.

16. Ibid., 37, 34.

17. J. Walter Thompson Education, "An Exploration of the Demand for Study Overseas from American Students and Employers: An analysis of how future employment considerations are likely to impact students' decisions to study overseas and employers' perceptions of candidates with overseas qualifications." This study, prepared for the Institute of International Education, the German Academic Exchange Service (DAAD), the British Council, and the Australian Education Office, is available online at http://www.iie.org/.

18. Ruth M. Sylte, e-mail correspondence, 5 April 1996.

19. John S. Brubacher and Willis Rudy, *Higher Education in Transition: A History of American Colleges and Universities,* 4th ed., with new chapters by Willis Rudy (New Brunswick, N.J., and London: Transaction Publishers, 1997), 287–304. In their earliest years, American institutions of higher learning offered a program of study following the traditional liberal arts model, defined by the classical European curriculum that included Greek, Latin, mathematics, philosophy, science, and English.

20. Boyer and Hechinger, *Higher Learning*, 11–13, 198.

21. Ibid., 143.

22. Sandra L. Singer, *Adventures Abroad: North American Women at German-Speaking Universities, 1868–1915,* Contributions in Women's Studies, Number 201 (Westport, Conn., and London: Praeger, 2003), 1–26. A good example is M. Carey Thomas, the first female Ph.D. degree recipient at Zurich, who returned to the United States to become the president of Bryn Mawr (xiii). Among others who sought education in Germany was W. E. B. Du Bois: see Hamilton Beck, "W. E. B. Du Bois as a Study Abroad Student in Germany, 1892–1894," in Frontiers, online at http://www.frontiersjournal.com/issues/vol2/vol2–03_Beck.htm/.

23. Singer, *Adventures Abroad*, xv, 2.

24. Solomon, *In the Company*, 80–87.

25. Some women worked for months and years toward Ph.D. degrees at German universities, only to be told in the end that the institution would not award the degree to a woman. One woman was told that the only reason

women wanted education was so they could become political subversives, although few actually entered politics. Ironically, American women continued to attend German institutions long after American males had stopped, because professional training doors, especially at the best schools in the United States, stayed shut to them. Singer, *Adventures Abroad*, 1–2, 10–11, 22–26.

26. Solomon, *In the Company*, 82.
27. Ibid., 78–87.
28. Page Smith, *Killing the Spirit: Higher Education in America* (New York: Viking Press, 1990), 92–93.
29. Ibid., 93.
30. Solomon, *In the Company*, 157–159; Horowitz, *Alma Mater*, 281–282. Also see Chapter 3 of this book.
31. Horowitz, *Alma Mater*, 295.
32. Ibid.
33. Solomon, *In the Company*, 83.
34. Ibid.
35. Ibid., 80–88.
36. Smith, *Killing the Spirit*, 97.
37. Pace, *Junior Year*, 15–16. The more recent Sweet Briar survey, reflecting participants between 1948 and 2004, found a similar pattern still: The majority of students attending the Sweet Briar program have chosen to major in the humanities or social studies, with the greatest number majoring in foreign languages (see Appendix, Table 4–1).
38. Fields of Study of U. S. Study Abroad Students, Selected Years 1985–86—2002/03, *Open Doors 2004*; Chin, ed., *Open Doors 2003*, 19, 61. In 1985–86, according to IIE's historical records, 20.3 percent of all U.S. students abroad majored in fields outside the liberal arts on their home campuses. That proportion rose to 34.6 percent in 2002–03, more than half (17.7% of the total) of whom were business and management majors. In contrast, in 1985–86, 67.4 percent of students overseas majored in the humanities and social sciences, down to 55.5 percent in 2002–03. A large part of that change may be attributed to the decline in foreign language majors registering in overseas programs.
39. Chin, *Open Doors 2003*, 19 , 61.
40. William Velivis, correspondence, 14 December 1998. Peterson's is unable to provide updated data gleaned in a fashion similar to that provided from its earlier database structure, according to Patricia Sheffer, Peterson's manager of mailing lists and services, e-mail correspondence, 23 July 2004 and 24 August 2004; phone conversation, 23 July 2004.
41. Hogan, e-mail correspondence, 9 August 2004.
42. Chin, ed., *Open Doors 2003*, 19.
43. Michel Foucault, *Discipline and Punish*, tr. Alan Sheridan (New York: Pantheon Books, 1977), 194; *Death and Labyrinth*, 164–165; Hubert L. Dreyfus and Paul Rabinow, *Michel Foucault: Beyond Structuralism and Hermeneutics*, 2nd ed. (Chicago: University of Chicago Press), 212; G. Burchell, C. Gordon, and P. Miller, *The Foucault Effect: Studies in Govern-*

mentality (Hemel, Hempstead: Harvester Wheatsheaf, 1991), 179; Mourad, *Postmodern Philosophical Critique*, 60–66.

44. Roy J. Honeywell, *The Educational Work of Thomas Jefferson* (Cambridge, Mass.: Harvard University Press, 1931), 94.

45. Dumas Malone, *The Sage of Monticello* (Boston: Little, Brown & Co., 1981), 409.

46. Philip G. Altbach, *Comparative Higher Education: Knowledge, the University, and Development* (Greenwich, Conn., & London: Ablex Publishing Corp., 1998), 77.

47. Goodwin and Nacht, *Abroad and Beyond*, 29–30.

48. Josef Mestenhauser, "In Search of a Comprehensive Approach," in *Rockin' in Red Square*, 206.

49. Hoffa, William W., "Learning about the Future World: International Education and the Demise of the Nation State," in *Rockin' in Red Square*, 59.

50. David Engberg and Madeleine F. Green, eds., *Promising Practices: Spotlighting Excellence in Comprehensive Internationalization* (Washington, D.C.: Center for Institutional and International Initiatives, American Council on Education, 2002), 13–14. This book was funded by the Carnegie Corporation of New York.

51. Benjamin Urbain de Winter, *Overcoming Barriers to Study Abroad: A Report of the New York State Task Force on International Education* (Ithaca, N.Y.: Cornell University, 1995), 59.

52. Goodwin and Nacht, *Abroad and Beyond*, 15.

53. Siaya and Hayward, *Mapping Internationalization*, viii.

54. Ibid., 9–10. This data represents an update of an earlier 1990s study, also reported by the American Council on Education, which found that at only 8 percent of all higher education institutions in the U.S. had more than one out of ten faculty members participated in overseas projects or consulting activities, and that at only 12 percent had more than one out of ten faculty members participated in international research projects. E. El-Khawas, *Campus Trends, 1992* (Washington: American Council on Education, 1993), cited in Joan Claffey, *Serving the World: International Activities of American Colleges and Universities* (Washington: Office for University Cooperation in Development).

55. Goodwin and Nacht, *Abroad and Beyond*, 4.

56. Ibid., 4–5.

57. Ibid., 55. When they asked college and university presidents to be more specific about their intentions to globalize their campuses, Goodwin and Nacht heard frequent references to "the short-sightedness and stinginess of the state legislature." One faculty member complained that his leader "does not put his resources where his rhetoric is" (56).

58. Question 1, How would you rate your institution's commitment to the development of international education? Council on International Educational Exchange, *Study Abroad Baseline Survey* (New York: CIEE, 1996), 1.

59. Question 17, Do you charge an administrative fee? Ibid., 9.

60. De Winter, *Overcoming Barriers*, 46.

61. Thomas H. Hoemeke, Maria Krane, Judy Young, and Gerald Slavin, *A Survey on Chief International Education Administrators, Their Institutions and Offices* (Buffalo, N.Y.: Committee on Campus Administration and Programs, Association of International Education Administrators, 1999), accessible online at http://wings.buffalo.edu/intled/aiea/ciea.pdf, 9–10. AIEA's membership represents the most senior international education administrators in the United States. Of respondents, 90 percent reported that they did receive institutional funds for their offices, which almost always conducted study abroad activities, but their funding was mixed, with over 50 percent also generating their own income from program fees. Other types of sources, rather than institutional funding, were reported as well. AIEA concluded that alternatives to institutional funding are linked to the future of international education development, with at least one-third of institutions surveyed seeking alternative funding currently. Also see Ketayoun Darvich-Kodjouri, *International Activity on State College and University Campuses, 1995* (Washington: American Association of State Colleges and Universities, 1995) and *Promising Practices,* 16.

62. Biddle, *Internationalization: Rhetoric or Reality,* 120.

63. The first NAFSA national task force reported "the lack of institutional commitment to a strong international dimension in undergraduate education" and found it a major inhibitor to "expansion and improved quality" in undergraduate study abroad (*A National Mandate,* 9). Responding to a spring 2004 survey of participants at Denmark's International Study Program's conference, "Study Abroad in a Globalized World," 62.3 percent reported that their campuses had no institutional policy about why or how to develop study abroad. Even more—78.3 percent—said their institution did not have a mandate for increasing the number of students going abroad (Claus Elhom Andersen, panel presentation, "DIS Response to Study Abroad Challenges of the 21st Century," DIS Quintennial International Educators Conference, Copenhagen, 24 June 2004). And a serious lack of support services for study abroad programming has significantly inhibited the growth and development of programs for undergraduate students, as William Hoffa noted in NAFSA's *Guide to Education Abroad* (Hoffa, Pearson, and Slind, *NAFSA's Guide* [1993], x). See also *A National Mandate,* 11; and study abroad adviser comments, "Working with DIS: Workshop on the Administration of Academic and Practical Matters," during "Study Abroad in a Globalized World," DIS Quintennial International Educators Conference.

64. Community colleges reported the least support, with 12 percent reporting an office dedicated to international education (*Mapping,* 33). Among comprehensive universities, 90 percent had an office charged at least in part with international initiatives (53). Among research universities, 48 percent reported a dedicated office and only 3 percent no office charged with an international mission. Thirty-one percent of research institutions also reported a senior appointment charged with international responsibility at the vice presidential or provost level (65). In 2004, NAFSA reports that 2,200 U.S. colleges are members, with 790 of them having at least one staff member identified as working in study abroad. Not all members identify

sectional affiliation, however (Sandy Schoeps Tennies, NAFSA associate director for education abroad & campus internationalization, 27 September 2004).

65. *Mapping,* 42. Eighty percent did report hosting administrative structures that included international issues as their mission.

66. Ibid., 51.

67. Goodwin and Nacht, *Abroad and Beyond,* 57. The 1996 CIEE Baseline Survey revealed that international education advisers and administrators near the end of the twentieth century believed that the most useful change to help their efforts would be to tie study abroad activities to the normalized and empowered components of the institution by creating a centralized administrative structure, closely connected with the institution's central administration (Question 17, If you could make any changes in how programs are administered or available, what would those changes be?, 7).

68. Jane I. Guyer, Foreword to Biddle, *Internationalization: Rhetoric or Reality,* v.

69. See Chapters 2 and 3 of this book for descriptions of the rise of the multifaceted American university and its new curriculum.

70. Patricia Olmsted, "Sixty Years of Study Abroad: A Backward Glance at the Profession," presentation at NAFSA Conference, Long Beach, Calif., U.S., May 1987, 4.

71. Ibid., 4.

72. Ibid., 15–16. See also John A. Garraty and Walter Adams, *From Main Street to the Left Bank: Students and Scholars Abroad* (East Lansing, Mich.: The Michigan State University Press, 1959), 9–10.

73. Bowman, *Educating,* 13.

74. Richard Lambert typified this ideal when, in a speech at CIEE's 41st Annual Conference, he noted that the "relatively brief period of time" students devote to study abroad often becomes an obstacle for effective learning (Lambert, "Study Abroad"). In a backhanded way, he was praising the earlier model, in which students spent a full year abroad.

75. Goodwin and Nacht, *Abroad and Beyond,* 35.

76. Engle and Engle, in *Rockin' in Red Square,* 36–37. These sentiments appear elsewhere in contemporary discourse, as in articles such as one that appeared in *USA Today* in February 2004. Originally titled "Study Abroad: The Short Course Students Like. Quick Studies, But Critics Question Their Direction," the article raised doubt about the quality of short-term study abroad (Mary Beth Marklein, "Study Abroad: The Short Course Students Like," *USA Today,* 2 February 2004, D-1; cited in Jenkins and Skelly, "Education Abroad Is Not Enough").

77. De Winter, *Overcoming Barriers,* 59.

78. Briggs and Burn, *Study Abroad,* 52–53.

79. Ibid., 55–56.

80. Madeleine Green, Peter Eckel, and Andris Barblan, *The Brave New (and Smaller) World of Higher Education: A Transatlantic View* (Washington, D.C.: American Council on Education, Center for International Initiatives, and European University Association, 2002), 22.

81. Ibid.

82. Duration of U. S. Study Abroad, Selected Years, 1985/86–2002/03, Chin, ed., *Open Doors 2003,* 18.
83. *A National Mandate,* 10.
84. Bowman, *Educating,* 33. Summarizing studies of foreign language study program participants, Bowman observed: "Eighty-five percent in the 1930s were language majors, 54 percent in the 1950s, 50–66 percent in the 1970s but only 22 percent in 1984" (ibid.).
85. *Promising Practices,* 9–10.
86. Fields of Study of U.S. Study Abroad Students, 2001/02 & 2002/03, *Open Doors 2004.*
87. James Pritchett, e-mail correspondence, 12 May 1997, 3 October 1997, and 6 October 1997. Of 1,540 programs listed by Peterson's, 909, or 59 percent, were taught in English.
88. According to CIEE program records kept by Cindy Sittler, director of campus relations, CIEE, for enrollments from 1973 through 1992 in all CIEE programs.
89. Hogan, e-mail correspondence, 9 August 2004.
90. Briggs and Burn, *Study Abroad,* 45.
91. David Maxwell and Nina Garrett, "Meeting National Needs," *Change,* Vol. 34, no. 3 (May/June 2002), 22.
92. Biddle, *Internationalization: Rhetoric or Reality,* 45, 112.
93. *Securing America's Future,* 5.
94. Engle and Engle in *Rockin' in Red Square,* 36–37.
95. Female enrollment levels have remained consistent even as more courses are taught in English (Pritchett, e-mail correspondence, 12 May 1997, 3 October 1997, and 6 October 1997).
96. Mestenhauser, interview, April 1989.
97. In the SECUSSA section—the study abroad professional section of NAFSA—the majority of practitioners in the field were women, did not have Ph.D.s, and earned under $40,000 per year (NAFSA, national membership survey, 1990; NAFSA, "Report on National Membership Survey," *NAFSA Newsletter,* Vol. 41, no. 3 [December/January 1990]).
98. "Survey Sheds Light on Members," *NAFSA Newsletter,* July/August 2002, 31. Further, only 11 percent of the membership stated that increasing the impact of international education on their campuses was their primary goal.
99. Tennies, e-mail correspondence, 31 August 2004.
100. Harlan N. Henson, director of the College Consortium for International Studies (CCIS), reported that study abroad-related salaries are often "abysmally low"—sometimes even below cost-of-living standards, and certainly lower than faculty salaries (personal interview, 30 April 2004).
101. Erin Strout, "Median Salaries of Midlevel College Administrators by Type of Institution, 2003–4," *Chronicle of Higher Education,* 2 April 2004, http://chronicle.com/weekly/v50/i30/30a03001.htm/.
102. Robin Wilson, "Faculty Salaries Rise 2.1%, the Lowest Increase in 30 Years," *Chronicle of Higher Education,* 23 April 2004, A-13. In all ranks, women faculty earned less than men, from 3.8 percent less at the least to 11.6 less at the greatest difference.

103. Strout, "Median Salaries."
104. Hoemeke et al., *A Survey,* 16, 12–13.
105. Ibid., 6–10. The AIEA report did indicate that the more senior the appointment for an international educator, the greater the likelihood of receiving resources, both personal, such as salary, and professional, such as institutional support.
106. Ibid., 6. Additionally, only 15 percent of respondents reported international education as a high priority in their institution's mission statement, though 48.4 percent said it was highly placed in the institution's strategic plan, and most of the schools represented did have such a plan (5). In 1989 Phi Beta Delta, the national honor society for study abroad participants, canvassed its membership of 2,400 administrators. Of them, 1,357 were women. Of those, only 206 held the title of "director" (Edward Blankenship [director of the Office of International Education, California State University], interviews, April 1989).
107. Hoemeke et al., *A Survey,* 12.
108. Mestenhauser, "In Search of a Comprehensive Approach," in *Rockin' in Red Square,* 179.
109. *Mapping,* 74. The first NAFSA task force report emphasized this point, stating that "We were struck repeatedly by the importance of a charismatic leader in galvanizing a campus to focus on and undertake study abroad" (*A National Mandate,* 9).
110. Panel and audience discussion, "Study Abroad as a Response to the Need for Globalization of Higher Education," 23 June 2004.
111. Briggs and Burn, *Study Abroad,* 51.
112. Goodwin and Nacht, *Abroad and Beyond,* 29–36, 57–59, 70–74, 112.
113. Ibid., 43.
114. *Mapping,* 75. See also *The Brave New,* 21–22.
115. *Promising Practices,* 10.
116. *Securing America's Future,* 8–9.
117. Burchell, Gordon, and Miller, *The Foucault Effect,* 79.
118. Mourad, *Postmodern Philosophical Critique,* 60–61.
119. Cohen, interview.
120. Foucault, *Archaeology,* 186–187. See Chapter 1 of this book.
121. Boyer and Hechinger, *Higher Learning,* 10.
122. Ibid., 5, 9–13.
123. Ibid., vii–18.
124. Cohen, interview; Mourad, *Postmodern Philosophical Critique,* 60.
125. Foucault, *Discipline,* 185, 187, 191–192.

NOTES TO CHAPTER FIVE

1. Foucault identifies "genealogy" as "the union of erudite knowledge and local memories which allows us to establish a historical knowledge of struggles and to make use of this knowledge tactically today" (Michel Foucault, "Genealogy and Social Criticism," in Steven Seidman, ed., *The Postmodern Turn: New Perspectives on Social Theory* [Cambridge: Cambridge

University Press, 1995]; and "Introduction" in D. C. Hoy, *Foucault: A Critical Reader* [New York: Basil Blackwell], 6–7). See also Michel Foucault, *Language, Counter-Memory, Practice: Selected Essays and Interviews,* Donald F. Bouchard, ed. (New York: Cornell University Press, 1977), 146–152.

2. Foucault, "The Discourse on Language," 215–237; Hubert L. Dreyfus and Paul Rabinow, *Michel Foucault: Beyond Structuralism and Hermeneutics,* 2nd ed. (Chicago: University of Chicago Press, 1983), 119.

3. Foucault, "Genealogy and Social Criticism"; Hoy, Introduction, *Foucault: A Critical Reader,* 6–7.

4. Bowman, *Educating,* 14.

5. R. W. Kirkbride, letter to Dr. Walter Hullihen, president, University of Delaware, 2 March 1923, Paris, France (provided by Andrew T. Hill, International Programs and Special Sessions Office, University of Delaware).

6. Francis M. Rogers, *American Juniors on the Left Bank* (Sweet Briar, Va.: Sweet Briar College, 1958), 10.

7. Bowman, *Educating,* 13–14. For a full description of the Delaware program, see Sketch of Foreign Study Plan, Scope and General Statement, University of Delaware Archives, Folder # 1 and Foreign Study section, Papers of Walter Hullihen, # 3/18, University of Delaware Archives.

8. John M. Clayton, Jr., *Foreign Study Plan Records, 1922–1948: An Inventory* (University of Delaware Archives, 16 March 1970), n.p.

9. John A. Munroe, interview, 7 February 1994.

10. Clayton, *Foreign Study Plan Records,* n.p. There is no indication in the records that in the first year, when the Delaware program enrolled only men, women applied and were turned away from the program.

11. Munroe, *University of Delaware,* 266.

12. Ibid.

13. Delfor Alumni Association, Committee on Foreign Study Survey (University of Delaware Archives, 26 January 1933, 33/0/8), n.p.

14. Clayton, Foreign Study Plan Records, n.p.

15. Bowman, *Educating,* 14.

16. Margaret Farrand Thorp, *Neilson of Smith* (New York: Oxford University Press, 1956), 129–149.

17. Ibid., 193–199.

18. Ibid., 1–59.

19. Ibid., 196.

20. Ibid., 197–199.

21. Hélène Cattanès, *Vers d'autres horizons, Mémento de l'année en France* (New York/Paris: Association of Former Juniors in France of Smith College, 1965), 10.

22. Ibid., 8–9.

23. Jean Collignon, "Le programme des études en France," in Cattanès, *Vers d'autres horizons,* 20.

24. Thorp, *Neilson of Smith,* 197.

25. Ibid., 193–199.

26. Emile Langlois, interview, 25 April 1994; Bowman, *Educating*, 15.
27. Martha Lou Lemmon Stohlman, *The Story of Sweet Briar College* (Sweet Briar, Va.: Alumnae Association of Sweet Briar College, 1956), 171–178, 182–183, 205.
28. Matthew, *Twenty-Five Years*, n.p.
29. Ibid.
30. Pace, *Junior Year in France*, 3.
31. Ibid., 3–4.
32. As noted on the Sweet Briar Junior Year in France Admissions website, http://www.jyf.sbc.edu.
33. Marion Macri and Patricia O'Callaghan, "A Review of the Marymount Schools in Paris, Rome and Elsewhere," in *Oriflamme*, Jubilee Number (Tarrytown, N.Y.: Marymount College, 1932).
34. Sister Rita Arthur, interview, 6 August 1997; Bowman, *Educating*, 15.
35. Arthur, interview.
36. Rosary College Bulletin, 1947 (University of Delaware Archives: Folder 418, AR64, 33/0/3, Rosary College General, General Correspondence, Box 20), 12.
37. Ibid.
38. See, for example, "American Assistants in French Lycees" *School and Society* 18 (25 October 1923), 497–498; "Student Exchanges & Peace," *School and Society* 18 (25 August 1923), 233–234; "Vacation Courses for Foreigners in French Universities," *School and Society* 20 (August 1924), 247–248; "Educational: American Students at Oxford University," *School and Society* 21 (10 June 1925), 40–41; "Delaware Foreign Study Plan on Intercollegiate Basis," *School and Society* 24 (3 July 1926), 14; "International Study," *School and Society* 20 (24 April 1926), 46–47; "American German Student Exchange Fellowships," *School and Society* 21 (10 June 1925), 40–41; "Foreign Study Scholarships of University of Delaware," *School and Society* 27 (9 June 1928), 686–687; "Institute of International Education & Student Exchange," *School and Society* 28 (14 July 1928), 38–39; "The Success of American Graduate Students in the University of London," *School and Society* 29 (26 January 1929), 121–123; "The Franco-American Student Exchange," *School and Society* 64 (9 November 1946), 327; and "Junior Year in Zurich," *School and Society* 66 (12 July 1947), 27–28. When the authors of these articles discussed purpose, they most often identified educating people competent to contribute to international peace.
39. Arcadia admission requirements available online at http://www.arcadia.edu. Information also from David Larsen, personal interview, June 1, 1995.
40. IES website, http://www.iesabroad.org/info/abouties.html.
41. Joan Gillespie and Carla Slawson, *IES Outcomes Assessment Project*, http://www.iesabroad.org/info/alumnioutcomes.pdf.
42. Question 31, *CIEE Baseline Survey*, 1996.
43. Kate Watkins [director of communications, Council on International Educational Exchange], personal interview, 27 May 2004. Also see http://www.ciee.org/about_ciee.cfm/.

44. Data confirming this statement were gathered by projecting program admission grade point averages (drawn from Sara J. Steen, ed., *Academic Year Abroad 1997–98* [New York: Institute of International Education, 1996]) onto a list of U.S. colleges and universities, ranked as to the number of study abroad participants as reported to Peterson's (William Velivis, correspondence, 14 December 1994). Among the 60 schools sending the greatest number abroad, only three report grade point admission requirements under 2.75. These data are just suggestive, though, since only 50 percent of schools reporting provided grade point average information.

45. Elinor G. Barber and Barbara B. Burn, eds., *Study Abroad: The Experience of American Undergraduates in Western Europe and in the United States* (Westport, Conn.: Greenwood Press, Inc., 1990); cited in Stephen Cooper and Mary Anne Grant, "The Demographics of Education Abroad," in Hoffa, Pearson, and Slind, eds., *NAFSA's Guide* (1993), 96.

46. Beatrice Beach Szekely and Maria Krane, "The Current Demographics of Education Abroad," in Hoffa and Pearson, *NAFSA's Guide*, 2nd ed., 162.

47. Pritchett, e-mail correspondence, 3 October 1997. In the directory, 1,335 programs were listed, of which 784 programs required a 2.5 GPA and 616 programs required a 2.75 GPA for admission.

48. Craufurd D. Goodwin, "Introduction," in Maranthi Zikopoulos, ed., *U.S. Students Abroad, Statistics on Study Abroad, 1985–86* (IIE Research Report Number 16 (New York: Institute of International Education, 1988), 5.

49. Foucault, "The Discourse on Language," 215–237; Dreyfus and Rabinow, *Foucault*, 119; Ralph Cohen, interview, 1 September 1999.

50. Wallace, "Characteristics of Programs for Study Abroad," 253.

51. Gruber, *Mars and Minerva*, 257.

52. Margaret Scouten [director of Sweet Briar College Junior Year in France], personal interview, 17 May 2004. Also see Sweet Briar College Junior Year in France website, online at http://www.jyf.sbc.edu/admission.html.

53. Harrison G. Gough and William A. McCormack, "An Exploratory Evaluation of Education Abroad," Cooperative Research Project No.S-440 (Berkeley, Calif.: University of California, 1967), 16.

54. Ibid., 26–28.

55. University of California Education Abroad Program, Foreign Language Options, online at http://eap.ucop.edu/eap/language/foreign.htm.

56. *Securing America's Future*, iv.

57. Ibid., 5.

58. Pritchett, e-mail correspondence, 12 May 1997.

59. Hogan, e-mail correspondence, 9 August 2004. Even with so many English-language programs, 57 percent of all CIEE students took courses taught in the host foreign language.

60. Pritchett, e-mail, 12 May 1997.

61. William W. Hoffa, "Learning about the Future World," in Grünzweig and Rinehart, eds., *Rockin' in Red Square*, 71.

62. Philip G. Altbach, "Higher Education Crosses Borders."

63. Undergraduate participation rate in study abroad is taken from U.S. Study Abroad Participation by Institution, 2002/2003, Appendix D, *Open Doors*

2004, http://opendoors.iienetwork.org/file_depot/0–10000000/0–10000/ 3390/folder/37269/SA_All+Institutions2.htm. School ranks and SAT scores are taken from *U.S. News and World Report's* 2003 Premium Online Edition of *America's Best Colleges,* http://www.usnews.com/usnews/edu/college/ rankings/rankindex_brief.php.

64. In their ongoing collaborative web-based project, *What Works in International Education,* the International 50 have created "a living and changing document," thematically organized to provide ongoing information on quality efforts at liberal arts institutions in support of international education. The What Works project, as it will hereafter be called in this book, focuses on a variety of internationalization case studies and projects at liberal arts institutions, including those with a substantial focus on study abroad. Beloit College continued its leadership role as an International 50 liberal arts college member, hosting the current International 50 and What Works websites and sponsoring an international education conference in fall 2004 in cooperation with the American Council on Education Internationalization Collaborative, a program of ACE's Center for Institutional and International Initiatives and the Associated Colleges of the Midwest, with science support from the Global Partners Project. See New Directions in International Education: Building Context, Connections and Knowledge, http://www.beloit.edu/~oie/conference/.

65. Engerman and Marden, *In the International Interest,* 35.

66. Ibid., 36–37. In their original study, the International 50 took pride in noting that while the total number of U.S. students seeking degrees in foreign languages and foreign area studies decreased by 38 percent between 1972 and 1988, the number of degree-seekers in those areas at International 50 colleges actually increased by 13 percent over the same period. More recently, in all liberal arts colleges, as the ACE *Mapping* study reported, commitment to foreign language learning remained important: 70 percent of liberal arts colleges stated a foreign language graduation requirement and 54 percent of liberal arts students (versus 34 percent nationally) reported foreign language study as part of their undergraduate curriculum. The *Mapping* study also reported that compared to others, more liberal arts students have had some type of college-sponsored overseas experience, though not necessarily study abroad, and that 23 percent of the study body of liberal arts colleges has engaged in some type of activity in another country (*Mapping,* 44–46).

67. Sara Rimer, "Committee Urges Harvard to Expand the Reach of Its Undergraduate Curriculum," *New York Times,* 27 April 2004, A-17.

68. Harvard University Faculty of Arts and Sciences, A Report on the Harvard College Curricular Review, April 2004, http://www.fas.harvard.edu/curriculum-review/HCCR_Report.pdf, 40.

69. Rimer, "Committee Urges Harvard."

70. Boyer and Hechinger, *Higher Learning,* vii-viii.

71. Ibid., vii.

72. Ibid., 9. Also see Zachary Karabell, *What's College For? The Struggle to Define American Higher Education* (New York: Basic Books, 1998), vii-viii, and John S. Brubacher, *On The Philosophy of Higher Education,* 4–6.

73. Boyer and Hechinger, *Higher Learning,* 3–5; Brubacher, *On The Philoso- phy of Higher Education* (San Francisco and London: Jossey-Bass Series in Higher Education, 1977), 5.

74. Brubacher, *On the Philosophy of Higher Education,* 5–7; Boyer and Hechinger, *Higher Learning,* 9–18.

75. Lincoln Steffens, "Sending a State to College," *American Magazine,* Febru- ary 1909, reprinted in James C. Stone and Donald P. DeNevi, eds., *Por- traits of the American University 1890–1910* (San Francisco: Jossey-Bass, 1971), 133. Cited in Boyer and Hechinger, *Higher Learning,* 13.

76. Boyer and Hechinger, *Higher Learning,* 12.

77. Brubacher, *On The Philosophy of Higher Education,* 1–8.

78. Boyer and Hechinger, *Higher Learning,* 11. Also see Frederick Rudolph, *The American College and University, A History* (New York: Vintage Books, 1962), 65.

79. Brubacher, *On The Philosophy of Higher Education,* 7.

80. John S. Brubacher and Willis Rudy, *Higher Education in Transition: A His- tory of American Colleges and Universities,* 4th ed., with new chapters by Willis Rudy (New Brunswick, N.J., and London: Transaction Publishers, 1997), 427.

81. Veysey, *Emergence,* 61.

82. James B. Conant, "America Remakes the University," reprinted from *Atlantic Monthly,* May 1946, in Brubacher and Rudy, *Higher Education,* 42.

83. Brubacher and Rudy, *Higher Education,* 426, quoting Merle E. Curti, "Intellectuals and Other People," *American Historical Review* 60 (January 1955).

84. Conant, "America Remakes," 42–43, in Brubacher and Rudy, *Higher Edu- cation,* 427.

85. Brubacher and Rudy, *Higher Education,* 427.

86. Ibid. As they put it, "American universities have demonstrated a much greater readiness to admit new and different fields of study as integral members of the academic family. Schools of journalism, education, engi- neering, pharmacy, nursing, business, public health, agriculture, library service, and public administration came in the United States to be accepted as proper and accredited parts of the academic structure."

87. Clayton, *Foreign Study Plan Records.*

88. Munroe, *University of Delaware,* 263.

89. John A. Munroe, interview, 7 February 1994. Details about how study abroad could contribute to international understanding were not devel- oped in the Delaware literature. The goals of peace and international understanding continued to be expressed through the end of the century in references to training students for "global competency" or to function effectively in the "'global society" (Council on International Educational Exchange, Annual Report 94–95 [New York: CIEE, 1995]). Such inten- tions have sometimes been linked to professional training in planning state- ments that mingle goals to train professionally proficient citizens with loosely stated goals to increase international understanding, as the

Delaware example illustrates. In other instances they are connected by the expression of interest in them by individuals who pursued professional lives to fulfill these goals. See, for example, President Martha Lucas, Sweet Briar College, in Emile Langlois, "Martha Lucas, President of Sweet Briar College," unpublished manuscript for panel presentation at NAFSA conference, Region VII and IX (16 November 1990), 2–3.

90. Munroe, *University of Delaware,* 263–264.
91. Walter H. Hullihen, "The Delaware Undergraduate Foreign Study Plan, or Junior Year Abroad," dated 1931 (University of Delaware Archives 33/0/5, Box 23 [AR67], folder 537), 4; also see Sketch of Foreign Study Plan in Hullihen's papers, University of Delaware Archives.
92. Ibid.
93. Clayton, *Foreign Study Plan Records,* opening commentary; also see Sketch of Foreign Study Plan, University of Delaware Archives.
94. Munroe, *University of Delaware,* 267.
95. Bowman, *Educating,* 14.
96. Munroe, interview, 7 February 1994.
97. Solomon, *In the Company,* 126–127.
98. Ibid., 128.
99. Rosary College Bulletin (1947).
100. Rogers, *American Juniors,* 27.
101. Patricia Olmsted, "Sixty Years of Study Abroad: A Backward Glance at the Profession," paper prepared for NAFSA Conference, Long Beach, Calif., May 1987, 3–4.
102. Ibid., 5.
103. Ibid., 6.
104. Ibid., 7, 9; Thorp, *Neilson of Smith,* 196–197.
105. Olmsted, "Sixty Years," 7.
106. "Special Correspondence: The New Oxford Summer Vacation Course," *School and Society* 14, no. 619 (6 November 1926), 580.
107. Virginia C. Gildersleeve, *Many a Good Crusade: Memoirs of Virginia Crocheron Gildersleeve* (New York: Macmillan Company, 1954), 129–134.
108. Ibid., 129.
109. Ibid., 143.
110. Solomon, *In the Company,* 115–116, 157.
111. Gildersleeve, *Many a Good Crusade,* 140–141. The uses of Reid Hall prior to World War I reflected discursive strands articulating female interest in the arts abroad.
112. Ibid., 405. Reid Hall continues today to be an important study abroad site for American programs in Paris. See, for example, Columbia University in Reid Hall, online at http://www.ce.columbia.edu/paris/ and Brunhilde Biebucyck, "Great Expectations: American Students in Paris," unpublished paper.
113. J. Stanley Lemons, *The Woman Citizen: Social Feminism in the 1920s* (Charlottesville and London: University Press of Virginia, 1990), viii-ix.
114. Stohlman, *Story of Sweet Briar,* 182–183.

115. Ibid., 171–178.

116. Rogers, *American Juniors,* 12.

117. Emile Langlois, unpublished manuscript for panel presentation at NAFSA conference, Region VII and IX (16 November 1990), 2.

118. Ibid., 2–3.

119. Ibid. Both Lucas and her husband, Maurice Pate, former director of UNESCO, pursued interest in international understanding and peace as a professional commitment.

120. Stohlman, *Story of Sweet Briar,* 198–205.

121. Langlois, interview, 1994. Like other colleges in the southern United States at the time, Sweet Briar was not racially integrated, but it agreed to continue to admit black students for study abroad. Ironically, therefore, from 1948 into the 1960s, when a lawsuit forced the issue, Sweet Briar's study abroad program was integrated but its home campus was not.

122. Langlois, unpublished manuscript, 2.

123. Ibid.

124. Sweet Briar College, Bulletin for Junior Year in France (February 1948).

125. Langlois, "Martha Lucas," 6.

126. David Larsen, personal interview, New Orleans, Louisiana, June 1, 1995.

127. John A. Wallace, *The Organization and Outcomes of a European Field Trip in Economics for 23 College Women* (Ed.D. dissertation. Philadelphia, Pa.: University of Pennsylvania, February 1949).

128. Ibid., 4.

129. From the 1948 Bulletin of Beaver College, page 7; cited in Wallace, "Characteristics of Programs for Study Abroad," 5. The Beaver statement is among the relatively few examples of discourse that articulate the value of cultural education as professional preparation.

130. Wallace, "Characteristics of Programs," 6–11.

131. Beaver College, Bulletin (1948), 6–7; cited in Wallace, 3–4.

132. Wallace, 1–11.

133. Barbara Burn, *Expanding the International Dimensions,* 1. On the Fulbright Program, see http://www.iie.org/FulbrightTemplate.cfm?Section= Fulbright_Program_Overview.

134. Wallace, "Characteristics," 254.

135. The combination of the Higher Education Act Title VI, originally passed in 1958 as the National Defense Education Act (NDEA) with Title VI called Language Development (Richard D. Scarflo, "The History of Title VI and Fulbright-Hays," in John N. Hawkins et al., eds., *International Education in the New Global Era: Proceedings of a National Policy Conference on the Higher Education Act, Title VI, and Fulbright-Hays Programs* [Los Angeles: International Studies and Overseas Programs, 1998], 23) and the ongoing Fulbright-Hays legislation "continue to be among the most significant federal programs supporting the development and maintenance of a higher education infrastructure," said Miriam A. Kazanjian of the Coalition for International Education ("Charge of the Conference," in Hawkins et al., eds., *International Education*). Also see proceedings of the research conference on Global Challenges and U.S. Higher Education, January 23–25, 2003, at Duke University

on behalf of the Coalition for International Education, http://www.duke.edu/web/cis/globalchallenges/research_papers.html/.

136. Paul Weaver, "Study Abroad and General Education," *Journal of General Education* 13:4 (January 1962), 250.

137. Council on International Educational Exchange, Annual Report (New York: CIEE, 1990).

138. Mikhailova, *History of CIEE.*

139. Cindy Sittler (representing the Council on International Educational Exchange), interview, August 1993, and Mikhailova, *History of CIEE,* 112–126.

140. CIEE, *CIEE A World of Opportunity.*

141. Engerman and Marden, *In the International Interest,* 17.

142. Ibid., 21. International 50 institutions continue their international education activities, including the New Directions in International Education conference, http://www.beloit.edu/~oie/conference/.

143. These terms can be seen reflected in study abroad literature, including, for example, Sven Groennings, *The Impact of Economic Globalization on Higher Education* (1987); and Norman L. Kauffmann et al., *Students Abroad, Strangers at Home—Education for a Global Society* (1992).

144. Hans de Wit, *Internationalization of Higher Education in the United States of America and Europe: A Historical, Comparative, and Conceptual Analysis* (Westport, CT: Greenwood Press, 2002), 89–101; see also Hans de Wit, *Strategies for the Internationalization of Higher Education: A Comparative Study of Australia, Europe and the United States of America* (Amsterdam: European Association for International Education, 1995).

145. Nancy L. Ruther, *Barely There, Powerfully Present: Thirty Years of U.S. Policy on International Higher Education* (New York and London: RoutledgeFalmer, 2002), 195. Area studies were included in these categories.

146. Also see chapter 3 of this book.

147. *Securing America's Future,* 4.

148. Ben L. Kedia and Shirley J. Daniel, "U.S. Business Needs for Employees with International Expertise," paper delivered at Global Challenges and U.S. Higher Education conference, Durham, N.C., 23–24 January 2004; http://www.duke.edu/web/cis/globalchallenges/research_papers.html/.

149. See *Securing America's Future* and "Educating for Peace, Working for Justice," panel presented at the NAFSA: Association of International Educators Conference, Thursday, 27 May 2004.

NOTES TO CHAPTER SIX

1. Craufurd D. Goodwin and Michael Nacht, *Missing the Boat: The Failure to Internationalize American Higher Education* (Cambridge: Cambridge University Press, 1991), 10.

2. Stowe, William W., *Going Abroad,* 161–162; see also Thorstein Veblen, *The Theory of the Leisure Class: An Economic Study of Institutions* (New York: Modern Library, 1934).

3. Mary Morris and Larry O'Connor, eds., *Maiden Voyages: Writings of Women Travelers* (New York: Vintage, 1993), xv-xxii.
4. John A. Garraty and Walter Adams, *From Main Street to the Left Bank: Students and Scholars Abroad* (East Lansing, Mich.: The Michigan State University Press, 1959), 8.
5. *Educating for Global Competence*, 8.
6. *Securing America's Future*, 17.
7. Yemi Akande and Carla Slawson, "Exploring the Long-term Impact of Study Abroad: A Case Study of 50 Years of Study Abroad Alumni," *International Educator Magazine*, Summer 2000, http://www.nafsa.org/. Also see Gillespie and Slawson, *IES Outcomes Assessment Project*.
8. Feinberg, "What Students Don't Learn Abroad."
9. Singer, *Adventures Abroad*, 3.
10. Olmsted, "Sixty Years," 12.
11. Ibid., 8.
12. Ibid., 8–9.
13. Ibid., 9.
14. Ibid.
15. Ibid., 10.
16. Clayton, Foreign Study Plan Records, 4.
17. Munroe, *The University of Delaware*.
18. Madeleine Forwood, interviewed by Myron L. Lazarus for the University of Delaware Oral History Project, 8 July 1970 (transcript page 14–15, University of Delaware Paris Program Class of 1931, AR97, 33/1/1, University of Delaware Archives).
19. Olmsted, "Sixty Years," 12.
20. Ibid.
21. Council on International Educational Exchange, Oral History Video Tape, 16 November 1994 (part of the CIEE Oral History Series).
22. Langlois, "Martha Lucas," n.p.
23. Ibid.
24. Olmsted, "Sixty Years," 15.
25. Jerry Johnson, personal interview, 22 February 1994.
26. See Appendix, Figure 6–1, Part 2, CIEE Study Abroad Programs in Spain (Undergraduate Only, 1973–84): Participation by Gender.
27. Female enrollment did drop substantially in the calendar year 1989, well after the terrorist incident, but male enrollment dropped then, too. That change could be attributed to that year's economic recession (Gerry Thompson [CIEE vice president], interview, 15 August 1991). See Appendix, Figure 6-1, Part 1, CIEE Study Abroad Programs in France.
28. Hogan, e-mail correspondence, 9 August 2004.
29. American Council on Education, *Public Opinion Poll*, 6.
30. Melissa Biermann, e-mail to SECUSSA, 21 April 2004. Biermann is a marketing communications specialist for Educational Directories Unlimited, Inc, Chester, PA, reporting on an online survey of students searching on its StudyAbroad.com program directory. Parents participating in the survey

did indeed report safety as their number one concern. Articles like Tamar Lewin's "War and Illness Cloud Prospects for Study Abroad" document the fears parents express about their children's safety overseas (*New York Times,* 9 April 2003, http://www.nytimes.com; also posted on the IIE News Service Announcement List, http://www.iienetwork.org/).

31. Profile of U.S. Study Abroad Students, 1993/94—2002/03, *Open Doors 2004.*
32. Ibid., 19. See Table 26, "U.S. Study Abroad Students, 1993–94–2001–2002."
33. Jennifer Jacobson, "Studying in Safety," *Chronicle of Higher Education,* 23 April 2004, 47.
34. Thorp, *Neilson of Smith,* 197.
35. Educational Reconstruction Conference (1949), cited in Bowman, *Educating,* 15.
36. Langlois, unpublished manuscript.
37. Ibid.
38. Ibid.
39. Ibid.
40. Ibid.
41. Ibid.
42. *A National Mandate,* 4; *Educating for Global Competence,* 5.
43. National Security Education Program, *Summary Report, Undergraduate Scholarships, 1994–1995 Competition Cycle* (New York: Institute for International Education, 1994).
44. Host Regions of Study Abroad Students, 1985/86—2002/2003, *Open Doors 2004.*
45. Ibid. Since these are IIE compilations, graduate students have been included in the count, so the actual percentage of undergraduates in nonconventional areas is lower.
46. Ibid., xxxvi. Also see Paul Desruisseaux, "15% Rise in American Students Abroad Shows Popularity of Non-European Destinations," *Chronicle of Higher Education,* 10 December 1999, A60.
47. The Council on International Educational Exchange conducted a survey of U.S. higher education institutions sponsoring programs in the Third World. The data, collected from the summer of 1987 to the spring of 1993, revealed 277 Third World study programs reported by the 57 responding institutions enrolling a total student population of 14,348 (CIEE, Report on Third World Study Abroad Programs [New York: CIEE, 1993], 1–4).
48. Hogan, e-mail correspondence, 9 August 2004.
49. NSEP considers its responsibility to undergraduate students to be "to provide American undergraduates with the resources and encouragement they need to acquire skills and experience and less commonly studied languages and cultures" (National Security Education Act, Summary Report, n.p.). Among the NSEP goals is support of diversified student participation in study abroad as well.
50. Ibid.

51. Christopher Powers [deputy director, U.S. Student Programs, IIE], e-mail correspondence, 25 January 2005. Powers grants that the table below, which he provided, does not include every applicant or recipient, since not everyone answered this question.

	Male	Female	Total
2004 Applicants	399 (46.1)	467 (53.9)	866
Recipients	90 (50.0)	91 (50.0)	181 (20.9)
2003 Applicants	346 (45.2)	419 (54.8)	765
Recipients	83 (45.4)	100 (54.6)	183 (23.9)
2002 Applicants	271 (39.8)	410 (60.2)	681
Recipients	84 (43.3)	110 (56.7)	194 (28.5)
2001 Applicants	156 (38.0)	255 (62.0)	411
Recipients	54 (41.2)	77 (58.8)	131 (31.9)
2000 Applicants	159 (38.3)	256 (61.7)	415
Recipients	52 (40.9)	75 (59.1)	127 (30.6)

52. Benjamin A. Gilman International Scholarships, http://www.iie.org/gilman. The program was founded under the Academic Opportunity Act of 2000. It is sponsored by the U.S. Department of State, Bureau of Educational and Cultural Affairs, and administered by the Institute of International Education.
53. This data was calculated from the list of awardees posted by name at http://www.iie.org/programs/gilman/stats/scholars.html. Of these names, 114 names were female and the balance male or indeterminate. Thus 67 percent of awardees could be confirmed as female. Thirty-four of the 170 students, or 20 percent, attended Western European programs.
54. Sarah Phillips [senior program coordinator, Gilman International Scholarship Program], e-mail correspondence, 25 August 2004.
55. Ruth M. Sylte, e-mail correspondence, 5 April 1996.
56. Ibid.
57. Council on International Educational Exchange, Study Abroad Facts and Myths, http://www.ciee.org/. Also see a similar listing in Peterson's study abroad guide, http://www.petersons.com/stdyabrd/abroad2.html.
58. *Mapping Internationalization*, 44. Sixty percent expressed strong interest in work or study abroad and believed it could enhance their resumes.
59. Ibid, 7.
60. Ibid, 44.
61. "Evaluation of Initiative," *Internationalizing the Curriculum*, 63–65.
62. Thorp, *Neilson of Smith*, 193–199.
63. Delfor Alumni Directories, 1933–35 (Box 53, AR 97, University of Delaware Archives). At that point in its history, the Society included 138 men and 245 women, according to Delfor Alumni Directories.
64. Edwin C. Byam, letter to alumni, 26 January 1933 (Alumni Questionnaire, AR 97, Folder 1639, Delfor, University of Delaware Archives).

65. Delfor Alumni Association, Committee on Foreign Study Alumni Survey, especially questions regarding Alumnae Occupations and Business Affiliations, Box 53, AR 97, 33/0/8, University of Delaware Archives.
66. Ibid.
67. Ibid.
68. Ibid.
69. Ibid.
70. "Delforean," Listing of Former Alumni, 1923–36 (unnumbered insert, *Record Book*. Box 52, AR 96, Folder 1645, University of Delaware Archives).
71. Mrs. Beatrice F. Davis, interview for the University of Delaware Oral History Project by Myron L. Lazarus, 15 July 1970, University of Delaware Paris Program Class of 1931, AR 97, 33/1/1, University of Delaware Archives), 29.
72. Pace, *Junior Year*; Rogers, *American Juniors*, 16.
73. Rogers, *American Juniors*, 21.
74. Sanders and Ward, *Bridges to Understanding*, 92.
75. Ibid.
76. Koester, *Profile*.
77. Ibid. When students who chose U.S.-sponsored programs abroad were asked, "What are your personal goals in taking this trip?," 38 percent answered "knowledge of country," 29 percent "improving language ability," and 18 percent "improving academic performance." In 1985, the option most frequently selected (by 38% of respondents) was "improving education." Twenty-two percent cited that their personal goal in taking the trip was "to improve foreign language ability," 21 percent "to improve their knowledge of the country" (24, 29). Fewer than 9 percent of students each year associated their goals with social travel, personal development, or pleasure. Sixty-nine percent of respondents were women (29).
    Of the students enrolling directly in foreign universities, 56 percent were female. In 1984, 34 percent of this group said they had pursued study abroad to improve foreign language ability; 31 percent to improve their knowledge of the host country. In 1985, within this same group, 42 percent indicated that they chose study abroad to "improve my education," 24 percent to "improve foreign language ability" (30–31).
    Among those who created independent study experiences, 60 percent were female. Of these students, in 1984, 34 percent were motivated to improve their knowledge of the country; 28 percent to improve their foreign language ability; and 21 percent to improve their academic performance. In 1985, 45 percent said they chose foreign study to improve their education; 19 percent to improve foreign language ability (38, 43). Even among students studying independently for credit, few associated study abroad with pleasurable travel, leisure travel, or interpersonal development.
    Of all the modes, the one most often associated with leisure is the study tour. Participants visit multiple sites, so study-tour opportunities emphasize travel. Koester's study found that answers from this group of

students differed markedly from others. Their primary goal was to improve knowledge of the country (57% in 1984, 45% in 1985). In 1985, furthermore, 29 percent of this group considered "improving education" an important goal (67, 72).

78. Ibid., 24–72.
79. Ibid.
80. Ibid.
81. Ayres et al., "CIEE Market Study."
82. Ibid., 18.
83. Ibid., 19.
84. Gillespie and Slawson, *IES Outcomes Assessment Project.*
85. Amy Ruhter McMillan and Gayly Opem, "Tips for the Road: Study Abroad, A Lifetime of Benefits," *Abroad View Magazine,* Spring 2004, http://www.abroadviewmagazine.com/spring_04/study.html.
86. Koester, *Profile,* 114.
87. Brian Whalen, "Summary of Study Abroad Alumni Research, Dickinson College," presentation at PACIE Conference, 28 November 2001, online at http://www.dickinson.edu/global/global_ed_research/index.html.
88. Mary Louise Tylor, "Study Abroad," in Asa S. Knowles, editor-in-chief, *International Encyclopedia of Higher Education,* vol. 4 (D-F) (San Francisco: Jossey Bass Publishers, 1977), 1518; cited in Briggs and Burn, *Study Abroad.* See also Hoffa, Pearson, and Slind, eds., *NAFSA's Guide* (1993).
89. Rudolph, *American College and University,* 87, 125–140, 157–171, 341; Mabel Newcomer, *A Century of Higher Education for American Women* (Washington: Zenger Publishing Co, 1959), 73, 74, 134, 176–179; Solomon, *In the Company,* 130–131.
90. Rudolph, *American College and University,* 87.
91. Margaret W. Rossiter, "Doctorates for American Women, 1868–1907," *History of Education Quarterly,* Summer 1982. Women's numbers eventually urged a "change in policy, which could now be seen as harmless, 'only fair,' long overdue, and quietly enacted" (161).
92. Solomon, *In the Company,* 134–135.
93. Ibid., 136.
94. Ibid., 138; see 132–140.
95. Rudolph, *American College and University,* 340–334; Brubacher and Rudy, *Higher Education,* 121–136, 198–210, 465–466, 447–449.
96. Newcomer, *A Century of Higher Education,* 79. The only exception to the 10 percent measure of maximum female participation in any of the disciplinary programs was pharmacy, where by 1956 10.7 percent of degree recipients were women.
97. Patricia A. Graham, "Expansion and Exclusion: A History of Women in American Higher Education," *Signs: Journal of Women in Culture and Society* 3, no. 4 (Summer 1978); reprinted in Goodchild and Wechsler, *ASHE Reader,* 417, citing statistics from Rudolph C. Blitz, "Women in the Professions, 1870–1970," *Monthly Labor Review,* no. 5 (May 1974), 37.
98. Solomon, *In the Company,* 126.
99. Ibid.

100. National education statistics reveal that in 2001–02, among thirteen broadly inclusive humanities, social science, and interdisciplinary areas, men exceeded women in only two areas: 1) philosophy and religion, and 2) theological studies and religious vocations. In contrast, among fourteen broadly inclusive science and technology areas, female degree recipients exceeded male in only one area: the health professions and related sciences, a category that included nursing. Women clearly dominated in degrees awarded in education and recreation. Interestingly, in the two categories representing business degrees, either more were awarded to women or women were not far behind, a change from the past. Laura G. Knapp et al., *Postsecondary Institutions in the United States: Fall 2002 and Degrees and Other Awards Conferred: 2001–02* (Washington, D.C.: National Center for Education Statistics, U.S. Department of Education, 2003), 38–40.

101. Ibid.

102. In 2002, for example, only 10.8 percent of all engineers, 30.6 percent of all doctors, and 29.2 percent of all lawyers were women (Barbara Wootton, "Gender Differences in Occupational Employment," *Monthly Labor Review,* April 1997, 16–17). Female faculty, too, report that the higher education environment remains discriminatory. In an example that recalls the voices of those in the later nineteenth and earlier twentieth centuries who worried that the presence of women in social science classrooms would devalue the worth of the emerging social sciences, reporter Robin Wilson questioned the outcome of a trend today. Women are emerging as the majority among anthropology graduate students and assistant professors, but, asked Wilson, "does the shift have a downside? If anthropology becomes a mostly female field, will it go the way of other female-dominated professions and lose prestige and pay?" Jane H. Hill, a professor of anthropology at the University of Arizona and a past president of the American Anthropological Association, commented, "It's not that I'm not delighted" by the influx of women, "but I do worry about the larger picture. Are we going to become the nursing of social science, with low salaries, low prestige, and discrimination? Women encounter all of those things in academia" (Robin Wilson, "The 'Feminization' of Anthropology," *Chronicle of Higher Education,* 18 April 2003, A-13; http://chronicle.com/ prm/weekly/v49/i32/32a01301.htm/).

103. *Statistical Abstract of the United States,* 123rd edition (Washington, D.C.: U.S. Bureau of the Census Table, 2003), Table 591, 387.

104. Newcomer, *A Century of Higher Education,* 178.

105. In her chapter, "The Promises of a Liberal Education—Forgotten and Fulfilled," Barbara Solomon wrote, "More women in the United States had gained access to higher education at the start of World War II than in other modern countries, yet this access did not ensure that they could use that education as fully as men could," wrote Solomon. "Liberal education had made a real difference in women's lives, but their choices were still limited by personal inhibitions as well as public barriers. The course of development of the educated woman did not become any simpler in the next four decades" (Solomon, *In the Company,* 186ff.).

106. For many women, particularly in the late nineteenth and early twentieth century, volunteerism was an avenue to meaningful work in spite of the perception of women as marital spouses, adjuncts, and servants to society (see Horowitz, *Alma Mater,* 209; Solomon, *In the Company,* 124, 172; Newcomer, *History of Higher Education,* 223, 227–30; Lemons, *The Woman Citizen,* viii- xi; and Daphne Spain, *How Women Saved the City* [Minneapolis: University of Minnesota Press, 2001]). The academic community has not considered volunteer work a bonafide professional use of education. Jacques Barzun described the path of the young college-educated woman who "topped off college with shorthand and typewriting in case of need" and found "semi-responsible office work." "A few," he granted, "are real executives or specialists," but most are full-time housewives and mothers, willing to volunteer but actually debilitated by their education: "Of these, the most energetic may work for the League of Women Voters, or some benevolent organization. But usually their college training never comes into play; indeed they are probably handicapped by four years of leisure and learning for the battle of life over crib and stove" (Jacques Barzun, *Teacher in America* (New York: Doubleday Anchor Books, 1954), 212.
107. Olmsted, *Sixty Years,* 5, 6.
108. Pace, *Junior Year,* 15, 16.
109. Matthew, *Twenty-Five Years,* 2–3.
110. Aureta E. Lewis, "Letters from a Junior in France" [1938], University of Delaware Archive 33/0/1, Box C, AR 44, Folder C-15, page 2.
111. Delfor Alumni Association, Alumni Questionnaire (1933), AR 97, Folder 1639, "Delfor," University of Delaware Archives.
112. Olmsted, "Sixty Years," 6.
113. *JYF,* 1974–1978, Sweet Briar Junior Year Abroad Alumni Newsletter (Sweet Briar, Va.: Sweet Briar College, 1979).
114. See Stephen Cooper and Mary Anne Grant, "The Demographics of Education Abroad," in Hoffa, Pearson, and Slind, eds., *NAFSA's Guide* (1993), 96; and Koester, *Profile,* 13.
115. Cited in Norman L. Kauffmann, Judith N. Martin, Henry D. Weaver, with Judy Weaver, *Students Abroad, Strangers at Home—Education for a Global Society* (Yarmouth, Maine: Intercultural Press, 1992), 113; see also the Carlson study (the abridged version of the Elinor Barber/Barbara Burn study): J. S. Carlson, B. B. Burn, J. Useem, and D. Yachimowicz, *Study Abroad: The Experience of American Undergraduates in Western Europe and in the United States* (Westport, Conn.: Greenwood Press, 1990).
116. Koester, *Profile,* 67, 38, 31, 24.
117. Gillespie and Slawson, *IES Outcomes Assessment Project.*
118. Fields of Study of U.S. Study Abroad Students, 1993/94—2002/03, *Open Doors 2004.*
119. *A National Mandate,* 4; Briggs and Burn, *Study Abroad,* 49.
120. Barbara Burn, "Progress Report: Education Abroad in the 1990s, Are We Moving in the Right Direction?," *Transitions Abroad* 17, no. 2 (September/October 1993), 67.

121. Cooper and Grant, "The Demographics," in Hoffa, Pearson, and Slind, *NAFSA's Guide* (1993), 94; they cite *NCISPA Newsletter,* U.S. Department of Education Centers for International Education, No. 2, Jan. 1990, 7–9.

122. Briggs and Burn, *Study Abroad,* 49. Domestic undergraduate enrollments grew 4.44 percent between 2001–02 and 2002–03, as calculated from projections of enrollments in four-year public plus four-year private schools for 2002 and 2003 (http://www.nces.ed.gov//programs/projections/tables/table_17.asp/). However, in the same period, study abroad enrollments increased by 8.5 percent"(Study Abroad Surging," press release, 15 November 2004, http://opendoors.iienetwork.org/?p=50138).

123. Todd Davis, e-mail correspondence, 20 May 1998; Pritchett, e-mail correspondence, 21 May 1998.

124. For 1991–1992 BUNAC data, see BUNAC, *Work in Britain,* Programme Handbook, 1994, 42. BUNAC data from 1993 to 2004 provided by Jill Tabuteau (e-mail, 31 August 2004).

125. Boston University International Programs, Programs with Internships, http://www.bu.edu/abroad/internships/.

126. Joseph Finkhouse [director of student affairs, Boston University International Programs], e-mail correspondence, 27 January 2005. Only suggestive pieces of information rather than comprehensive data are currently available to analyze the extent of student interest or the gender proportions of that interest in internship placements overseas.

127. Fields of Study of U.S. Study Abroad Students, 1993/94–2002/03, *Open Doors 2004.* In this period, enrollment grew from 1.1 percent to 2.4 percent of majors choosing study abroad.

128. Peter Schiffman, "Science Education Abroad: The Perspective of a Study Abroad Director at a Large Research University," panel presentation, NAFSA: Association of International Educators Conference, Baltimore, MD, 27 May 2004; and, earlier, Jorge Fontana, "Disciplinary Points of View: A Science and Technology," in Allaway and Shorrock, *Dimensions of International Higher Education,* 76.

129. Goodwin and Nacht, *Missing the Boat,* 29–31.

130. Schiffman, "Science Education Abroad."

131. Paul W. Davis, personal interview, Beloit, Wisconsin, 29 October 2004.

132. Al Balkcum, personal interview, Copenhagen, Denmark, 24 June 2004.

133. Niels Gottlieb, "Introduction and Update on DIS: Philosophy, Programs, Services, and Quality Assurance System," panel presentation, "Study Abroad in a Globalized World," Denmark's International Study Program Quintennial International Education Conference, Copenhagen, 23 June 2004.

134. Hogan, e-mail correspondence, 9 August 2004.

135. "Report Sees Widening of College Gender Gap," *Chronicle of Higher Education,* 27 June 2003, A-30.

136. See Undergraduate Degree Programs Most Offered by U.S. Members, AACSB International, the Association to Advance Collegiate Schools of Business, http://www.aacsb.edu/publications/enewsline/archive_data/UG_Degree_Pgm.jpg. Only 41.7 percent of AACSB schools have international business programs.

137. Laura G. Knapp et al., *Postsecondary Institutions in the United States.*
138. U.S. Department of Education, *Digest of Educational Statistics, 1998* (Washington: National Center for Educational Statistics, 1998). See Table 253 in chapter 3: Postsecondary Education.
139. Briggs and Burn, *Study Abroad,* 52.
140. Foucault, *Discipline and Punish,* 194.
141. Ibid. Also see 180–194.
142. Foucault, *Archaeology,* 16.
143. Foucault, *Discipline and Punish,* 183–184; Michel Foucault, "What is Enlightenment?," in Paul Rabinow, ed., *The Foucault Reader* (New York: Pantheon Books), 39.
144. Foucault, *Archaeology,* 172–173; Mourad, *Postmodern Philosophical Critique,* 60; Cohen, interview.

NOTES TO CHAPTER SEVEN

1. Philip G. Altbach, "Resource Review: Perspectives on International Higher Education," *Change,* Vol. 34, no, 3 (May-June 2002), 29–31; http://pqasb.pqarchiver.com/change/.
2. Biddle, *Internationalization: Rhetoric or Reality.*
3. Michel Foucault, *Politics, Philosophy, Culture: Interviews and Other Writings 1977–1984,* trans. Alan Sheridan et al., ed. Lawrence D. Kritzman (New York and London: Routledge, 1988), 155.
4. Ibid.
5. Merquior, *Foucault,* 35.
6. Foucault, *Order of Things,* 50.
7. In *The Archaeology of Knowledge,* Foucault says beliefs can undergo transformation through changes in discursive practices (209).
8. Foucault, *Archaeology,* 16, 192; Foucault, *Birth of the Clinic,* xix. See also Foucault, *Archaeology,* 172–173; Foucault, *Order of Things,* 31; Michel Foucault, "Intellectuals and Power," in *Language, Counter-Memory, Practice,* 207–208; and "Truth and Power" in *Power/Knowledge: Selected Interviews and Other Writings 1972–1977 by Michel Foucault,* Colin Gordon, ed. (New York: Random House, 1980), 126–133.
9. Foucault, *Archaeology,* 16; Cohen, interview, 1 September 1999; Foucault, *Politics, Philosophy, Culture,* 14.
10. Jaclyn Rosebrook-Collignon, e-mail correspondence to SECUSSA, 3 May 2002.
11. For policy authors, resource persons, and advisers, see *Educating For Global Competence,* v; *A National Mandate,* 21–24; *Securing America's Future,* vi.
12. Foucault, *Politics, Philosophy, Culture,* 14.
13. Foucault, *Discipline and Punish,* 218–227; Burchell, Gordon, and Miller, *The Foucault Effect,* 79; Michel Foucault, *Technologies of the Self,* ed. Luther H. Martin, Huck Gutman, and Patrick H. Hutton (Amherst: University of Massachusetts Press, 1988), 19; and Foucault, *Order of Things,* 170.
14. Foucault, *Order of Things,* xxii; Cohen, interview.
15. *Educating for Global Competence,* 9.

16. *A National Mandate*, 13.
17. *Securing America's Future*, 7.
18. Ibid., 2
19. *A National Mandate*, 13.
20. *Securing America's Future*, 10.
21. Lambert, "Study Abroad," 14.
22. Briggs and Burn, *Study Abroad*, 52.
23. Ibid., 39.
24. Ibid.
25. *Securing America's Future*, 2.
26. Ibid., 7.
27. *A National Mandate*, 2.
28. *Securing America's Future*, 2, 7, 9–10.
29. *Educating for Global Competence*, 8.
30. *A National Mandate*, 2.
31. Ibid., 8.
32. *Securing America's Future*, 9.
33. Ibid., 10.
34. Brown, "U.S. Students Abroad," 74.
35. *Educating for Global Competence*, 9.
36. *A National Mandate*, 2.
37. *Securing America's Future*, 13–14.
38. Ibid., 15.
39. Ibid., 2. The report did, however, encourage the study of infrequently taught languages.
40. Munroe, *University of Delaware*, 263, 266–267.
41. *A National Mandate*, 15; *Securing America's Future*, 15.
42. *Securing America's Future*, 11–12. Some of the arguments presented to encourage support for study abroad and, most especially, to appeal to the federal government for support may themselves have run aground amidst the dominant discourse, which so often overlooks serious functional purposes for study abroad. The alternative discourse points to study abroad as a means to achieve international peace and understanding or even to train adequately for the global marketplace, still perceived much better done in domestic classrooms.

When the policy reports argued that study abroad contributes to U.S. economic and political security issues, they did address a discourse about international education which, according to Nancy Ruther, author of *Barely There, Powerfully Present: Thirty Years of U.S. Policy on International Higher Education*, appears to resonate most effectively within the federal government. Ruther argued that economic security and national security motivate successful federal legislation, while loosely defined citizenship arguments are more frequently overlooked (195). For example, the two federally funded scholarship programs supporting undergraduate study abroad connect to this more persuasive dialogue: the National Security Education Program, whose name clearly states the premise, and the Gilman Scholarship which, though not described in security terms, is

housed within the U.S. Department of State (http://exchanges.state.gov/
education/educationusa/abroadgilman.htm#Looking/). Legislation in support of study abroad still remains limited, however.

Security is the focus of the newest task force report, evident in its
very title, *Securing America's Future*, and in its primary argument that
"Americans need enhanced international skills and knowledge to guarantee our national security and economic competitiveness" (4). However, in the policy reports, including sometimes in the most recent, most
arguments for governmental support did not refer to security, either
physical or economic, but instead to the creation of a more internationally competent citizenry. For example, in the 2003 task force report, the
reference to security quoted above was followed by this statement: "An
educational opportunity outside the United States can be among the
most valuable tools for preparing a student to participate effectively in
an increasingly interconnected international community that demands
cross-cultural skills and knowledge" (ibid.).

Without question the task force authors connected the general
motives of peace and international understanding to the more specific
goal of national security. They may have been reacting to the federal
government's apparently persistent exclusion of those motives as sufficient reason to support international education. Sheila Biddle suggested
abandoning altogether the rhetoric of "developing the global citizen"—a
rhetoric that she deems vague and insubstantial (*Internationalization:
Rhetoric or Reality*, 119). It is a rhetoric that has not been validated
within U.S. higher education as a reason to promote study abroad and,
left uncontextualized, it appears insufficient to motivate the federal government as well.

43. *A National Mandate*, 3.
44. Ibid., 4.
45. *Securing America's Future*, 5.
46. Herrin, "It's Time for Advancing Education Abroad," 3.
47. *A National Mandate*, 12.
48. Ibid., 10.
49. *Educating for Global Competence*, 8.
50. *Securing America's Future*, 2.
51. *Educating for Global Competence*, 14.
52. *A National Mandate*, 4, 10.
53. *Securing America's Future*, 8.
54. Carl Herrin, personal interview, April 30, 2004.
55. *Securing America's Future*, 16.
56. Ibid., ii.
57. Mourad, Jr., *Postmodern Philosophical Critique*, 61.
58. Foucault, "Intellectuals and Power," 180–194.
59. Michel Foucault, *The History of Sexuality, Vol. 2: Uses of Pleasure*, transl.
    Robert Hurley (New York: Pantheon Books, 1985), 8; Foucault, *Archaeol-
    ogy*, 16.
60. *Educating for Global Competence*, 17.

61. Stated among the Forum's top goals are "Encouraging outcomes assessment and other research" and "Facilitating data collection" (Forum on Education Abroad, http://www.forumea.org).

62. Foucault, *Politics, Philosophy, Culture,* 155.

63. De Wit, *Internationalization of Higher Education in the United States of America and Europe,* 213.

64. Michel Foucault, "The Eye of Power," in *Power/Knowledge,* 159.

65. Ibid., 212.

66. Herrin, "It's Time for Advancing Education Abroad," 3–4.

67. *The Brave New,* 25.

68. Ibid.

69. "Lay boards and strong presidents, certainly strong by comparison with their counterparts elsewhere, command large administrative staffs located inside the institutions rather than in some central ministry or governmental agency," wrote Martin Trow in "American Higher Education: Past, Present, and Future," in Goodchild and Wechsler, eds., *ASHE Reader,* 618.

70. Brubacher, *On the Philosophy of Higher Education,* 26–27. Also see Kerr, *The Uses of the University,* 25–26.

71. Herrin, "It's Time for Advancing Education Abroad," 3–4.

72. *A National Mandate,* 17.

73. Ibid., 18.

74. *Educating for Global Competence,* vii.

75. Ibid., 15.

76. Carl Herrin, e-mail, 6 May 2004.

77. Madeleine F. Green and Christa Olson, *Internationalizing the Campus: A User's Guide* (Washington, D.C.: American Council on Education Center for Institutional and International Initiatives, 2003), 81.

78. Barbara B. Burn and Ralph H. Smuckler, *A Research Agenda for the Internationalization of Higher Education in the United States: Recommendations and Report* (New York: Association of International Education Administrators, 1995).

79. Margaret Kidd, e-mail correspondence, 13 April 1998; http:\\aieaworld.org.

80. Ned Quigley, interview, 8 June 1998. Today *Frontiers* is housed at Dickinson College and is sponsored by a consortium of colleges, including Arcadia University, Binghamton University, Butler University, Dickinson College, Grinnell College, Harvard University, Macalester College, Middlebury College, Partnership for Global Education of Hobart and William Smith Colleges and Union College, Pomona College, Rutgers University, The School for International Training, Southwest Missouri State University, Tufts University, the University of Southern California, Villanova University, Yale University. *Frontiers* is a strategic partner of the Forum on Education Abroad, http://www.frontiersjournal.com/index-pf.htm/.

81. See http://www.forumea.org/chartermem_opps.html#whatdoes/.

82. Janet Grunwald, personal interview, 19 June 1998; JoAnn McCarthy, personal interview, 9 June 1998.

83. Annmarie Whalen, e-mail correspondence, 21 May 2004.

84. *Journal of Studies in International Education,* http://www.ciee.org/journal.cfm?subnav=journal/. As of June 2004, members included: AIEA: Association of International Education Administrators; CBIE: Canadian Bureau for International Education; CIEE: Council on International Educational Exchange; EAIE: European Association for International Education; IDP: Education Australia; IEASA: International Education Association of South Africa; NAFSA: Association of International Educators; NUFFIC: Netherlands Organization for International Cooperation in Higher Education; UKCOSA: The Council for International Education (United Kingdom); WES: World Education Services.

85. Council on International Educational Exchange, "Association for Studies in International Education (ASIE)," *Journal of Studies in International Education,* http://www.ciee.org/journal.cfm?subnav=journal/.

86. Ibid.

87. The *Journal* circulates primarily to an audience with international education interest, though it is promoted to a general education market and there may be some circulation beyond the international education community, according to Bernie Folan [senior marketing manager at SAGE Publications, London], e-mail correspondence, 27 January 2005. Sage does not release distribution figures.

88. For example, NAFSA's "most recent mailing of *International Educator* was 9,510 copies. Of that, 280 were complimentary subscriptions, 56 were non-NAFSA member paid subscriptions, and the balance went to the NAFSA membership" (Jan Steiner, e-mail correspondence, 17 May 2004). See online at http://www.nafsa.org/content/ProfessionalandEducationalResources/Publications/IE/IeHome.htm.

89. See online at http://www.iienetwork.org/?p=34243/. IIE prints 5,000 copies of the *IIENetworker Magazine,* of which approximately 3,500 go to IIE members (including U.S. study abroad advisers, international student advisers, international education professionals around the world, university presidents, and others in the educational community). The remaining 1,500 are distributed to subscribers and at international education conferences (Daniel Obst [managing editor, *IIENetworker Magazine*], e-mail correspondence, 28 October 2004.

90. David Comp, SECUSSA Research Committee Annual Report, e-mail correspondence, 14 May 2004). Kidd, e-mail correspondence, 13 April 1998.

91. Ann Kelleher, with Lance Schachterle and Francis C. Lutz, co-eds., *Learning from Success: Campus Case Studies in International Program Development* (New York: Peter Lang, 1996), 417. Kelleher notes that her research reinforces similar findings by Joseph S. Johnston, Jr., and Richard J. Edelstein in *Beyond Borders: Profiles in International Education* (Washington: Association of American Colleges, 1993), whose final chapter argues that one of the most important factors in building successful programs is to engage faculty.

92. Ibid.

93. See "Publications" on the AACSB website, http://www.aacsb.edu/publications. The organization's publications include *BizEd and Enewsline,* superseding the paper edition of *NEWSLINE.* All AACSB publications are archived online. See also G. Tomas M. Hult and Elvin C. Lashbrooke, eds., *Study Abroad: Perspectives and Experiences from Business Schools* (Amsterdam & Boston: JAI, 2003).

94. http://www.abet.org/about.html.

95. See report online at http://center.acs.org/stratplan/strategicplan04.pdf.

96. Division of Chemical Education, http://divched.chem.wisc.edu/index.html.

97. Geoffrey Davies, "Experiential, Cooperative, and Study Abroad Education," *Journal of Chemical Education,* vol. 73, no. 5 (May 1996), 438. Online abstract at http://www.jce.divched.org/Journal/Issues/1996/May/abs438.html.

98. As stated during open discussion forums by Nigel Rogers during a preconference workshop, "Overcoming Barriers to Study Abroad for Science Students: Strategies and Success," CIEE Conference at Atlanta, Georgia, 6 November 2002, and, more recently, during Schiffman's talk, "Science Education Abroad: Who What When Where How and Why." Also voicing such observations during the same CIEE workshop was Lawrie Davidson, both during the same CIEE workshop and in papers written as chair of the CIEE Working Party, "Study abroad for science and engineering students: Barriers to students and strategies for change," Progress Report of the CIEE Working Party on Science Study Abroad, 17 March 2003, revised for distribution 10 July 2003.

99. Peter Hudleston, Plenary Session, "Internationalizing the Curriculum." See also http://www.abet.org/about.html.

100. See Task Force and Sounding Board Organizations in *A National Mandate,* 21–22.

101. Foucault, *Archaeology,* 3–17.

102. Mestenhauser, "In Search of a Comprehensive Approach," 167. One limitation to future research, especially that which is grounded in history, is the lack of material chronicling study abroad program development. To date, no comprehensive history of the development of study abroad in the United States has been completed. Few program records have been archived. It is still possible to develop a documentary field for investigation, however, for example through library archives or private program collections; individual programs records, which offer a wealth of material, although often uncatalogued; and surveys to collect relevant research data.

   Fruitful research topics might include issues reflecting shared ideals and commonly identified needs between those who participate in the academy's dominant discourse devaluing study abroad and those who voice the alternative vision of its worth. For example, both groups are concerned with the role of globalization in the higher education curriculum, including implications of increasing web-based technologies for domestic and foreign education. For examples of topics held in common, see Marshall McLuhan and Bruce R. Powers, *The Global Village: Transformation in the World Life and Media in the 21st Century* (New York: Oxford University Press, 1989); Marshall

McLuhan and Quentin Fiore, produced by Jerome Gael, *The Medium is the Massage* (New York: Touchstone, 1989, 1967); Marshall McLuhan and Quentin Fiore, coordinated by Jerome Agel, *War and Peace in the Global Village: An Inventory of Some of the Current Spastic Situations that could be Eliminated by more Feedforward* (New York: McGraw-Hill, 1968); Manuel Castells (editor), Ramon Flecha, Paulo Freire, Henry A. Giroux, Peter McLaren, *Critical Education in the New Information Age* (Maryland: University Press of America, Critical Perspectives Series, 1999); Manuel Castells, *The Information Age: Economy, Society, and Culture,* three volumes (Oxford: Blackwell, 1996–1998; 2nd edition, 2000); Richard W. Riley, "The Growing Importance of International Education"; Philip G. Altbach, "Higher Education Crosses Borders," *Change,* Vol. 36, no. 2 (March/April 2004), http://pqasb.pqarchiver.com/change/; Hayward and Siaya, *Public Experience, Attitudes, and Knowledge,* 43 n1; Jane Knight and Hans de Wit, *Internationalisation of Higher Education in Asia Pacific Countries* (Amsterdam: European Association for International Education, 1997), 6; Philip Altbach, "Resource Review: Perspectives on International Higher Education," *Change,* Vol. 34, no. 3 (May/June 2002), http://pqasb.pqarchiver.com/change/; *Journal of Studies in International Education* (suggested by Bernie Folan, e-mail correspondence, 18 June 2004); and Manuel Castells, *The Internet Galaxy: Reflections on Internet, Business, and Society* (London & New York: Oxford University Press, 2001).

Both constituencies may be concerned about gender issues in education. On this see, for example, Elizabeth A. Duffy, with Idana Goldberg, *Crafting a Class: College Admissions and Financial Aid, 1955–1994* (Princeton: Princeton University Press, 1998); Ann Diller, with Maryann Ayim and Kathryn Morgan, *The Gender Question in Education: Theory, Pedagogy, and Politics* (Boulder: Westview Press, 1996); Judith Glazer-Raymo, *Shattering the Myths: Women in Academe* (Baltimore: Johns Hopkins University Press, 1999); American Association of University Women, *How Schools Shortchange Girls* (Washington: AAUW Educational Foundation, National Education Association, 1992); and Sheena Erskine and Maggie Wilson, eds., *Gender Issues in International Education: Beyond Policy and Practice,* vol. 1162, Garland Reference Library of Social Science (New York: Falmer Press, 1999). Erskine and Wilson's publication is a study in cross-cultural gender and education issues. Greater exploration is needed about male conceptions of study abroad: Why do men go abroad? How do they identify their role in a female-dominated educational setting?

Joint research might be also encouraged in arenas such as culture study, an emerging topic for discussion among domestic educators, and the curricular core of study abroad programs. Only passing commentary exists in the historical literature about culture study. See, for example, W. F. Hull, W. H. Lemke, and R. T. Houang, "Introduction" in *The American Undergraduate, Off Campus and Overseas: A Study of the Educational Validity of Such Programs* (New York: CIEE, 1977); John A. Wallace, "Characteristics of Programs for Study Abroad," 255; Manuel Castells's trilogy, *The Information Age;* E. D. Hirsch, Jr., *Cultural Literacy: What Every American Needs to Know* (New York: Vintage Books, 1988); and Michael Peters, ed., *After the Disciplines: The Emergence of Cultural Studies* (Westport, Conn.: Bergin & Garvey, 1999).

Common goals for international peace and understanding, global competency skills, and now political and economic security—all are likewise arenas for study. On this topic, see John Paul Lederach, *Preparing for Peace: Conflict Transformation Across Cultures* (Syracuse, N.Y.: Syracuse University Press, 1996); Elise Boulding, *Building a Global Civic Culture: Education for an Interdependent World* (Syracuse, N.Y.: Syracuse University Press, 1990); Munroe, *University of Delaware,* 263; Rogers, *American Juniors,* 12; Stohlman, *The Story of Sweet Briar College,* 198–205.

Finally, the role of liberal education in preparing undergraduate students for the world of work clearly needs further study. See, for example, William G. Durden, "The Liberal Arts as a Bulwark of Business Education," *Chronicle of Higher Education,* 18 July 2003, http://chronicle.com/prm/weekly/v49/i45/45b02001.htm/. The topics of curriculum development and quality assurance in study abroad also deserve further consideration. See, for example, Joan Gillespie, "Colleges Need Better Ways to Assess Study-Abroad Programs," *Chronicle of Higher Education,* B20, 5 July 2002, and *Securing America's Future,* 15.

Appendix
Supplementary Charts and Tables

Table 2–1: Sweet Briar Alumni Survey, Question 18
Identify the Primary Reason for Women Participating in Study Abroad

If you are a woman who participated in study abroad, do you see the primary reason for women participating in study abroad being:	Yes	No
a. Their cultural interests	93.2%	6.3%
b. Their desire to grow independently	75.1%	24.3%
c. Their career interests	42.9%	56.4%
d. Their desire to find a more supportive educational environment than they experienced at home	7.5%	91.8%

No. of responses	a.	b.	c.	d.
Yes	177	130	92	12
No	12	42	70	146
Total	189	172	162	158

Table 2–2: Sweet Briar Alumni Survey, Question 10
Why More Women than Men?

Why do you think it has been more frequently undergraduate women than men from the United States who have studied abroad?*	Males	Females
a. Men need to stay in the U.S. and focus on job training in their college education.	54.1%	41.9%
b. Women more frequently than men are interested in understanding and supporting art and culture.	88.9%	87.5%
c. Women are more capable of learning foreign languages.	21.9%	31.1%
d. Women feel overseas living and study is an important opportunity for self-development and independence which men can usually attain within their U.S. environment.	55.2%	57.3%
e. Women have fewer opportunities for experimentation and growth than men on the U.S. campus.	32.3%	26.5%
f. None of the above	0.0%	64.7%
g. Other	100%	100%

	a.	b.	c.	d.	e.	f.	g.
Males	20	32	7	16	10	0	11
Females	75	161	55	98	44	11	47
Total no. of respondents	216	220	209	200	197	18	58

* Note: respondents could choose more than one response. Cross-tabulations refer to those who responded 'yes' to a-g.

Table 2–3: Sweet Briar Alumni Survey, Question 13, Reasons for Study Abroad.

Did you go abroad to:	Males	Females
a. enhance career skills	82.4%	76.0%
b. broaden your cultural horizon	100%	99.0%
c. develop your independence	100%	88.1%
d. other	85.7%	53.2%

	a.	b.	c.	d.
Males	14	39	22	12
Females	79	191	119	33

Table 2–4: University of Delaware Foreign Study Plan
Paris Program Gender Analysis, 1923–24 to 1939–40

	Total number	Men	Women	Unidentified
1923–24	7	7	0	0
1924–25	5	4	1	0
1925–26	13	7	6	0
1926–27	43	15	28	0
1927–28	39	12	27	0
1928–29	61	16	42	3
1929–30	65	14	50	1
1930–31	56	13	42	1
1931–32	88	18	66	4
1932–33	60	12	43	5
1933–34	42	8	31	3
1934–35	34	6	26	2
1935–36	38	8	30	0
1936–37	34	8	26	0
1937–38	52	10	41	1
1938–39	51	9	40	2
1939–40	40	12	26	2
TOTALS	728	179	525	24

This is a count of all participants identified through Delfor, the University of Delaware Foreign Study Alumni Association. This analysis is done by name identification—identifying
female names, male names, other (unidentified by gender) names.

Source: Delfor Alumni Association, Foreign Study Plan Records, Box 52 (AR52) (AR96),
Folder 1623, 33/0/8.

Table 3–1: Summary of Sweet Briar Junior Year in France Groups
1948–49 to 2003–04

Group	Women	Men	Total	Colleges represented in enrollment
1. 1948–49	34	33	67	32
2. 1949–50	53	20	73	33
3. 1950–51	60	19	79	31
4. 1951–52	57	23	80	34
5. 1952–53	70	16	86	35
6. 1953–54	62	19	81	30
7. 1954–55	61	22	83	38
8. 1955–56	59	27	86	41
9. 1956–57	61	26	87	42
10. 1957–58	55	29	84	44
11. 1958–59	65	26	91	49
12. 1959–60	62	28	90	44
13. 1960–61	63	34	97	22
14. 1961–62	76	26	102	51
15. 1962–63	67	43	110	45

Table 3–1: Summary of Sweet Briar Junior Year in France Groups (continued)

Group	Women	Men	Total	Colleges represented in enrollment
16. 1963–64	63	42	105	45
17. 1964–65	73	36	109	51
18. 1965–66	72	38	110	45
19. 1966–67	72	34	106	49
20. 1967–68	68	33	101	40
21. 1968–69	62	40	102	51
22. 1969–70	65	34	99	45
23. 1970–71	73	29	102	51
24. 1971–72	71	35	106	40
25. 1972–73	82	25	107	47
26. 1973–74	96	27	123	50
27. 1974–75	95	27	122	47
28. 1975–76	100	24	124	44
29. 1976–77	93	30	123	35
30. 1977–78	83	31	114	40
31. 1978–79	79	31	110	36
32. 1979–80	86	29	115	34
33. 1980–81	92	25	117	37
34. 1981–82	92	25	117	34
35. 1982–83	89	27	116	30
36. 1983–84	90	28	118	37
37. 1984–85	92	30	122	33
38. 1985–86	87	31	118	31
39. 1986–87	96	19	115	42
40. 1987–88	107	29	136	41
41. 1988–89	115	23	138	52
42. 1989–90	111	21	132	49
43. 1990–91	101	24	125	38
44. 1991–92	101	18	119	38
45. 1992–93	75	18	93	36
46. 1993–94	85	19	104	37
47. 1994–95	81	17	98	31
48. 1995–96	78	14	92	26
49. 1996–97	98	11	109	33
50. 1997–98	76	15	91	28
51. 1998–99	77	20	97	26
52. 1999–00	60	7	67	27
53. 2000–01	72	25	97	26
54. 2001–02	86	15	101	30
55. 2002–03	80	10	90	30
56. 2003–04	102	12	114	30
TOTAL	4,381	1,419	5,800	

As of February 2004
Provided by Dr. Margaret Scouten, Director, Sweet Briar Junior Year in France Program.

Table 3–2: Sweet Briar Alumni Survey, Question 10, Written Responses

Question 10: Why do you think it has been more frequently undergraduate women than men from the United States who have studied abroad?

- A romanticization of foreign cultures based on childhood fantasy and personal dreams.
- I found in studying French that most men find French to be a "sissy language."
- I think many are more enamored by the idea of spending time in a foreign country than men.
- I think with French specifically, men consider it a "gay," therefore undesirable, language to study.
- I think, for this age group (20–22), women for the most part are more focused on long-term goals.
- It is more accepted (culturally) for the female gender to have an interest in arts and culture.
- Men do not generally prefer what is foreign to them.
- Men do not tend to study foreign languages with the depth necessary for study abroad.

- Men focus on studies that do not involve going abroad . . .
- Men get too comfortable in the cocoons of frats and sports. They tend to follow the easy path.
- Men see language study as not being a male-type course. Men are more devoted to sports.
- More difficult to complete a degree in math/science/engineering on time and do study abroad.
- Perhaps women are more adventurous when it comes to creating a new group of friends.
- Specifically, French is considered a more feminine language.
- Women are more comfortable taking risks in experiences that might affect their identity.
- Women are more open in general. They have tolerance. They are dreamers and would like adventures.

Table 3–3: Sweet Briar Alumni Survey, Question 20
Impediments to Study Abroad

Did you encounter beliefs which impeded your study abroad pursuits?
Question 20, part 2, for those who said "Yes" in part 1.
What were those impediments?

	Males	Females
c. Faculty belief that your discipline could best be studied in the U.S.	43%	52%
d. Faculty belief that study abroad was not serious	29%	52%
e. Faculty suspicion of study abroad	43%	34%
f. Faculty perception (contrary to reality) that you had no career goals	29%	31%

	c.	d.	e.	f.
Males	3	2	3	2
Females	15	15	10	9

Table 3–4: Sweet Briar Alumni Survey, Question 11
Socioeconomic Status at Time of Study

How would you define your socio-economic status at the time of your participation in study abroad?	Males	Females
a. Upper class	4.4%	10.2%
b. Upper middle class	35.6%	48.8%
c. Middle class	44.4%	33.7%
d. Lower middle class	8.9%	5.4%
e. Upper/lower class	4.4%	0.5%
f. Lower class	0%	0.5%
g. other	2.2%	1.0%

	a.	b.	c.	d.	e.	f.	g.
Males	2	16	20	4	2	0	1
Females	21	100	69	11	1	1	2

Table 3–5: Sweet Briar Alumni Survey, Question 12
Financing Study Abroad

How did you finance your study abroad experience?	Males	Females	Total
a. Family paid	48.0%	75.5%	70.8%
b. You worked and paid	20.0%	11.0%	14.4%
c. You received scholarship support which was necessary in order to be able to afford study abroad	30.0%	9.5%	14.8%
d. You received financial aid in the form of federal or state loan programs, work study, etc.	16.0%	10.5%	12.8%
e. Combination of the above	34.0%	30.5%	32.0%
f. Other	2.0%	1.0%	2.8%

	a.	b.	c.	d.	e.	f.
Males	24	10	15	8	17	1
Females	151	22	19	21	61	2

*Note: This table is calculated from all students surveyed, not from students answering the question.

Table 4–1: Sweet Briar Alumni Survey, Question 15
Student Majors Prior to Study Abroad

Prior to your study abroad experience what was your planned or declared academic major?	Male	Female
a. Humanities	22.2%	11.9%
b. Social Science	13.3%	5.4%
c. Foreign Language	33.3%	57.5%
d. Science	11.1%	3.0%
e. Political Science	2.2%	7.9%
f. Engineering	2.2%	0%
g. Business	0%	2.0%
h. Pre-Law	6.7%	2.9%
i. Other	8.9%	9.9%

	a.	b.	c.	d.	e.	f.	g.	h.	i.
Male	10	6	15	5	1	1	0	3	4
Female	24	11	116	6	16	0	4	5	20

Table 5–1: Sweet Briar Alumni Survey, Question 19: Deciding Factors

Were any of these factors important in helping you decide to go abroad?*	Males	Females
a. your ethnic background and your desire to explore your roots	6.7%	8.8%
b. previous travel	48.9%	58.0%
c. your family's interest in international issues and preferences	37.8%	36.6%
d. your friendship with foreign individuals	22.2%	29.3%
e. your academic interests	68.9%	74.6%
f.a. A male faculty member who encouraged you	35.6%	17.1%
f.b. A female faculty member who encouraged you	4.4%	21.0%
g. other	20.0%	24.4%

	a.	b.	c.	d.	e.	f.a.	f.b.	g.
Males	3	22	17	10	31	16	2	9
Females	18	119	75	60	153	35	43	50

* Note: Respondents could choose more than one response. Cross-tabulations refer to those who responded "yes" to a–g. (n=250)

Table 5–2: Sweet Briar Alumni Survey, Question 23
Source of Information on Program

How did you hear about the Sweet Briar program?	Male	Females
a. From a study abroad advisor	15.6%	22.4%
b. From a faculty member	53.3%	46.5%
c. From a friend/peer who had attended the program	22.2%	15.6%
d. From a friend/peer who had heard about the program	6.7%	6.3%
e. From a parent or other adult relative	0%	9.3%
f. From a poster	2.2%	2.4%
g. From program literature	17.8%	23.4%
h. Other	6.7%	5.4%

	a.	b.	c.	d.	e.	f.	g.	h.	Total
Males	7	24	10	3	0	1	8	9	45
Females	46	95	32	13	19	5	48	11	205

Table 6–1: Sweet Briar Alumni Survey, Question 1
Intentions for Graduate Study, Professional Study, or a Career

Question 1: Before you did your study abroad program, did you hope to pursue a graduate or professional study or a career after graduation?	Male	Female
a. yes	88.9%	80.8%
b. no	8.9%	14.8%
c. other	2.2%	4.4%

	Yes	No	Other
Males	40	4	1
Females	164	30	9

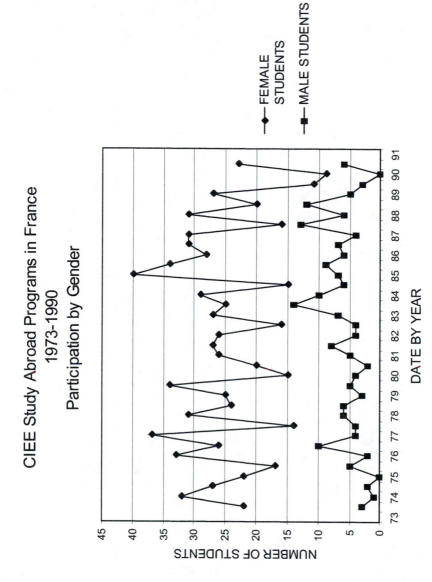

Figure 6-1: Part 1

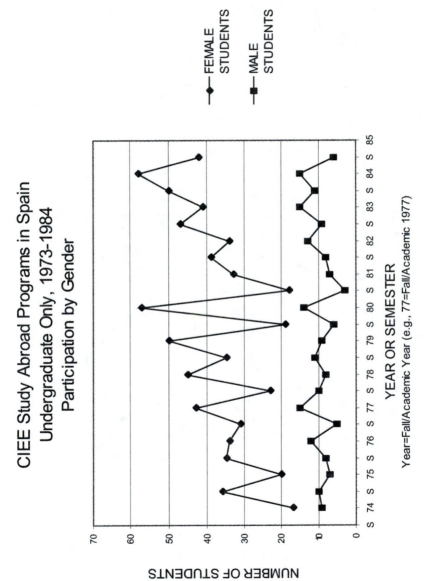

Figure 6-1: Part 2

Table 6–2: Sweet Briar Alumni Survey, Question 2
Study Abroad as Preparation for Graduate or Professional Study or a Career

Did you feel your study abroad experience could better prepare you for graduate or professional school or a career?		Males	Females
a.	yes	75.0%	68.5%
b.	no	6.8%	6.0%
c.	maybe	2.3%	5.5%
d.	other	0%	2.0%

	Yes	No	Maybe	Other
Males	33	3	1	0
Females	137	12	11	4

Table 6–3: Sweet Briar Alumni Survey, Questions 3 and 5
Professional Study or Career Goals

Question 3: Did your study abroad experience change your graduate or professional education or career goals?		Males	Females
a.	yes	37.8%	27.0%
b.	no	51.1%	53.5%
c.	maybe	11.1%	19.5%

	Yes	No	Maybe
Males	17	23	5
Females	54	107	39

Question 5: Was your study abroad experience directly connected to your graduate, professional or work experiences after you graduated from college?		Males	Females
a.	yes	44.2%	50.2%
b.	no	55.8%	49.3%

	Yes	No
Males	19	24
Females	101	99

Table 6–4: Sweet Briar Alumni Survey, Question 4
Pursuits after College

After college did you pursue:	Males	Females
a. graduate or professional study	90.2%	78.3%
b. a professional or full-time job	73.3%	73.5%
c. a full-time job in a non-professional category	27.8%	35.5%
d. part-time professional work	16.7%	26.3%
e. part-time non-professional work	0%	25.9%
f. volunteer activities	45.0%	70.9%

	a.	b.	c.	d.	e.	f.
Males	37	22	5	3	0	9
Females	141	119	44	31	28	100

*Note: respondents could choose more than one response. Cross-tabulations refer to those who responded 'yes' to a-f.

Bibliography

"2004 Public Policy Priorities: International Education and the Search for Security." *Newsletter, NAFSA: Association of International Educators*, vol. 55, no. 2 (March/April 2004).

Abrams, Irwin, and W. R. Hatch. *Study Abroad, New Dimensions in Higher Education*, No. 6, U.S. Department of Health, Education and Welfare and Office of Education. Washington, D.C.: U.S. Government Printing Office, 1962.

Akande, Yemi, and Carla Slawson. "Exploring the Long-term Impact of Study Abroad: A Case Study of 50 Years of Study Abroad Alumni." *International Educator Magazine*, Summer 2000. http://www.nafsa.org/Template.cfm?NavMenuID=227&Template=/Source/ProfessionalandEducationalResources/Publications/IE/50years%2Ehtm&Preview=True.

Allaway, William. "The American Campus Moves Abroad," in Mathies and Thomas, *Overseas Opportunities: Perspectives and Possibilities*.

—— and Hallam C. Shorrock. *Dimensions of International Higher Education*. The University of California Symposium on International Education Abroad. Boulder, Colo., and London: Westview Special Studies in Education, 1985.

Allen, Henry J. *Student Magellan*. New York: Stanley D. Woodard, 1927.

Altbach, Philip G. *Comparative Higher Education: Knowledge, the University, and Development*. Greenwich, Conn., & London: Ablex Publishing Corp., 1988.

——. "Resource Review: Perspectives on International Higher Education." *Change*, Vol. 34, no. 3 (May/June 2002). http://pqasb.pqarchiver.com/change/.

——. "Higher Education Crosses Borders." *Change*, Vol. 36, no. 2 (March/April 2004). http://pqasb.pqarchiver.com/.

—— and Hans de Wit. "International Higher Education: America Abdicates Leadership." *International Higher Education*, Journal of the Boston College Center for International Higher Education, 1995.

Altschuler, Glenn C. "College Prep: La Dolce Semester." *New York Times*, 8 April 2001, sec. 4A, p. 17, col. 1.

"American Assistants in French Lycees." *School and Society* 18 (25 October 1923).

American Association of University Women. *How Schools Shortchange Girls*. Washington, D.C.: AAUW Educational Foundation, National Education Association, 1992.

American Council on Education. *Campus Trends, 1986.* Higher Education Panel Report No. 73 (August 1986).

———. *Educating Americans for a World in Flux: Ten Ground Rules for Internationalizing Higher Education.* Washington, D.C.: American Council on Education, 1995.

———. *Beyond September 11: A Comprehensive National Policy on International Education.* Washington, D.C.: American Council on Education, 2002.

———. "Higher Education Groups Propose National Policy on International Education." *Higher Education and National Affairs* (online edition), Vol. 51, No. 9, 13 May 2002. http://www.acenet.edu/hena/issues/ 2002/05-13-02/international.ed.cfm

———, Higher Education Panel. *What We Can't Say Can Hurt Us: A Call for Foreign Language Competence by the Year 2000.* Washington, D.C.: American Council on Education, 1989.

"American German Student Exchange Fellowships." *School and Society* 21 (10 June 1925).

Andersen, Claus Elhom. "DIS Response to Study Abroad Challenges of the 21st Century." Panel presentation, "Study Abroad in a Globalized World." Denmark's International Study Program Quintennial International Educators Conference. Copenhagen, 24 June 2004.

Arnold, David. Interview, 15 October 1990.

Arthur, Sister Rita. Interview, 6 August 1997.

Ayres, H. Fairfax III, Andrea Brennan, Michael Clancy, Timothy Cronin, John Druitt, Julie Gibbons, Lois Lynch, Kevin Marks, Debra Stinchfield, Kathryn Young; James Rubin, faculty advisor; Christopher Gale, project supervisor. "CIEE Market Study: Motivations for Study Abroad." Charlottesville, Va.: Darden School of Graduate Business Studies, University of Virginia, May 1996.

Balkcum, Al. Personal interview, 24 June 2004.

Ball, S. J., editor. *Foucault and Education: Disciplines and Knowledge.* London: Routledge, 1990.

Barber, Elinor G., and Barbara B. Burn, editors. *Study Abroad: The Experience of American Undergraduates in Western Europe and in the United States.* Westport, Conn.: Greenwood Press, Inc., 1990.

Barker, Philip. *Michel Foucault, An Introduction.* Edinburgh: Edinburgh University Press, 1998.

Barnett, Vincent M., Jr., editor. *The Representation of the United States Abroad,* revised edition. New York: Frederick A. Praeger, 1965.

Barron's. *Profiles of American Colleges,* 22nd edition. Hauppage, N.Y.: Barron's Educational Series, Inc., 1997.

Bartlett, Thomas. "Academics Discuss How to Explain the Value of the Liberal Arts to Those Who Pay the Bills." *Chronicle of Higher Education,* Today's News, 26 January, 2004. Online at http://chronicle.com/daily/2004/01/2004012605n.htm.

Barzun, Jacques. *Teacher in America.* New York: Doubleday Anchor Books, 1954.

Battle, Edward. Interview, July 1993.

Beaver College Admissions Service. Interview, 30 September 1997.

————————. *1948 Bulletin.* Glenside, Penn.: Beaver College, 1948.

Beck, Hamilton. "W. E. B. Du Bois as a Study Abroad Student in Germany, 1892-1894." In *Frontiers,* online at http://www.frontiersjournal.com/issues/vol2/vol2-03_Beck.htm.

The Bedford Bibliography for Teachers of Writing. http://www.bedfordbooks.com/bb/contents.html

Bennett, Milton J. "Intercultural Communication: A Current Perspective." In Bennett, Milton J., ed. *Basic Concepts of Intercultural Communication: Selected Readings.* New York: Intercultural Press, 1998.

Bernauer, James, and David Rasmussen, editors. *The Final Foucault.* Cambridge, Mass., and London: The MIT Press, 1988.

Bernstein, Elizabeth. "Study-Abroad Programs Grow in Uncertain Times," *Wall Street Journal,* 7 February 2003.

Biddle, Sheila. *Internationalization: Rhetoric or Reality.* ACLS Occasional Paper, No. 56. New York: American Council of Learned Societies, 2002.

Biebucyck, Brunhilde. "Great Expectations: American Students in Paris." Unpublished paper.

Biermann, Melissa. E-mail to SECUSSA discussion list, 21 April 2004.

Biesta, Gert J. J. "Pedagogy Without Humanism: Foucault and the Subject of Education." *A Quarterly Review of Education* 29, 1 (1998). Dordrecht/Boston/London: Kluwer Academic Publishers.

Blankenship, Edward. Director of the Office of International Education, California State University, Long Beach, California. Interviews, April 1989.

Blitz, Rudolph C. "Women in the Professions, 1870-1970." *Monthly Labor Review,* no. 5 (May 1974).

Booth, Jon. Interview, 12 May 1997.

Boulding, Elise. *Building a Global Civic Culture: Education for an Interdependent World.* Syracuse, N.Y.: Syracuse University Press, 1990.

Bowman, John E. *Educating American Undergraduates Abroad: The Development of Study Abroad Programs by American Colleges and Universities.* CIEE Occasional Papers, series no. 24 (1987).

Boyer, Ernest L., and Fred M. Hechinger. *Higher Learning in the Nation's Service.* Washington, D.C.: The Carnegie Foundation for the Advancement of Teaching, 1981.

Brecht, Richard D., and Jennifer L. Robinson. "Qualitative Analysis of Second Language Acquisition in Study Abroad: The ACTR-NFLC Project." National Foreign Language Center and University of Maryland, 1993.

Briggs, Asa, and Barbara Burn. *Study Abroad: A European and an American Perspective, Organization and Impact of Study Abroad.* No. 1, European Institute of Education and Social Policy (Paris, 1985).

Brooks, David. "Yanks go home, Europe's a bore." *The Sunday Times.* 7 July 1996, section 3, page 9.

Brown, Jean F. Personal interview, 7 February 1994.

Brown, M. Archer. "U.S. Students Abroad." In Hugh M. Jenkins and Associates, *Educating Students from Other Nations.*

Brubacher, John S. *On the Philosophy of Higher Education.* San Franciso and London: Jossey-Bass Series in Higher Education, 1977.

————, and Willis Rudy. *Higher Education in Transition: A History of American Colleges and Universities.* New York: Harper & Row, Publishers, Inc. 1976. Reprinted in Wechsler, Harold S., and Lester F. Goodchild. *ASHE Reader on the History of Higher Education.* New York: Ginn Press, 1989.

————. *Higher Education in Transition: A History of American Colleges and Universities.* 4th edition, with new chapters by Willis Rudy. New Brunswick, N.J., and London: Transaction Publishers, 1997.

Bulletin of the University of Delaware. Vol. XXVI, new series, no. 6 (November 1931).

BUNAC (British University's North America Club). *Work in Britain.* Programme Handbook, 1994.

Burchell, G., C. Gordon, and P. Miller. *The Foucault Effect: Studies in Governmentality.* Hemel, Hempstead: Harvester Wheatsheaf, 1991.

Burn, Barbara. *Expanding the International Dimensions of Higher Education,* San Francisco: Jossey-Bass, 1980.

————. "Strength through Wisdom: The Report of the President's Commission on Foreign Language and International Studies." *Independent School* 40, 1 (October 1980).

————. *The Contribution of International Exchange to the International Education of Americans: Projections for the Year 2000.* Occasional Paper, Council on International Educational Exchange. New York: Institute of International Education, 1990.

————. "Progress Report: Education Abroad in the 1990s, Are We Moving in the Right Direction?" *Transitions Abroad* 17, no. 2 (September/October 1993).

————. *The Contribution of International Educational Exchange to the International Education of Americans: My 1990 Forecasts Revisited.* American Institute for Foreign Study. http://www.aifs.org/aifsfoundation/burn.htm. Also published in in Martin Tillman, ed., *Study Abroad: A 21st Century Perspective,* Volume I.

———— and Ralph H. Smuckler. *A Research Agenda for the Internationalization of Higher Education in the United States: Recommendations and Report.* New York: Association of International Education Administrators, 1995.

Byam, Edwin C. Letter to alumni, 26 January 1933. University of Delaware Archives, Alumni Questionnaire, AR 97, Folder 1639, "Delfor."

Carlson, J. S., B. B. Burn, J. Useem, and D. Yachimowicz. *Study Abroad: The Experience of American Undergraduates in Western Europe and in the United States.* Westport, Conn.: Greenwood Press, 1990.

Castells, Manuel. *The Information Age: Economy, Society and Culture. Vol. I: The Rise of the Network Society.* Malden, Mass.: Blackwell Publishers, 1996.

————. *The Information Age: Economy, Society and Culture. Vol. II: The Power of Identity.* Malden, Mass.: Blackwell Publishers, 1997.

————. *The Information Age: Economy, Society and Culture. Vol. III: End of the Millennium.* Malden, Mass.: Blackwell Publishers, 1998.

————. *The Internet Galaxy: Reflections on Internet, Business, and Society.* London and New York: Oxford University Press, 2001.

———— (editor), Ramon Flecha, Paulo Freire, Henry A. Giroux, and Peter McLaren. *Critical Education in the New Information Age* (Critical Perspectives Series). Maryland: University Press of America, 1999.

Cattanès, Hélène. *Vers d'autres horizons, Mémento de l'année en France.* New York/Paris: Association of Former Juniors in France of Smith College, 1965.

Center for Institutional and International Initiatives, American Council for Education. "One Year Later: Attitudes about International Education since September 11," *Public Opinion Poll,* September 2002. http://www.acenet.edu /bookstore/pdf/2002_one-year-later.pdf

Chancey, Edward. *The Grand Tour and the Great Rebellion: Richard Lassels and "The Voyage of Italy" in the Seventeenth Century.* Geneva: Slatkine, 1985.

Chandler, Alice. "Paying the Bill for International Education: Programs, Partners, and Possibilities at the Millennium." *NAFSA Newsletter,* May/June 1999.

Chin, Hey-Kyung Koh. E-mail correspondence, 3 March 2003.

————, ed. *Open Doors 2003: Report on International Educational Exchange.* New York: Institute of International Education, 2003.

Citron, James L. "U.S. Students Abroad: Host Culture Integration of Third Culture Formation?" in Grünzweig and Rinehart, eds., *Rockin' in Red Square.*

Clayton, John M., Jr. *Foreign Study Plan Records, 1922-1948: An Inventory.* University of Delaware Archives, 16 March 1970.

Cleveland, Harlan, Gerard J. Mangone, and John Clarke Adams. *The Overseas Americans.* New York: McGraw-Hill Book Co., Inc., 1960.

Coalition for the Advancement of Foreign Languages and International Studies (CAFLIS). *Reforming Education for the International Century.* Washington, D.C.: CAFLIS, 1989.

Cohen, Ralph. Interview, 1 September 1999.

"The College Cruise Around the World." University Travel Association, 1928.

College Facts. Annual chart, 37th edition, 1992-93. Spartanburg, S.C.: National Beta Club, 1992.

Collignon, Jean. "Le programme des études en France." In Hélène Cattanès, *Vers d'autres horizons, Mémento de l'année en France.*

Commager, Henry Steele. *The American Mind: An Interpretation of American Thought and Character since the 1880's.* New Haven: Yale University Press, 1950.

Comp, David. SECUSSA Research Committee Annual Report. E-mail correspondence, 14 May 2004.

Conant, James B. "America Remakes the University." In John S. Brubacher and Willis Rudy, eds., *Higher Education in Transition: History of American Colleges and Universities.* New York: Harper & Row, Publishers, Inc., 1976. Reprinted from *Atlantic Monthly* (May 1946).

Cooper, Stephen, and Mary Anne Grant. "The Demographics of Education Abroad." In William Hoffa, John Pearson, and Marvin Slind, eds. *NAFSA's Guide to Education Abroad for Advisers and Administrators* (1993).

Council on International Educational Exchange. Oral History Video Tape, December 1993. Part of CIEE Oral History Series.

————. Report on Third World Study Abroad Programs. New York: CIEE, 1993.

————. "Analyzing the 1991-92 Open Doors Survey: Are We There Yet?" *Council on International Educational Exchange Update,* vol. 16, no. 2 (March 1994).

————. Oral History Video Tape, November 1994. Part of CIEE Oral History Series.

————. *Study Abroad Baseline Survey.* New York: CIEE, 1996.

————. "Association for Studies in International Education (ASIE)." Document distributed during 54th Annual CIEE Conference, 11-15 November 1999, Chicago, Ill.

————. *CIEE A World of Opportunity* (2003 Annual Report). New York: CIEE, 2003.

Cremin, Lawrence A. "College." Excerpted from his book, *American Education: The Colonial Experience* (1970), and reprinted in Goodchild, Lester F., and Harold Wechsler, eds. *ASHE Reader on the History of Higher Education.* Needham Heights, Mass.: Ginn Press/Simon & Schuster, 1989.

Cross, Barbara M. *The Educated Woman in America.* Classics in Education, no. 25. New York: Teachers College Press, 1965.

Curti, Merle E. "Intellectuals and Other People," *American Historial Review* 60 (Jan. 1955). In John S. Brubacher and Willis Rudy, *Higher Education in Transition: History of American Colleges and Universities.* New York: Harper & Row, Publishers, Inc., 1976.

Darvich-Kodjouri, Ketayoun. *International Activity on State College and University Campuses, 1995.* Washington, D.C.: American Association of State Colleges and Universities, 1995.

Davies, Geoffrey. "Experiential, Cooperative, and Study Abroad Education," *Journal of Chemical Education,* vol. 73, no. 5 (May 1996), 438. http://www.jce.divched.org/Journal/Issues/1996/May/abs438.html.

Davis, Mrs. Beatrice F. Interview for the University of Delaware Oral History Project by Myron L. Lazarus, 15 July 1970. University of Delaware Archives, Paris Program Class of 1931, AR 97, 33/1/1.

Davis, Paul W. Personal interview, 29 October 2004.

Davis, Todd, ed. *Open Doors 1995/96: Report on International Exchange.* New York: Institute of International Education, 1996.

————, ed. *Open Doors 1996/97: Report on International Exchange.* New York: Institute of International Education, 1997.

————, ed. *Open Doors 2000/01: Report on International Exchange.* New York: Institute of International Education, 2001.

"Delaware Foreign Study Plan on Intercollegiate Basis." *School and Society* 24 (3 July 1926).

Delfor Alumni Association. Committee on Foreign Study Survey, 26 January 1933. AR 97, 33/0/8, "Delfor," University of Delaware Archives.

————. Alumni Questionnaire, 1933. AR 97, Folder 1639, "Delfor," University of Delaware Archives.

————. Foreign Study Plan Records, 1922-48. Box 52 (AR 52) (AR 96) Folder 1631, 33/0/8, University of Delaware Archives. Delfor Alumni Address list from Group I, 1923-24, through Group XVII, 1939-40.

Delfor Alumni Directories, 1933-35. University of Delaware Archives, Box 53, AR 97.

"Delforean." Listing of Former Alumni, 1923-36. Unnumbered insert, *Record Book.* University of Delaware Archives, Box 52, AR 96, Folder 1645.

Desruisseaux, Paul. "Lack of Funds Threatens Future of Academic Exchanges, Report Warns." *Chronicle of Higher Education,* 2 April 1999: A53.

———. "15% Rise in American Students Abroad Shows Popularity of Non-European Destinations." *Chronicle of Higher Education*, 10 December 1999, A60.

De Beauvoir, Simone. *The Second Sex,* translated by H. M. Parshley. New York: Vintage Books, 1952, 1974.

De Winter, Benjamin Urbain. *Overcoming Barriers to Study Abroad. A Report of the New York State Task Force on International Education.* Ithaca, N.Y.: Cornell University, 1995.

De Wit, Hans. *Internationalization of Higher Education in the United States of America and Europe: A Historical, Comparative, and Conceptual Analysis.* Westport, CT: Greenwood Press, 2002.

———. *Strategies for the Internationalization of Higher Education: A Comparative Study of Australia, Europe and the United States of America.* Amsterdam: European Association for International Education, 1995.

Dictionary of the History of Ideas: Studies of Selected Pivotal Ideas. New York: Charles Scribners' Sons, 1973.

Diller, Ann, with Maryann Ayin and Kathryn Morgan. *The Gender Question in Education: Theory, Pedagogy, and Politics.* Boulder, Colo.: Westview Press, 1996.

Dillman, Don. *Mail and Telephone Surveys: The Total Design Method.* New York: John Wiley, 1978.

Dreyfus, Hubert L., and Paul Rabinow. *Michel Foucault: Beyond Structuralism and Hermeneutics,* 2nd ed. Chicago: University of Chicago Press, 1983.

Duffy, Elizabeth A., with Idana Goldberg. *Crafting a Class: College Admissions and Financial Aid, 1955-1994.* Princeton: Princeton University Press, 1998.

Duke University. Conference, "Global Challenges & U.S. Higher Education," January 2003. http://www.duke.edu/web/cis/globalchallenges.

Durden, William G. "The Liberal Arts as a Bulwark of Business Education." *Chronicle of Higher Education,* 18 July 2003. http://chronicle.com/prm/weekly/v49/i45/45b02001.htm.

Dye, Richard W. Testimony presented before the subcommittee on international operations, U.S. House Committee on Foreign Affairs, 1 August 1990.

Educating Americans for a World in Flux: Ten Ground Rules for Internationalizing Higher Education. Washington, D.C.: American Council on Education, 1995.

"Educational: American Students at Oxford University." *School and Society* 21 (10 June 1925).

El-Khawas, E. *Campus Trends, 1992.* Washington, D.C.: American Council on Education, 1993. Cited in Joan Claffey, *Serving the World: International Activities of American Colleges and Universities.* Washington, D.C.: Office for University Cooperation in Development, 1993.

Engberg, David, and Madeleine F. Green, eds. *Promising Practices: Spotlighting Excellence in Comprehensive Internationalization.* Washington, D.C.: Center for Institutional and International Initiatives, American Council on Education, 2002.

Engerman, David C., and Parker G. Marden. *In the International Interest: The Contributions and Needs of America's International Liberal Arts Colleges.* Beloit, Wisconsin: The International Liberal Arts Colleges, 1992.

Engle, John, and Lilli Engle. "Neither International Nor Educative: Study Abroad in the Time of Globalization." In Grünzweig and Rinehart, eds., *Rockin' in Red Square.*

Erskine, Sheena, and Maggie Wilson, editors. *Gender Issues in International Education: Beyond Policy and Practice* (vol. 1162, Garland Reference Library of Social Science). New York: Falmer Press, 1999.

Feinberg, Ben. "What Students Don't Learn Abroad." *Chronicle of Higher Education.* 3 May 2002. http://chronicle.com/prm/weekly/v48/i34/34b02001.htm.

Feltman, Paul. Interview, New York, 15 February 1995.

Finkhouse, Joseph. E-mail correspondence, 27 January 2005.

Folan, Bernie. E-mail correspondence, 18 June 2004.

Fontana, Jorge. "Disciplinary Points of View: A Science and Technology." In William H. Allaway and Hallam C. Shorrock, *Dimensions of International Higher Education.*

"Foreign Study Scholarships of University of Delaware." *School and Society* 27 (9 June 1928).

Forwood, Madeleine. Interviewed by Myron L. Lazarus for the University of Delaware Oral History Project, 8 July 1970. University of Delaware Archives, Paris Program Class of 1931, AR 97, 33/1/1.

Foucault, Michel. *Madness and Civilization: A History of Insanity in the Age of Reason,* translated by Richard Howard. New York: Mentor Books, 1965. Translation of *Histoire de la folie à l'age classique.* Paris: Gallimard, 1964.

———. *The Order of Things,* translated by Alan Sheridan. New York: Random House, 1970. Translation of *Les Mots et les Choses.* Paris: Editions Gallimard, 1966.

———. *The Archaeology of Knowledge,* translated by A. M. Sheridan Smith. New York: Pantheon Books, 1972. Translation of *L'Archéologie du Savoir.* Paris: Editions Gallimard, 1969.

———. "The Discourse on Language." In Foucault, *The Archaeology of Knowledge.*

———. *Madness and Civilization: The History of Insanity in the Age of Unreason,* translated by Richard Howard. New York: Pantheon Books, 1973.

———. *Discipline and Punish,* translated by Alan Sheridan. New York: Pantheon Books, 1977. Translation of *Surveiller et Punir; Naissance de la Prison.* Paris: Editions Gallimard, 1975.

———. *Language, Counter-Memory, Practice: Selected Essays and Interviews,* edited by Donald F. Bouchard. Ithaca, N.Y.: Cornell University Press, 1977.

———. *The Birth of the Clinic: An Archaeology of Medical Perception,* translated by A. M. Sheridan. New York: Vintage Books, 1978.

———. *The History of Sexuality. Vol. 1: An introduction,* translated by Robert Hurley. New York: Vintage Books, 1978.

———. "The Eye of Power." In Michel Foucault, *Power/Knowledge: Selected Interviews and Other Writings, 1972-1977.*

———. *Power/Knowledge: Selected Interviews and Other Writings, 1972-1977,* edited by Colin Gordon. New York: Random House, 1980.

———. "Omnes et Singulatim: Toward a Criticism of 'Political Reason.'" In the Tanner Lectures of Human Values, II. Salt Lake City, Utah: University of Utah Press/Cambridge University Press, 1981.

———. "The Subject and Power." Afterword in Hubert L. Dreyfus and Paul Rabinow, *Michel Foucault: Beyond Structuralism and Hermeneutics*, 2nd ed. Chicago: University of Chicago Press, 1983.

———. "What is Enlightenment?" In Paul Rabinow, ed. *The Foucault Reader*. New York: Pantheon Books, 1984.

———. "Space, Knowledge and Power." In Paul Rabinow, ed. *The Fouault Reader*. New York: Pantheon Books, 1984.

———. *The History of Sexuality. Vol. 2: Uses of Pleasure,* translated by Robert Hurley. New York: Pantheon Books, 1985.

———. *Death and Labyrinth: The World of Raymond Roussel,* translated by Charles Ruas. New York: Doubleday and Co., 1986.

———. *The History of Sexuality. Vol. 3: Care of the Self,* translated by Robert Hurley. New York: Random House, 1986.

———. "Governmentality," *Ideology and Consciousness* 6 (Summer 1986).

———. *Politics, Philosophy, Culture: Interviews and Other Writings 1977-1984,* translated by Alan Sheridan et al., edited with an introduction by Lawrence D. Kritzman. New York and London: Routledge, 1988.

———. *Technologies of the Self,* edited by Luther H. Martin, Huck Gutman, and Patrick H. Hutton. Amherst: University of Massachusetts Press, 1988.

———. *Résumé des cours, 1980-1982.* Paris: Conférences, essais et leçons du college de France/Juilliard, 1989.

———. "The Minimalist Self." In *Politics, Philosophy, Culture: Interviews and Other Writings 1977-1984*, edited by Lawrence D. Kritzman. New York: Routledge, 1990.

———. "Genealogy and Social Criticism," in Steven Seidman, ed. *The Postmodern Turn: New Perspectives on Social Theory*. Cambridge, U.K.: Cambridge University Press, 1995. Reprinted from Michel Foucault, *Power/Knowledge: Selected Interviews and Other Writings, 1972-1977*.

"The Franco-American Student Exchange." *School and Society* 64 (9 November 1946).

Freeman, Stephen A. *The Middlebury College Foreign Language Schools, 1915-1970*. Middlebury, Vt.: Middlebury College Press, 1975.

Garraty, John A., and Walter Adams. *From Main Street to the Left Bank: Students and Scholars Abroad*. East Lansing, Mich.: The Michigan State University Press, 1959.

Gildersleeve, Virginia C. *Many a Good Crusade: Memoirs of Virginia Crocheron Gildersleeve*. New York: Macmillan Company, 1954.

Gillan, Garth. "Foucault's Philosophy." In James Bernauer and David Rasmussen, eds. *The Final Foucault*. Cambridge, Mass., and London: The MIT Press, 1988.

Gillespie, Joan. "Colleges Need Better Ways to Assess Study-Abroad Programs." *Chronicle of Higher Education*, B20, 5 July 2002.

——— and Carla Slawson. *IES Outcomes Assessment Project*. Presentation at NAFSA Conference 2003, Salt Lake City, UT. http://www.iesabroad.org/info/alumnioutcomes.pdf.

Gjerlufsen, Helle. Data analysis documents, Denmark International Studies, Copenhagen, Denmark.

Glazer-Raymo, Judith. *Shattering the Myths: Women in Academe.* Baltimore: Johns Hopkins University Press, 1999.

Goodman, Allan. "Opening Doors and Opening Minds: Why Both Are Needed for the 21st Century." Speech at USIA/ETS Conference on International Education, September 1998. Reprinted in NAFSA Newsletter, January/February 1999.

Goodwin, Craufurd D. "Introduction," *U.S. Students Abroad, Statistics on Study Abroad, 1985-86,* Maranthi Zikopoulos, ed. IIE Research Report Number 16. New York: Institute of International Education, 1988.

——— and Michael Nacht. *Abroad and Beyond: Patterns in American Overseas Education.* Cambridge, U.K.: Cambridge University Press, 1988.

———. *Missing the Boat: The Failure to Internationalize American Higher Education.* Cambridge, U.K.: Cambridge University Press, 1991.

Gordon, Colin, ed. *Power/Knowledge: Selected Interviews and Other Writings 1972-1977 by Michel Foucault.* New York: Random House, 1980.

Gore, Joan, Karen Keim (Lehigh University), David Portlock (Lafayette University), and Sara Dumont (Duke University). "Tuition Drain and Financial Strain." Panel presentation at NAFSA: Association of International Educators National Conference, May 1994.

Gore, Joan Elias. *Discourse and Traditional Belief: An Analysis of American Undergraduate Study Abroad.* Doctoral dissertation, University of London, 2000.

Gottlieb, Niels. "Introduction and Update on DIS: Philosophy, Programs, Services, and Quality Assurance System." Panel presentation, "Study Abroad in a Globalized World." Denmark's International Study Program Quintennial International Educators Conference. Copenhagen, 23 June 2004.

Gough, Harrison G., and William A. McCormack. "An Exploratory Evaluation of Education Abroad." Cooperative Research Project No. S-440. Berkeley, Calif.: University of California, 1967.

Graham, Patricia A. "Expansion and Exclusion: A History of Women in American Higher Education." *Signs: Journal of Women in Culture and Society* 3, no. 4 (Summer 1978). Reprinted in Lester F. Goodchild and Harold Wechsler, eds. *ASHE Reader on the History of Higher Education.* Needham Heights, Mass.: Ginn Press/Simon & Schuster, 1989.

Green, Madeleine, Peter Eckel, and Andris Barblan. *The Brave New (and Smaller) World of Higher Education: A Transatlantic View.* Washington, D.C.: American Council on Education, Center for International Initiatives, and European University Association, 2002.

Green, Madeleine F., and Christa Olson. *Internationalizing the Campus: A User's Guide.* Washington, D.C.: American Council on Education Center for Institutional and International Initiatives, 2003.

Gregory, Marshall. "A Liberal Education Is Not a Luxury," *Chronicle of Higher Education,* 12 September 2003, B16.

Grimes, Sara. 1994. "World Class: The Leading Personality in International Exchange Pulls No Punches." *Massachusetts,* Winter 1994.

Groennings, Sven. *The Impact of Economic Globalization on Higher Education.* Staff Paper Number III, New England Board of Higher Education, Boston, Mass. (1987).

Gruber, Carol S. *Mars and Minerva: World War I and the Uses of Higher Learning in America*. Baton Rouge, La.: Louisiana State University Press, 1976.

Grunwald, Janet. Interview, 19 June 1998.

Grünzweig, Walter, and Nana Rinehart, eds. *Rockin' in Red Square: Critical Approaches to International Education in the Age of Cyberculture*. Washington, D.C./Münster, Germany: Lit-Verlag, 2002.

———. "International Understanding and Global Interdependence: Towards a Critque of International Education." In Grünzweig and Rinehart, eds., *Rockin' in Red Square*.

Gwin, Mary Elizabeth Conway. *Study Abroad Advising: Information Delivery and Quality Assessment in Computer-Assisted Advising on Study Abroad Opportunities*. Doctoral dissertation, University of Mississippi, 1985.

———. Interview, 3 June 1992.

Hakim, Hossein, Worcester Polytechnic Institute, Worcester, Mass.. Unpublished letter, 21 May 1993.

Haley, Frances. *Reforming Education for the International Century. Report on the Recommendations and Findings of the Coalition for the Advancement of Foreign Languages and International Studies: Working Group on State and Local Initiatives*. New York: Coalition for the Advancement of Foreign Languages and International Studies, 1989.

Haro, Carlos. Review of Hawkins et al., eds., *International Education in the New Global Era*. Posted on AIEA-LIST@listserv.acsu.buffalo.edu, viewed 7 March 2002.

Harvard University Faculty of Arts and Sciences. "A Report on the Harvard College Curricular Review," April 2004. http://www.fas.harvard.edu/curriculum-review/HCCR_Report.pdf/.

Haskins, Charles Homer. *The Rise of Universities*. Ithaca and London: Cornell University Press, 1987, second edition; New York: H. Holt and Co., 1923.

Hawkins, John N., Carlos Manuel Haro, Miriam A. Kazanjian, Gilbert W. Merkx, and David Wiley, eds. *International Education in the New Global Era: Proceedings of a National Policy Conference on the Higher Education Act, Title VI, and Fulbright-Hays Programs*. http://www.isop.ucla.edu/ pacrim/title6/. Los Angeles: UCLA International Studies and Overseas Programs, 1998.

Hayward, Fred M., and Laura M. Siaya, *Public Experience, Attitudes and Knowledge: A Report on Two National Surveys About International Education*. Washington, D.C.: American Council on Education, 2001.

Healey, Joseph F. *Statistics: A Tool for Social Research*, 3rd edition. Belmont, Calif.: Wadsworth Publishing Company, 1993.

Henson, Harlan N. Interview, 30 April 2004.

Herrin, Carl. "It's Time for Advancing Education Abroad," *International Educator*, Vol. XIII, no. 1 (Winter 2004), 3.

———. Interview, CCIS (College Consortium for International Studies) Conference, Miami Beach, Florida, April 30, 2004.

———. E-mail correspondence, 6 May 2004.

"Higher Education Associations." American Council on Education, 1996.

Hirsch, E. D., Jr., *Cultural Literacy: What Every American Needs to Know*. New York: Vintage Books, 1988.

Hochhauser, Gail A. "Demographic Factors Redefining Education Abroad." In Martin Tillman, ed., *Study Abroad: A 21ˢᵗ Century Perspective,* vol. II.

Hoemeke, Thomas H., Maria Krane, Judy Young, and Gerald Slavin. *A Survey on Chief International Education Administrators, Their Institutions and Office.* Buffalo, N.Y.: Committee on Campus Administration and Programs, Association of International Education Administrators, 1999. Online at http://wings.buffalo.edu/intled/aiea/ciea.pdf.

Hoffa, William. E-mail to SECUSS-L Discussion List on History Project, 9 August 2000.

———. E-mail to SECUSS-L members, 18 April 2002.

———. "Study Abroad: not a Guy Thing?" ForumEA.org, The Forum on Education Abroad Message Board, http://forum.forumea.org/. 22 July 2004,

———. "What Are Participation Rates . . . And Why Should Anybody Care?," http://www.iienetwork.org/?p+41566/.

———, John Pearson, and Marvin Slind, eds. *NAFSA's Guide to Education Abroad for Advisers and Administrators.* Washington, D.C.: NAFSA: Association for Foreign Student Affairs, 1993.

——— and John Pearson, eds. *NAFSA's Guide to Education Abroad for Advisers and Administrators,* 2nd edition. Washington, D.C.: NAFSA: Association for Foreign Student Affairs, 1997.

Hogan, Martin. E-mail correspondence, 9 August 2004.

Honeywell, Roy J. *The Educational Work of Thomas Jefferson.* Cambridge, Mass.: Harvard University Press, 1931.

Horowitz, Helen Lefkowitz. *Alma Mater: Design and Experience in the Women's Colleges from their Nineteenth-Century Beginnings to the 1930s.* New York: Alfred A. Knopf, 1984.

Hoy, D. C. *Foucault: A Critical Reader.* New York: Blackwell, 1986.

Hudleston, Peter. Plenary session, *Internationalizing the Curriculum.*

Hull, W. F., W. H. Lemke, and R. T. Houang. *The American Undergraduate, Off Campus and Overseas: A Study of the Educational Validity of Such Programs.* Occasional Papers Series no. 20. New York: CIEE, 1977.

Hullihen, Walter H. "The Delaware Undergraduate Foreign Study Plan, or Junior Year Abroad." Dated 1931. University of Delaware Archives 33/0/5, Box 23 (AR67), folder 537.

Hult, G. Tomas M., and Elvin C. Lashbrooke, eds. *Study Abroad: Perspectives and Experiences from Business Schools.* Amsterdam and Boston: JAI, 2003.

Institute of International Education. *Foreign Study for U.S. Undergraduates.* New York: IIE, 1958.

———. *Transplanted Students: A Report of the National Conference on Undergraduate Study Abroad.* New York: Institute of International Education, 1961.

———. *Report on NSEP Undergraduate Allocations.* Washington, D.C.: IIE, 1994.

———. *NSEP: Undergraduate Scholarships for Study Abroad—Preparing for the Future.* New York: IIE, 1994.

———. "National Security Education Program, Undergraduate Scholarships, 1994-1995," *Competition Cycle Summary Report.* Washington, D.C.: IIE, 1995.

———. "Open Doors 1997/98 IIE's Annual Report on International Educational Exchange." Press release, 7 December 1998. http://www.iie.org/open-doors/od98text.htm

———. *50 Years of Open Doors.* CD-ROM. New York: IIE, 2001.

———. *Open Doors 2001.* http://opendoors.iienetwork.org/.

———. *Open Doors 2002.* http://opendoors.iienetwork.org/.

———. *Open Doors 2003.* http://opendoors.iienetwork.org/.

———. *Open Doors 2004.* http://opendoors.iienetwork.org/.

———. "The Impact of September 11 on International Education Exchange," IIE Network Online Survey Summary of Results, 18 November 2002. http://opendoors.iienetwork.org/.

———. "More American are studying abroad." Press release, 18 November 2002. http://www.iie.org.

———. "Study Abroad Surging Among American Students: After Sept. 11, interest in study abroad continues to grow rapidly." Press release, 15 November 2004. http://opendoors.iienetwork.org/?p=50138/.

———. Selected Open Doors Reports, provided to author by HeyKyung Koh. E-mail, 6 March 2003.

"Institute of International Education & Student Exchange." *School and Society* 28 (14 July 1928).

International 50. *What Works in International Education.* http://www.beloit.edu/~i50/whatworks.html.

"International Study." *School and Society* 20 (24 April 1926).

Internationalizing the Curriculum. Conference program and resource notebook, International Conference on Study Abroad Curriculum Integration, 15–17 April 2004, Minneapolis, Minnesota.

Jacobson, Jennifer. "Studying in Safety: In a post-9/11 world, colleges struggle to protect students abroad." *Chronicle of Higher Education,* 23 April 2004, 47.

Jenkins, Hugh M., and Associates. *Educating Students from Other Nations.* San Francisco/Washington/London: Jossey-Bass, 1983.

Jenkins, Karen. Interview, 19 November 1998.

———, and James Skelly. "Education Abroad Is Not Enough." *International Educator,* vol. 13, no. 2 (Winter 2004).

Jensen, Hans Peter (President of Denmark's Technical University), Helle Gjerlufsen (Field Director, Denmark's International Study Programme), and William W. Anthony (Director, Office of Study Abroad, Northwestern University). Interview, 11 November 1999.

Johnson, Jerry. Interview, 22 February 1994.

Johnson, Marlene M. "Advancing U.S. International Education: Leading by Example." *International Educator,* Vol. XII, no. 1 (Winter 2003).

Johnson, Vic. "From the Front Lines: International Education as a National Security Issue." *Newsletter, NAFSA: Association of International Educators* 53, no.4 (May/June 2002).

Johnston, Joseph S., Jr., and Richard J. Edelstein. *Beyond Borders: Profiles in International Education.* Washington, D.C.: Association of American Colleges, 1993.

"Junior Year in Zurich." *School and Society* 66 (12 July 1947).

Jurow, Susan, Kirk D. Beyer, and Management Compensation Services, a Division of Hewitt Associates, LLC. *Administrative Compensation Survey, College and University Personnel Association, 1996-97.* Washington, D.C.: College and University Personnel Association, 1997.

J. Walter Thompson Education. *An Exploration of the Demand for Study Overseas from American Students and Employers: An analysis of how future employment considerations are likely to impact students' decisions to study overseas and employers' perceptions of candidates with overseas qualifications.* Online at http://www.iie.org.

JYF. Sweet Briar College Junior Year Abroad Alumni Newsletter, 1974-78.

Kaplan, Deborah. E-mail correspondence, 29 August 2002.

Karabell, Zachary. *What's College For? The Struggle to Define American Higher Education.* New York: Basic Books, 1998.

Kauffmann, Norman L., Judith N. Martin, Henry D. Weaver, with Judy Weaver. *Students Abroad, Strangers at Home—Education for a Global Society.* Yarmouth, Maine: Intercultural Press, 1992.

Kazanjian, Miriam A. "Charge of the Conference." In Hawkins, John N., et al., *International Education in the New Global Era.*

Kedia, Ben L., and Shirley J. Daniel. "U.S. Business Needs for Employees with International Expertise." Paper delivered at Global Challenges and U.S. Higher Education Conference, Duke University, Durham, N.C., January 23-24, 2004. Online at http://www.duke.edu/web/cis/globalchallenges/research_papers.html, accessed 1 June 2004.

Kee, Arnold M. "The Force of Work." *Statistical Abstract of the U.S* http://www.poppolitics.com/articles/2000-10-02-laborstates.shtml.

Kelleher, Ann, with Lance Schachterle and Francis C. Lutz, co-editors. *Learning from Success: Campus Case Studies in International Program Development.* Vol. 15, Worcester Polytechnic Institute Studies in Science, Technology and Culture. New York: Peter Lang, 1996.

Kerr, Clark. "Introduction." In Allaway and Shorrock, *Dimensions of International Higher Education.*

————. *The Uses of the University.* Cambridge, Mass.: Harvard University Press, 1963.

Kidd, Margaret. E-mail correspondence, 13 April 1998.

Kirkbride, R. W. Letter to Dr. Walter Hullihen, President, University of Delaware. 2 March 1923, Paris, France. Provided by Andrew T. Hill, International Programs and Special Sessions Office, University of Delaware.

Knapp, Laura G., et al. *Postsecondary Institutions in the United States: Fall 2002 and Degrees and Other Awards Conferred: 2001-02.* Washington, D.C.: National Center for Education Statistics, U.S. Department of Education, 2003.

Knight, Jane, and Hans de Wit. *Internationalisation of Higher Education in Asia Pacific Countries.* Amsterdam: European Association for International Education, 1997.

Koester, Jolene. *A Profile of U.S. Students Abroad—1984 and 1985.* New York: Council on International Educational Exchange, 1987.

Lambert, Richard D. "Language Policy: An International Perspective." NFLC Occasional Papers, National Foreign Language Center. Baltimore: The Johns Hopkins University, 1990.

————. *Points of Leverage: An Agenda for a National Foundation for International Studies.* New York: Social Science Research Council, 1984.

————. "Study Abroad: Where We Are, Where We Should Be." In *Proceedings of the 41st Annual Conference on International Educational Exchange*, Cannes, France, November 1988.

————. *International Studies and the Undergraduate, A Special Report.* Washington, D.C.: American Council on Education, 1989.

Langlois, Emile. "Martha Lucas, President of Sweet Briar College." Unpublished manuscript and panel presentation at NAFSA conference, Region VII and IX, 16 November 1990.

————. Interviews, 17 February 1993 and 25 April 1994.

————. Unpublished computer analysis and summary of Junior Year in France groups (July 1994), Sweet Briar College, Sweet Briar, Va.

————. Unpublished financial aid records (Spring 1996), Sweet Briar College, Sweet Briar, Va.

Larsen, David. Interview, 1 June 1995.

Leadership Conference on Civil Rights. "The Wage Gap by Education." January 2004. http://fairchance.civilrights.org/research_center/details.cfm?id=18076/.

Lederach, John Paul. *Preparing for Peace: Conflict Transformation Across Cultures.* Syracuse, N.Y.: Syracuse University Press, 1996

Lemons, J. Stanley. *The Woman Citizen: Social Feminism in the 1920s.* Charlottesville and London: University Press of Virginia, 1990.

Levine, Lawrence, and Margaret Byrne. *The Opening of the American Mind: Canons, Culture, and History.* Boston: Beacon Press, 1996.

Lewin, Tamar. "War and Illness Cloud Prospects for Study Abroad." *New York Times,* 9 April 2003, http://www.nytimes.com.

Lewis, Aureta E. "Letters from a Junior in France" [1938]. University of Delaware Archives 33/0/1, Box C, AR 44, Folder C-15.

Liaison Group for International Educational Exchange. *Exchange 2000: International Leadership for the Next Century.* Washington, D.C.: Liaison Group for International Educational Exchange, 1990.

Liebhardt, Paul. "The History of Shipboard Education." *Steamboat Bill, Number 227*, vol. 55, no. 3 (Fall 1998).

Lipka, Sara. "Feminine Critique." *Chronicle of Higher Education*, Vol. 50, no. 37 (21 May 2004), A35. http://chronicle.com/prm/weekly/v50/i37/ 37a03501.htm.

Macri, Marion, and Patricia O'Callaghan. "A Review of the Marymount Schools in Paris, Rome and Elsewhere." *Oriflamme*, Jubilee Number. Tarrytown, N.Y.: Marymount College, 1932.

Malone, Dumas. *The Sage of Monticello.* Boston: Little, Brown and Co., 1981.

Marklein, Mary Beth. "Study Abroad: The Short Course Students Like." *USA Today,* 2 February 2004, D-1.

Mathies, Larraine, and William G. Thomas, eds. *Overseas Opportunities for American Educators: Perspective and Possibilities.* New York: CCM Information Corporation, 1971.

Matthew, R. John. *Twenty-Five Years on the Left Bank.* Sweet Briar, Va.: Sweet Briar College, 1973.

Maxwell, David, and Nina Garret. "Meeting National Needs." *Change,* vol. 34, no. 3 (May/June 2002).

Maza, Herbert. "Backlash in Education Abroad." In Mathies and Thomas, eds., *Overseas Opportunities for American Educators: Perspective and Possibilities.*

McCarthy, JoAnn. "Connecting the International Office to Campus and Curriculum Internationalization Strategy." Presentation at Association of International Educators Conference, San Jose, Costa Rica, 21 February 1997.

———. Interview, 9 June 1998.

McLuhan, Marshall, and Quentin Fiore, produced by Jerome Agel. *The Medium is the Massage.* New York: Touchstone, 1967, 1989.

———, coordinated by Jerome Agel. *War and Peace in the Global Village: An Inventory of Some of the Current Spastic Situations that could be Eliminated by More Feedforward.* New York: McGraw-Hill, 1968.

McLuhan, Marshall, and Bruce R. Powers. *The Global Village: Transformation in the World Life and Media in the 21st Century.* New York: Oxford University Press, 1989.

McMillan, Amy Ruhter, and Gayly Opem. "Tips for the Road: Study Abroad, A Lifetime of Benefits." *Abroad View Magazine,* Spring 2004. http://www.abroadviewmagazine.com/spring_04/study.html.

McNeal, R. A. *Nicholas Biddle in Greece: The Journals and Letters of 1806.* University Park, Penna.: Pennsylvania State University Press, 1993.

Menand, Louis. "Everybody Else's College Education." *The New York Times Magazine,* 20 April 1997.

Merkx, Gilbert W. "The Two Waves of Internationalization in U.S. Higher Education." *International Educator,* Vol. XII, no. 1 (Winter 2003), 8-12.

Merquior, J. G. *Foucault.* London: Fontana Modern Masters, Fontana Press/HarperCollins, 1991.

Mestenhauser, Josef A. Interview, April 1989.

———. "In Search of a Comprehensive Approach to International Education: A Systems Perspective," in Walter Grünzweig and Nana Rinehart, eds., *Rockin' in Red Square.*

Miel, Jan. "Ideas or Epistemes: Hazard versus Foucault." *Yale French Studies* 49 (1973).

Mikhailova, Liudmila K. *The History of CIEE: Council of International Educational Exchange and its role in international education development: 1947-2002.* Master's thesis, University of Minnesota, 2003. http://www.lib.umn.edu/articles/proquest.phtml/.

Moore, Ann. Interview, August 1993.

Morison, Samuel Eliot. *Three Centuries of Harvard 1636-1936.* Cambridge, U.K.: Cambridge University Press, 1936.

Morris, Mary, and Larry O'Connor, eds. *Maiden Voyages: Writings of Women Travelers.* New York: Vintage Departures Original, 1993.

Mourad, Roger P., Jr. *Postmodern Philosophical Critique and the Pursuit of Knowledge in Higher Education.* Critical Studies in Education and Culture Series, edited by Henry A. Giroux. Westport, Conn., and London: Bergin and Garvey, 1997.

Munroe, John A. *The University of Delaware: A History.* Newark, Del.: University of Delaware, 1986.

———. Interview, 7 February 1994.

NAFSA: Association of International Educators. National Membership Survey, August 1990.

———. "Report on National Membership Survey." *NAFSA Newsletter* vol. 41, no. 3 (December/January 1990).

———. *NAFSA Directory*. New York: NAFSA: Association of International Educators, 1994.

———. *NAFSA Membership Directory, 1997-98*. New York: NAFSA: Association of International Educators, 1997.

———. About NAFSA, http://www.nafsa.org/Template.cfm?Section=Inside-Nafsa&NavMenuID=4/.

———. Strategic Task Force on Education Abroad: Mission and Scope. http://www.nafsa.org/.

———. Strengthening the Association for the 21st Century, March 2004. http://www.nafsa.org/strengthening/.

National Center for Educational Statistics. *Digest of Education Statistics, 1990*. Washington, D.C.: U.S. Department of Education, 1991.

———. *Digest of Education Statistics, 1993-94*. Washington, D.C.: U.S. Department of Education, 1996.

———. *Digest of Education Statistics, 1998*. Washington, D.C.: U.S. Department of Education, 2000. http://nces.ed.gov/pubs99/digest 98/chapter3.html/.

———. *Digest of Education Statistics, 2001*. Washington, D.C.: U.S. Department of Education, 2002. http://nces.ed.gov/pubs2002/digest2001/.

———. *Digest of Education Statistics, 2002*. Washington, D.C.: U.S. Department of Education, 2003. http://nces.ed.gov/programs/digest/d02/index.asp/.

———. Integrated Postsecondary "Completions" Survey. U.S. Department of Education, http://nces.ed.gov/pubs99/digest 98/chapter3.html/.

———. *Projection of Education Statistics to 2013*. http://www.nces.ed.gov//programs/projections/tables/table_27.asp/.

National Commission on Excellence in Education. *A Nation at Risk: The Imperative for Educational Reform*. Washington, D.C.: U.S. Department of Education, 1983.

National Governors Association Task Force on International Education. *America in Transition: The International Frontier*. Washington, D.C.: National Governors Association, 1989.

A National Mandate for Education Abroad: Getting on with the Task. Report of the National Task Force on Undergraduate Education Abroad. Washington, D.C.: NAFSA: Association for International Educators, May 1990.

National Security Education Program. *Summary Report, Undergraduate Scholarships, 1994-1995 Competition Cycle*. New York: Institute for International Education, 1994.

Newcomer, Mabel. *A Century of Higher Education for American Women*. Washington, D.C.: Zenger Publishing Co, 1959.

Nolting, William E. E-mail to SECUSS-L members, 26 November 2002.

NSEP: Undergraduate Scholarships for Study Abroad, Preparing for the Future. New York: Institute of International Education, 1994.

Obst, Daniel. E-mail correspondence, 13 April 1998.

Olmsted, Patricia. "Sixty Years of Study Abroad: A Backward Glance at the Profession." Paper presented at NAFSA Conference, Long Beach, Calif., U.S., May 1987.

O'Sullivan, Marie, ed. *IIE Passport: Academic Year Abroad, The Most Complete Guide to Planning Academic Year Study Abroad,* 33rd edition. New York and Chester, Penna.: Institute of International Education, 2004.

———, ed. *IIE Passport: Short-Term Study Abroad,* 54th edition. New York: Institute of International Education, 2004).

Pace, Robert C. *The Junior Year in France: An Evaluation of the University of Delaware-Sweet Briar College Program.* Syracuse, N.Y.: Syracuse University Press, 1959.

Parmelee, Donna. E-mail to SECUSS-L members, 28 January 2003.

Peters, Courtney. E-mail correspondence, 6 May 2004.

Peters, Michael, editor. *After the Disciplines: The Emergence of Cultural Studies.* Westport, Conn.: Bergin & Garvey, 1999.

Petersen, Andrea. "Sex, Drugs and Junior Year Abroad: Doctors Work to Protect Travelers." *Wall Street Journal,* 31 July 2003.

Peterson's Study Abroad 1993: A Guide to Semester and Year Abroad Academic Programs. Princeton, N.J.: Peterson's, 1993.

Peterson's Study Abroad 1995: A Guide to Semester and Year Abroad Academic Programs. Princeton, N.J.: Peterson's, 1994.

Peterson's Study Abroad 1997: A Guide to Semester and Year Abroad Academic Programs. Princeton, N.J.: Peterson's, 1997.

Phillips, Sarah. E-mail correspondence, 25 August 2004.

Pirog, Ronald. Panel discussion, NAFSA Region IX Conference on History of Study Abroad, Norfolk, Virginia, 17 November 1990.

Powers, Christopher. E-mail correspondence, 25 January 2005.

President's Commission on Foreign Language and International Studies. *Strength Through Wisdom: A Critique of U.S. Capability.* Washington, D.C.: Government Printing Office, 1979.

Pritchett, James. E-mail correspondence, 21 May 1998; 12 May 1997; 3 October 1997; 6 October 1997.

Putnam, Ivan, editor. *Study Abroad: A Handbook for Advisers and Administrators.* Washington, D.C.: National Association of Foreign Student Affairs, 1979.

Quigley, Ned. Interview, 8 June 1998.

Record Book on Delforians, 1923–1936. University of Delaware Archives, Box 52, AR 96, Folder 1645.

Redford, Bruce. *Venice and the Grand Tour.* New Haven: Yale University Press, 1966.

Reilly, Kathleen M. Unpublished paper, 1995.

"Report Sees Widening of College Gender Gap." *Chronicle of Higher Education.* 27 June 2003, A-30. http://chronicle.com/prm/weekly/v49/i42/42a03003.htm.

Rhodes, Gary. "Exploring the Framework for Entrepreneurial Growth in Study Abroad." In Todd Davis, *Open Doors 1996/97: Report on International Exchange.* New York: Institute of International Education, 1997.

Riley, Richard W. "The Growing Importance of International Education." Presented at La Maison Francaise, Washington, D.C., 19 April 2000.

Reported on U.S. Department of Education's website, http://www.ed.gov/Speeches/04-2000/000419.html/.

Rimer, Sara. "Committee Urges Harvard to Expand the Reach of Its Undergraduate Curriculum." *New York Times,* 27 April 2004, sec. A, p. 17.

Ritchie, Daniel L. "Global Beat Syndicate." http://www.nyu.edu/globalbeat/syndicate/ritchie092903.html/.

Rogers, Francis M. *American Juniors on the Left Bank.* Sweet Briar, Va.: Sweet Briar College, 1958.

Rogers, Nigel. "Overcoming Barriers to Study Abroad for Science Students: Strategies and Success." Preconference workshop, CIEE Conference, Atlanta, Ga., 6 November 2002.

Rooney, Megan. "Keeping the Study in Study Abroad." *Chronicle of High Education,* 22 November 2002. http://chronicle.com/prm/weekly/v49/i13/13a06301.htm/.

Rosary College. *The Rosary College Foreign Study Plan,* no. 1 (March 1947), River Forest, Ill. University of Delaware Archives, Rosary College General, Folder 418, AR64, 33/0/3 General Correspondence, Box 20.

Rosary College Bulletin, 1947. University of Delaware Archives, Rosary College General, Folder 418, AR64 33/0/3, General Correspondence, Box 20.

Rosebrook-Collignon, Jaclyn. E-mail correspondence to SECUSSA, 3 May 2002.

Rossiter, Margaret W. "Doctorates for American Women, 1868-1907." *History of Education Quarterly,* Summer 1982.

Roy, Gilbert. Interview, 23 July 1994.

Rudolph, Frederick. *The American College and University, A History.* New York: Vintage Books, 1962.

Ruther, Nancy L. *Barely There, Powerfully Present: Thirty Years of U.S. Policy on International Higher Education.* New York and London: Routledge Falmer, 2002.

Sanders, Irwin T. and Jennifer C. Ward. *Bridges to Understanding: International Programs of American Colleges and Universities.* New York: McGraw-Hill, 1970.

Sartre, Jean-Paul. *Existentialism and Humanism,* translated by Philip Mairet. London: Methuen & Co., Ltd., 1948.

Scarflo, Richard D. "The History of Title VI and Fulbright-Hays." in Hawkins, John N., et al., eds., *International Education in the New Global Age.*

Schiffman, Peter. "Science Education Abroad: The Perspective of a Study Abroad Director at a Large, Research University." Panel presentation at the NAFSA: Association of International Educators Conference, Baltimore, Md., 27 May 2004.

Schneider, Alison. "Stanford Revisits the Course that Set Off the Culture Wars." *Chronicle of Higher Education,* 9 May 1997: A10-A12.

Schrag, Francis. "Why Foucault Now." *Journal of Curriculum Studies* 31, http://www.ed.uiuc.edu/jcs/vol13.

Scott, Julie. E-mail correspondence, 9 June 2004.

Scouten, Margaret. E-mail correspondence, 22 July 2004.

Seaman, Barrett, et al. *The Best College for You.* New York: Time Inc., 1997.

Securing America's Future: Global Education for a Global Age, Report of The Strategic Task Force on Education Abroad. Washington, D.C.: NAFSA: Association of International Educators, 2003.

SECUSS-L. Survey initiated by William Hoffa on SECUSS-L Listserv, NAFSA: Association of International Educators, 30 November 1993.

Seyffer, Sherry. Interview, 13 April 2000.

Sheffer, Patricia. E-mail correspondence, 23 July 2004 and 24 August 2004.

Siaya, Laura, and Fred M. Hayward. *Mapping Internationalization on U.S. Campuses: Final Report*. Washington, D.C.: American Council on Education, 2003.

Sideli, Kathleen. "When It Comes to U. S. Education Abroad, Everybody Counts." http://www.iienetwork.org/?p+41589/.

Singer, Sandra L. *Adventures Abroad: North American Women at German-Speaking Universities, 1868-1915*. Contributions in Women's Studies, Number 201. Westport, Conn., and London: Praeger, 2003.

Sittler, Cindy. Interviews, December 1992 and August 1993.

The Sixth Annual Floating University World Voyage. New York: University Travel Association, 1936.

Smallwood, Scott. "Women Still Feel Marginalized at MIT, Study Finds." *Chronicle of Higher Education,* 5 April 2002, A9. http://chronicle.com/prm/weekly/v48/i30/30a00901.htm.

Smith, Page. *Killing the Spirit: Higher Education in America*. New York: Viking Press, 1990.

Smith, Stephen G., ed. *America's Best Colleges*. Washington, D.C.: U.S. News and World Report, 1999.

Solomon, Barbara Miller. *In the Company of Educated Women: A History of Women and Higher Education in America*. New Haven and London: Yale University Press, 1985.

Spain, Daphne. *How Women Saved the City*. Minneapolis: University of Minnesota Press, 2001.

"Special Correspondence: The New Oxford Summer Vacation Course." *School and Society* 14, no. 619 (6 November 1926).

Steen, Sara J., ed. *Academic Year Abroad 1992-93*. New York: Institute of International Education, 1993.

————, ed. *Academic Year Abroad 1997-98*. New York: Institute of International Education, 1996.

————., ed. *Vacation Study Abroad 1997-98*. New York: Institute of International Education, 1996.

Steffens, Lincoln. "Sending a State to College." *American Magazine,* February 1909. Reprinted in James C. Stone and Donald P. deNevi, eds., *Portraits of the American University 1890-1910*. San Francisco: Jossey-Bass, 1971.

Stein, Gertrude. *Paris and France*. New York: Charles Scribners' Sons, 1940.

Steinberg, Jacques. "Parlez-Vous Français? But Why Bother?" *New York Times,* 27 December 1998: WK-3.

Steinberg, Michael. E-mail correspondence, 5 August 2004.

Steiner, Jan. E-mail correspondence, 17 May 2004.

Stimpson, Catherine R. "Colleges in the U.S. Beginning to Ask, 'Where Have All the Men Gone?,'" *New York Times,* 6 December 1998: A38.

Stoffel, Meredith. "Gender difference in study abroad: BC sends more women than men abroad." *The Heights*, Boston College, Boston, Mass., 3 February 2004, 1. http://www.bcheights.com/news/2004/02/03/Features/Gender. Difference.In.Study.Abroad-594562.shtml?page=1

Stohlman, Martha Lou Lemmon. *The Story of Sweet Briar College*. Sweet Briar, Va.: Alumnae Association of Sweet Briar College, 1956.

Stowe, William W. *Going Abroad: European Travel in Nineteenth-Century American Culture*. Princeton, N.J.: Princeton University Press, 1994.

"Strategic Task Force on Education Abroad Formed, Begins Work." *Newsletter, NAFSA: Association of International Educators* 53, no.5 (July/August 2002), 15.

Strout, Erin. "Median Salaries of Midlevel College Administrators by Type of Institution, 2003-4." *Chronicle of Higher Education*, 2 April 2004. http://chronicle.com/weekly/v50/i30/30a03001.ht.

Stubbs, Nancy. "Financial Aid." In William Hoffa, *NAFSA's Guide to Education Abroad for Advisers and Administrators* 2nd edition.

"Student Exchanges & Peace." *School and Society* 18 (25 August 1923).

Study Abroad. Syracuse, N.Y.: Syracuse University Division of International Programs Abroad, 1993.

Study Abroad Baseline Survey. Unpublished report, Council on International Educational Exchange, 1996.

"Study Abroad in a Globalized World." Denmark's International Study Program Quintennial International Educators Conference. Copenhagen, Denmark, 24 June 2004.

"The Success of American Graduate Students in the University of London." *School and Society* 29 (26 January 1929).

Sweet Briar College. Bulletin for Junior Year in France (February 1948).

Sweet Briar College. *Sweet Briar College Junior Year in France* [catalog], 1993-94. Sweet Briar, Va.: Sweet Briar College, 1993.

Sylte, Ruth M. E-mail correspondence, 5 April 1996.

Szekely, Beatrice Beach, and Maria Krane. "The Current Demographics of Education Abroad." In William Hoffa and John Pearson, eds., *NAFSA's Guide to Education Abroad for Advisers and Administrators*, 2nd edition.

Tabuteau, Jill. E-mail correspondence, 31 August 2004.

Task Force on International Education, Committee on Education and Labor, U.S. House of Representatives, John Brademas, Chairman. *International Education: Past, Present, Problems, and Prospects: Selected Reading to Supplement H.R. 1464*. Washington, D.C.: U.S. Government Printing Office, 1966.

Tennies, Sandy Schoeps. E-mail correspondence, 31 August 2004.

Thiel, Kari. E-mail correspondence, 10 May 2004.

Thompson, Gerry. Interview, 15 August 1991.

Thorp, Margaret Farrand. *Neilson of Smith*. New York: Oxford University Press, 1956.

Tillman, Martin, ed. *Study Abroad: A 21st Century Perspective*. Washington, D.C.: American Institute for Foreign Study, 2001. Also at http://www.aifs.org/aifsfoundation/burn.htm/.

Tomas, G., M. Hult, and Elvin C. Lashbrooke, eds. *Study Abroad: Perspectives and Experiences from Business Schools*. Amsterdam & Boston: JAI, 2003.

Trease, Geoffrey. *The Grand Tour*. New York: Holt, Rinehart & Winston, 1967.

Trivedi, Bijal V. "Survey Reveals Geographic Illiteracy." *National Geographic Today*, 20 November 2002. http://news.nationalgeographic.com/news/2002/11/1120_021120_GeoRoperSurvey.html

Trow, Martin. "American Higher Education: Past, Present, and Future." In Lester F. Goodchild and Harold S. Wechsler, editors, *ASHE Reader on the History of Higher Education*, ASHE Reader Series. Needham Heights, Mass.: Ginn Press, 1989.

Tylor, Mary Louise. "Study Abroad." In Asa S. Knowles, editor-in-chief. *International Encyclopedia of Higher Education*, vol. 4 (D-F). San Francisco: Jossey Bass Publishers, 1977.

"Undergraduate Degree Programs Most Offered by U.S. Members." Association to Advance Collegiate Schools of Business, AACSB International. http://www.aacsb.edu/publications/.

University of Delaware Archives. Sketch of Foreign Study Plan, Scope and General Statement. University of Delaware Archives, Folder # 1 and Foreign Study section. Papers of Walter Hullihen, # 3/18. University of Delaware Archives.

U.S. Bureau of the Census. *Statistical Abstracts*, Table 617, 1996.

U.S. Congress. House Report 108-10. *Making Further Continuing Appropriations for the Fiscal Year 2003, and for other purposes, accompanying H.J. Res. 2, Consolidated Appropriations Resolution*, 2003.

U.S. Department of Education. *Digest of Educational Statistics, 1998*. Washington, D.C.: National Center for Educational Statistics, 1998.

U.S. Department of Education. Educational Statistics, U.S. Department of Education Publications. http://www.ed.gov/pubs/statss.html/.

U.S. News and World Report. *America's Best Colleges*, premium online edition, 2003.

"Vacation Courses for Foreigners in French Universities." *School and Society* 20 (August 1924).

Vaughn, Harold. "International Activity on State College and University Campuses." Discussion list posting, 7 May 1996.

Vaughn, Harold. "Connecting the International Office to Campus and Curriculum Internationalization Strategy." Presentation at Association of International Educators Conference, San Jose, Costa Rica, 21 February 1997.

———. Interview, 7 May 1997.

Veblen, Thorstein. *The Theory of the Leisure Class: An Economic Study of Institutions*. New York: Modern Library, 1934.

Veysey, Laurence R. *The Emergence of the American University*, third edition. Chicago and London: University of Chicago Press, 1974.

Von Klemperer, Lily. Oral history interview by Tom Roberts, Spring 1990. Sponsored by NAFSA: Association of International Educators.

Wagoner, Jennings L., Jr., and Wayne J. Urban. *American Education: A History*. New York: McGraw-Hill, 1996.

Wallace, John A. *The Organization and Outcomes of a European Field Trip in Economics for 23 College Women*. Ed.D. dissertation, University of Pennsylvania, February 1949.

———. "Characteristics of Programs for Study Abroad," *Journal of General Education*, vol. 13, no. 4 (January 1962).

Watkins, Kate. Interview, 27 May 2004.

Watson, Paul. Personal correspondence, 13 April 2004.

Weaver, Henry. Interview, CIEE Oral History Video Series, 1 June 1994.

Weaver, Paul. "Study Abroad and General Education." *Journal of General Education*, vol. 13, no. 4 (January 1962).

Weaver, Richard M. *Ideas Have Consequences*. Chicago and London: University of Chicago Press, 1971.

Whalen, Annmarie. E-mail correspondence, 21 May 2004.

Whalen, Brian. "Summary of Study Abroad Alumni Research, Dickinson College." Presentation at PACIE Conference, 28 November 2001. http://www.dickinson.edu/global/global_ed_research/index.html.

What Works in International Education. http://www.beloit.edu/~i50/whatworks.html/.

Whorf, Benjamin Lee. "Science and Linguistics." In Bennett, Milton J., ed. *Basic Concepts of Intercultural Communication: Selected Readings*. New York: Intercultural Press, 1998. Originally published in *Language, Thought, and Reality: The Selected Writings of Benjamin Lee Whorf*, ed. J. B. Carroll. Cambridge, Mass.: MIT Press, 1956.

Wilson, Robin. "How Babies Alter Careers for Academics." *Chronicle of Higher Education*, 5 December 2003, A-1. http://chronicle.com/prm/weekly/v50/i15/15a00101.htm.

———. "The 'Feminization' of Anthropology." *Chronicle of Higher Education*, 18 April 2003, A-13. http://chronicle.com/prm/weekly/v49/i32/ 32a01301.htm.

———. "Faculty Salaries Rise 2.1%, the Lowest Increase in 30 Years." *Chronicle of Higher Education*, 23 April 2004, A-13.

Woodard, Colin. "Exchange Group Accused of Placing Profits over its Mission of Promoting Foreign Study." *Chronicle of Higher Education*, 22 May 1998: A50.

Woodberry, L. Robert. "Sunday Forum: Internationalize University Curriculum with Exchanges." *Sunday* [Lewiston, Maine], 21 October 1990: 3D.

Woody, Thomas. *A History of Women's Education in the United States*, 2 vols. New York: The Science Press, 1929.

Woolf, Michael. "International Education and the Question of Quality." *International Educator*, Vol. 13, no. 2 (Spring 2004).

Wootton, Barbara. "Gender Differences in Occupational Employment." *Monthly Labor Review*, April 1997.

"Working with DIS: Workshop on the Administration of Academic and Practical Matters." International Educators Workshop, Denmark's International Study Program. Fall 2003, Copenhagen, Denmark.

Zeigler, A. Lee. "History of SECUSSA." Panel presentation, NAFSA: Association of International Educators National Conference, 28 May 1998.

Index